THE
WARREN BUFFETT
PHILOSOPHY *of*
INVESTMENT

THE
WARREN BUFFETT
PHILOSOPHY *of*
INVESTMENT

How a Combination of Value Investing and Smart Acquisitions Drives Extraordinary Success

ELENA CHIRKOVA

New York   Chicago   San Francisco   Athens   London   Madrid
Mexico City   Milan   New Delhi   Singapore   Sydney   Toronto

1 2 3 4 5 6 7 8 9 0   QFR/QFR   1 2 1 0 9 8 7 6 5

ISBN 978-0-07-181932-9
MHID 0-07-181932-0

e-ISBN 978-0-07-181933-6
e-MHID 0-07-181933-9

Library of Congress Cataloging-in-Publication Data
Chirkova, Elena
    The Warren Buffett philosophy of investment : how a combination of value investing and smart acquisitions drives extraordinary success / Elena Chirkova.
        pages cm
    ISBN 978-0-07-181932-9 (hardback) — ISBN 0-07-181932-0 (hardback)   1. Buffett, Warren.   2. Finance.   3. Investments.   I. Title.
    HG172.B84C45 2015
    332.6—dc23
                                                                        2015001176

McGraw-Hill Education books are available at special quantity discounts to use as premiums and sales promotions or for use in corporate training programs. To contact a representative, please visit the Contact Us pages at www.mhprofessional.com.

This title was originally published in Russia in 2008 but has been updated significantly for this current edition.

Contents

Preface

Is it possible to add to the portrait of Buffett, given all the books that have been written about him? The purpose of my book is to assemble all the factors that have played a role in Buffett's success, including those that go beyond his investment principles, which are well known and rather traditional if described from the point of view of value investors, to which group Buffett undoubtedly belongs. The ideas of my book are also discussed in my earlier article, "Why Is It That I Am Not Warren Buffett?" [Chirkova, 2012].

My book has eleven chapters. Two of them (Chapters 2 and 3) are devoted to Buffett's investment principles, and four (Chapters 7, 8, 9, and 10) to the tactics that Buffett uses when acquiring companies, making portfolio investments, or positioning Berkshire as a white knight and "the right home for the right people."

I begin by discussing Buffett's intellectual forebears, Ben Graham and Philip Fisher, whom Buffett regards as his teachers (Chapter 1). I don't share the view that Buffett adheres rigidly to their ideas, and I discuss where Buffett's principles differ from those of Graham and Fisher. Buffett's departure from some of Graham's ideas, which are considered to be controversial within the modern investor community, contributed positively to Buffett's success.

I also analyze Buffett's views on how the financial markets function and his position on key corporate finance issues (Chapter 5). To the best of my knowledge, these issues have not been assessed analytically in the available literature. I compare Buffett's views on corporate finance with mainstream concepts that are the current consensus among scholars.

I find that Buffett's better conceptual foundation is the cornerstone of his successful strategy. I review other scholars' analyses of the extent of Buffett's outperformance, as his investment success has recently become the subject of study by economists and financial theorists.

My book not only provides an analysis of Buffett's investment principles but also discusses how his different principles are logically interconnected; for instance, how Buffett's concept of risk, where he disagrees with its traditional interpretation as volatility, or his suspicions about investing in technology companies and his long-term investment horizon are linked to one another. I also compare Buffett's investment approach with the approaches used by Peter Lynch, a great investor who could be described as similar to Buffett in spirit, and by Robert Merton, a Nobel Prize–winning financial theorist who could be viewed as the antithesis of Buffett. These comparisons I make in Chapter 4 help crystallize the understanding of Buffett's investment principles.

Buffett's results are often compared with the returns delivered by investment funds, but Berkshire Hathaway is not a fund but a joint stock company, and this is one of the critical factors behind his success. The structural organization of an investment business set up as a corporation is beneficial only in terms of a specific investment strategy in which a long-term investment horizon is a key component. I discuss this issue in detail. Also, Berkshire's structural organization and Buffett's extensive, but intelligent, involvement in the insurance business allow the company to obtain practically cost-free leverage. Chapter 6 is devoted to a detailed analysis of Berkshire's use of leverage.

Last, but not least, Buffett's exceptional investment abilities cannot be overlooked, nor can the contribution from his alter ego, Charlie Munger. These are discussed in Chapter 11.

I am very grateful to all the authors and scholars who have written on the subject, for I have been inspired by the very valuable contributions made by others to the development of a deeper understanding of Buffett's investment practices. I would like to mention here some books that have proved to be priceless sources for my research (mentioning all of them would be prohibitively lengthy for a preface; nevertheless, the work of all these other scholars was absolutely indispensable to me, and I refer to them throughout my book).

James Altucher's book *Trade Like Warren Buffett* [Altucher, 2005] is close to my understanding of Buffett's investment strategy in spirit in that its author was the first, to the best of my knowledge, to have observed that Warren Buffett's investment principles are far more complicated than they seem at first sight and than they are described in most books on Buffett's investment success. Andrew Kilpatrick's excellent volume (currently two volumes) *Of Permanent Value: The Story of Warren Buffett* [Kilpatrick, 2005] is a unique collection of facts and stories about Warren Buffett and his deals and investments, many of which are not available in other sources. Alice Schroeder, who wrote *The Snowball*—a brilliant biography of Buffett with his participation [Schroeder, 2008], gives an illuminating account of his life. The magnificent *Buffett: The Making of an American Capitalist*, by Roger Lowenstein [Lowenstein, 1996], reviews many of Buffett's deals from the point of view of his interpersonal skills. *The Warren Buffett CEO: Secrets from the Berkshire Hathaway Managers* [Miles, 2002], written by Robert Miles on the basis of interviews with Berkshire's managers, many of whom are the former owners of the businesses that they had sold to Buffett, was also an invaluable resource in which I found information on the motivation of the business sellers that was not discussed in the mass media. Miles's book helped me write about the behavioral aspects of Buffett's business strategy, and it is in Miles's book that I found perhaps, in my view, the best insight into Buffett's attitude toward M&A. This insight was formulated by Ralph Schey, the CEO of Scott Fetzer Company: Buffett sells an illusion of ownership without ownership itself. If I had to pick one sentence that best illustrates the key driving force behind Buffett's success, I would probably choose these words.

Acknowledgments

I WOULD LIKE TO THANK MY FRIEND LEV GELMAN, THE OWNER OF A consulting company, who advised me to read Warren Buffett's letters to Berkshire's shareholders. Lev has regarded the letters as exemplary in terms of economic and investment thinking. The idea for this book came to me immediately upon opening the letters. I am also grateful to Tatiana Doump, my agent, who had faith that the book would find a publisher. Tatiana took on the endeavor of looking for one as I looked on without hope. I thank Donya Dickerson, executive editor at McGraw-Hill Education, who chose to believe in the book and who was extraordinarily patient with my seemingly endless reworking of it. I would also like to thank Daina Penikas, senior editing supervisor at McGraw-Hill Education, and copyeditor Alice Manning, who have been of considerable assistance during the production and copyediting process. I give my heartfelt thanks to my sister, Anna, who not only did the translation but also gave her intellectual support and creativity to the project, and owing to her advice and extensive assistance, the book has been much improved.

THE
WARREN BUFFETT
PHILOSOPHY *of*
INVESTMENT

Introduction

Who Is Warren Buffett?

To achieve satisfactory investment results is
easier than most people realize; to achieve
superior results is harder than it looks.
—BENJAMIN GRAHAM [GRAHAM, 2003, P. 524]

WARREN BUFFETT ONCE REMARKED THAT HE HAD THOUGHT ABOUT making money since before he was born. Perhaps he meant to say that he had contemplated financial success from as far back as he could remember. One of Buffett's biographers observed that he "was always telling vignettes from his career; he seemed to have a compulsion to tell and retell, to mythologize his past . . . to depict his success as partly the result of serendipity, rather than his intense, lifelong drive to get rich" [Lowenstein, 1996, pp. 277–278]. Was Buffett mythologizing when he talked about his earliest memories? Is his success indeed the result of serendipity?

When he was hospitalized at seven years old, Warren told his nurse: "I don't have much money now, but some day I will, and I'll have my picture in the paper" [cited in Boroson, 2008, p. 18]. At the age of 11, Buffett declared that he would become a millionaire by the age of 35. After graduating from business school, Buffett joined his father's brokerage firm. When asked whether the company would be renamed "Buffett & Son," he rather seriously replied that the firm's name would be changed to "Buffett & Father" [Lowenstein, 1996, p. 46]. In 1957, at the age of 27, when his wealth amounted to $200,000 (nearly $1.5 million in today's money), he wrote in a letter to a friend that he did not know what to do with his legacy and he did not want to leave it to his children. He felt: "It is easier to create money than to spend it" [cited in Lowe, 2007, p. 60]. It seems that Buffett might not be quite mythologizing when he talks about this particular aspect of his past. As for whether Buffett's success is the result of serendipity, this is one of the questions that I attempt to answer in this book.

Buffett's childhood vision became reality. In 1995, *Time* magazine published an article titled "How Smart Is Warren Buffett?" The author noted: "We've seen oil magnates, real estate moguls, shippers and robber barons at the top of the money heap, but Buffett is the first person to get there just by picking stocks" [Rothchild, 1995]. With his fortune valued at $250 million, Buffett appeared on the first *Forbes* list, published in 1982. His ascent on the *Forbes* list started from a relatively modest level. Gradually he rose through the ranks and reached the top position in 1993 with a fortune of $8.2 billion. Throughout 2001–2007 and in 2009, Buffett was in second place (after Bill Gates). In 2008, he again reached first place with a fortune of $62 billion; throughout 2010–2012, he remained in third place (by that time he had transferred some of his fortune to a charitable fund); and in 2013, he was in fourth place.

Buffett is "just" an investor. He began his career with a small amount of starter capital that he had accumulated while working as a newspaper delivery boy. Eventually he became internationally famous, widely regarded as the "investor of the century" and an "economic rock star." Berkshire Hathaway is comparable in size (market capitalization, revenue, and profit) to General Electric, one of the world's largest conglomerates. In 2013, Berkshire's revenue reached $182 billion, and its net profit reached $19.5 billion. The company's market capitalization currently (as of the time of this writing in November 2014) exceeds $355 billion. It is believed that Buffett and his company have created much more wealth for a much larger number of people than any mutual fund, partnership, hedge fund, or public company.

Buffett created his wealth without any financial assistance from others. When he was a young and unknown investor in need of funds, he never relied on his father, a wealthy congressman. When his father died in 1964, Warren did not inherit anything from him. In his will, Buffett's father wrote that he had made no arrangements for his son not because of any absence of affection between them, but because Buffett already had substantial assets in his own right and had requested that his father not bequeath him anything [Kilpatrick, 2005, p. 119]. Owing to Buffett's refusal to accept an inheritance, his investment success is entirely a personal achievement—a clean experiment untainted by any external financial infusions.

In 2000, Berkshire Hathaway started publishing data on asset book value performance. Details have included average annual returns since 1965, the time when Buffett took control of the company. Since 2002, the data have been presented on the title page of Warren Buffett's letter to shareholders. The results are impressive. The average annual asset growth rate from 1965 to 2013 was 19.7 percent, when the return on the S&P index, adjusted for dividends, was 9.8 percent. Thus, Buffett has delivered a return that is 9.9 percentage points higher than that of the index. From 1977 onward, profit has grown at an average annual rate of 20.6 percent [Buffett, 1977–2013]. Berkshire's asset book value per share rose approximately 7,265 times during this period, while the S&P with dividends included rose by around 93.4 times. Berkshire's revenue grew 4,500 times.

Buffett reports its results as the annualized growth rate of the *book value of assets*. To the best of my knowledge, except for one occasion, he has never commented on the market price of Berkshire's shares so as not to encourage speculation in company stock. For a number of accounting and other reasons, in many industries the book value of assets usually grows at a slower rate than the market price of the company stock. The rise in Berkshire's stock price between 1965 and 2013 is even greater than that of its asset book value—9,184 times (from $19 at year-end 1965 to $174,500 at year-end 2013), or 20.9 percent annually. Buffett's preferred method of presentation in effect diminishes his results.

This performance was delivered over an extraordinarily long period of time—49 years. Successful investors are usually able to sustain their performance over a much shorter time horizon—approximately 10 years. Berkshire's asset value per share fell for the first time in 2001, when the collapse of the Internet bubble caused a broader market fall. The return on the S&P, adjusted for dividends, was nearly negative 12 percent, while the return on the book value of Berkshire's assets was negative 6.2 percent. Berkshire's asset book value fell for the second time in 2008, when it decreased by 9.6 percent, while the S&P, adjusted for dividends, returned a negative 37 percent. Berkshire's asset book value outperformed the market over 39 out of 49 years. During these years, as Buffett commented, there took place the long and costly Vietnam War, wage and price controls, the oil shocks, the resignation of a president, the collapse of the Soviet Union and large single-day moves in the stock market [Buffett, 1977–2013, 1994].

Buffett's successful track record is even longer if we consider his performance prior to his acquisition of Berkshire. While a student at Columbia Business School, Buffett managed his personal capital (his savings at the start of his studies in 1950 amounted to $9,800). He grew his money by more than 61 percent a year [Schroeder, 2008, p. 200] until he created Buffett Partnership in 1956. Between 1957 and 1969, Buffett Partnership produced phenomenal returns of 29 percent annually—23.8 percentage points higher than the Dow Jones. Overall, $10,000 invested in the Partnership in 1957 would have increased to $270,000 by 1969 [Buffett, 1984]. In total, Buffett's successful track record covers more than 60 years.

What is the true scale of Buffett's success? Is his achievement as significant as it seems when one glances at the front pages of his letters to shareholders? Let us consider whether it is meaningful to contrast the performance of asset *book value* and market dynamics. An assessment based on the *market price* of Berkshire shares demonstrates that Buffett beat the market in 30 out of 48 years (as opposed to 39 out of 49 for asset book value). Since Berkshire's share price outperformed the market in fewer years than the asset book value did, the share price performance, in some sense, is less stable than the book value performance, although, as discussed earlier, Berkshire's shares appear to deliver better returns than the asset book value. It is difficult to judge which assessment is more insightful.

Buffett does not analyze Berkshire's share price for philosophical reasons. He believes that markets are not rational and that the market value of the shares of any company is more volatile than the company's real performance. He views the market price of its shares as about the least informative piece of information about a company. On the other hand, the book value of assets may not be an accurate reflection of the company's ability to generate profit. It is also possible to argue that book value analysis, while it seems more appropriate in some ways, might overestimate the number of years in which Buffett has outperformed the market.

It is indisputable that the average annual returns are startling. However, they reflect the results of those who invested in Berkshire in 1964. How widely known was Buffett at that time? His original investors were family members, friends, and a small group of clients whom Buffett had inherited from Benjamin Graham, his teacher and first employer. The wider investing public started joining Buffett's venture later. On October 12, 1986, a journalist from the *Omaha World-Herald* telephoned a company and advised it that its shares had been acquired by Warren Buffett. He received the response: "Who is Warren Buffett?" People were still asking that question when Buffett became chairman of Salomon Brothers in 1991 [Kilpatrick, 2005, p. 881]. It is now believed that the first book that was published about Buffett, *The Warren Buffett Way*, by Robert Hagstrom [Hagstrom, 2005], released in 1995, triggered a wider recognition of his success. The book sold one million copies.

Returns on an investment in Berkshire Hathaway at the end of 2013 as a function of the time of *entry* into the investment are diminishing (see Figure I.1). If the entry point is prior to 1979, then the average annual return is greater than 20 percent. If the entry point is between 1979 and

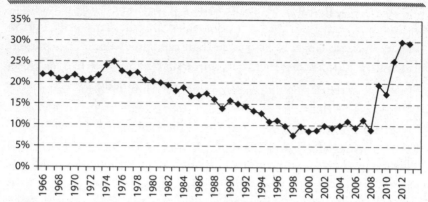

FIGURE I.1 Average Annual Return on Berkshire Hathaway Shares from the Year of Entry to 2014 for any Given Year of Entry (Calculated from the Year-End of the Entry Year to the End of 2014).

1988, then the average annual return is greater than 15 percent. For an entry point between 1989 and 1996, it is higher than 10 percent. Starting in 1997, the average annual return is lower than 10 percent unless you invested in 2009 or later. Investors who joined the company at the end of the 1980s, when the wider investing public began to hear about Buffett, earned approximately 13 to 17 percent annually. Those who joined at the end of 1995, after the publication of Hagstrom's best-seller, earned approximately 10.8 percent a year, while the S&P, dividends adjusted, delivered only 2.6 percentage points less—8.2 percent. Those who bought Berkshire shares in 2000, when Berkshire first published data about average annual historical returns in the company's annual report, earned 8.6 percent annually (importantly, the S&P, adjusted for dividends, returned only 4.8 percent during this period).

There is no downside to publishing historical returns data. Even if, in future, Buffett no longer beats the index, his results and the index returns, averaged since 1965, will probably never converge. For instance, if from 2015 on, Berkshire's asset growth rate stabilizes at 9 percent a year (roughly equivalent to the average annual American stock market return, adjusted for dividends, over a very long time horizon[1]), then Berkshire's returns, averaged since 1965, will fall only by 0.2 to 0.3 percentage points a year. For the foreseeable future, Berkshire's averaged returns will decrease relatively insignificantly. Buffett created such considerable odds in his favor in the early years that, under these assumptions, returns on an investment in Berkshire averaged since 1965 will be greater than the same returns on the S&P for another 50 to 70 years. Buffett earned high returns at the earlier stages of his career, when he managed a relatively smaller amount of capital. Later, when he started managing vast sums, he earned a return that was only slightly above average, although a superficial glance at the returns data gives the impression of high returns for all investors—old and new. Importantly, in his letter to shareholders for 2013, Buffett tells his audience that it is possible that in the future, Berkshire will be outperforming the S&P only in years when the market is either down or moderately up [Buffett, 1977–2013, 2013].

The data on Buffett's results are reliable, and his performance is very well documented. Several questions arise: "Is this a result of Buffett's application of his methodology, or did it happen by chance?" "Is it possible to replicate this achievement?" and "What is required for replication?" The question of whether financial success is achieved by chance or through application of a methodology is the central point of discussion on the rationality and efficiency of financial markets.

From the middle of the 1970s to the middle of the 1990s, the academic financial world was dominated by the conviction that no investment strategy would outperform the market systematically—markets

---

1 There are many studies that assess the stock market return over long intervals. The various calculations are consistent. They indicate that the long-term annual return on the U.S. stock market is around 8 to 10 percent in nominal terms and 6.5 to 7 percent in real terms. Roger Ibbotson and Rex Sinquefield calculated that over the 1926–1974 period, the annual return on the S&P index in nominal terms, including dividends, amounted to 8.5 percent, which is 6.3 percentage points higher than the return on U.S. Treasury bonds [Ibbotson and Sinquefield, 1976]. The annual inflation over this period amounted to 2.2 percent. Rajnish Mehra and Edward Prescott calculated that the annual return on the S&P over the 1889–1978 period amounted to 7 percent in real terms [Mehra and Prescott, 1985]. Elroy Dimson, Paul Marsh, and Mike Staunton calculated that for the period from 1900 to 2000, the real annual return on the U.S. stock market was 6.7 percent [Dimson, Marsh, and Staunton, 2002].

were regarded as efficient. Eugene Fama, who published "Efficient Capital Markets: A Review of Theory and Empirical Work" [Fama, 1970] in 1970, is considered to be the father of the efficient market hypothesis. According to the hypothesis, share prices do not depend on historical trends, as prices always take into account all relevant information, whether publicly available or insider.[2] Predictions based on past dynamics are meaningless. It is possible to obtain a return that is greater than average only if one takes greater risk, where risk is defined as volatility of market returns. We examine the volatility of Berkshire shares later in the Introduction. Roger Lowenstein comments that Buffett's attitude toward the substance of this hypothesis could be described by: "If you are so smart, how come I'm so rich?"[3] [cited in Lowenstein, 1996, p. 307]. Perhaps Buffett was familiar with Nobel Prize–winning economist Paul Samuelson's words about another Nobel Prize–winning financial theorist Robert Merton: "When today's associate professor of security analysis is asked, 'Young man, if you're so smart, why ain't you rich,' he replies by laughing all the way to the bank or to his appointment as a high-paid consultant to Wall Street" [Samuelson, 1992]. We discuss Robert Merton in Chapter 4.

In practical application, the hypothesis would suggest keeping one's savings in a bank account or investing in an index tracking fund. However, in the 1950s, when Buffett was not widely known as an investor, such famous economists, followers of the efficient market hypothesis, as Paul Samuelson [Setton, 1998] and Armen Alchian had already invested a large amount of money in Warren Buffett's fund. For a long time, data that would have discredited the efficient market hypothesis were simply disregarded. But the facts mounted, and at some point the dikes burst. Buffett's success was one of the phenomena that contributed to the deterioration of the hypothesis' authority.

Recognition of Buffett's superior investment skill was as slow as the retreat of the hypothesis' influence. In the early 1990s, Michael Lewis, the author of *Liar's Poker* (in response to Buffett, who, as Lewis

---

2 Different forms of the hypothesis stipulate different degrees of information inclusion.
3 This is a paraphrase of Kurt Vonnegut in *Slaughterhouse-Five*: "If you're so smart, why ain't you rich?"

writes, "regularly ridicules skeptical professors with a vaguely thuggish if-you're-so-smart-why-am-I-so-rich routine"), stated that "the reason he is rich is simply that random games produce big winners," and added: "but pity the business school professor on fifty grand a year who tries to argue with a billionaire" [Lewis, 1992]. Perhaps it is the other way around. It is difficult for billionaires to argue with university professors, as it is the university professors who set the intellectual tone in the world of financial theory. A buffettologist once remarked that had Buffett decided to become a finance professor, chances are that his career would have ended long ago [Janjigian, 2008, p. 17]. Robert Merton once attempted to explain Buffett-style phenomenal success with the help of probability theory and chance. I attended one of his lectures at Harvard Business School. During the lecture, he commented: If a million analysts devote their time to predicting the movement of the stock market in any particular year, then one-half of them will guess the movement correctly. Of these, 250,000 will be right the next year; of those, 125,000 will be right the third year. In 10 years, there will be 1,953 "seers," and in 21 years, there will be just 1. In Merton's view, this analysis explains why a guru always comes forward and then that figure eventually fades away.

When an example of a long-term outperformance appears, scholars always undertake to understand its true mechanism. Financial theorist William Sharpe (a famous pupil of Armen Alchian) attempted to tweak the notion of a sigma event from probability theory into an explanation of the Buffett phenomenon. Sigma is a standard deviation from the mean. He called Buffett a "three-sigma event"—this is such a strong deviation from the likely outcome that the event is practically impossible to encounter in reality, and therefore this event should be disregarded. Eventually, Buffett was called a "five-sigma event" [Loomis, 1988] and then a "six-sigma" one. Buffett once recounted Charlie Munger's words on the subject: "As the record gets longer, it is easier to add a sigma than it is to reevaluate the theory" [cited in Buffett, 1991b].

In some sense, defining Buffett's performance as a "statistically rare occurrence" was a recognition of the uniqueness of his accomplishment. At the same time, this definition casts a skeptical light on the possibility of his achievement being the result of the application of his methodology, as the explanation emphasizes the likelihood of Buffett's success being an accident. Buffett strongly disputed this logic: "The improbable happens, five-sigma events are not five-sigma events" [cited in Kilpatrick, 2005, p. 1409]. In essence, Buffett had declared that black swans exist far earlier than Nassim Taleb developed and popularized his breakthrough idea. Buffett is a positive black swan.

Recent studies indicate that Buffett's investment success cannot be explained entirely as an accident.[4] This is one of the conclusions in, for example, Martin and Puthenpurackal [2008]. The authors place Buffett's performance of beating the market in 28 out of 31 years (from 1976 to 2006) in the 99.99th percentile. Once they incorporate the magnitude of Berkshire's outperformance, they find that the "luck" explanation is not feasible even if they take the ex post selection bias into account. The authors also find that Berkshire's performance cannot be explained by assuming that Berkshire's investment strategy is high risk. They find that Berkshire's portfolio is relatively less risky than the market. Therefore, it is possible to argue that Warren Buffett possesses an investment skill—an ability to beat the market systematically. Frazzini, Kabiller, and Pedersen analyzed Buffett's results from 1976 to 2011 [Frazzini, Kabiller, and Pedersen, 2012]. They found that the volatility of Berkshire shares was somewhat higher than that of the stock market (24.9 percent and 15.8 percent, respectively) over the period from 1976 to 2011, but the excess positive return was far greater than the excess volatility. The authors assessed the Sharpe and information ratios of Berkshire shares.[5] The higher these ratios are, the better. Berkshire Hathaway's Sharpe ratio was 0.76, which is two times higher than that of the market as a whole; however, as the authors comment, it "is very good, but not unachievably good."

Berkshire's Sharpe ratio compares positively with those of mutual funds and public companies. Among the 3,479 mutual funds that

---

4 Scholars were able to show the same thing with regard to another outstanding investor, Peter Lynch, who demonstrated abnormal returns comparable to Buffett's, but over a shorter time horizon [Marcus, 1990]. We talk about Lynch's strategy in Chapter 4.

5 The Sharpe ratio is defined as the excess return of the portfolio (above the risk-free rate) divided by the standard deviation of the portfolio return. The information ratio is a modernized version of the Sharpe ratio in which the risk-free rate is replaced by another benchmark that is closer to the portfolio (in this case, the return on a diversified stock portfolio).

existed between 1976 and 2011, Berkshire occupies the 88th position, which is in the top 2.5 percent. Among 23,390 public companies that have existed since 1926, Berkshire's position is 1,360th (within the top 7.7 percent). Berkshire has the first position among all mutual funds (140) that were "alive in 1976 and 2011." Among 598 "stocks alive in 1976 and 2011," Berkshire also has the top position. The company's information ratio rating is only slightly weaker [Frazzini, Kabiller, and Pedersen, 2012, p. 25]. These statistics suggest that Berkshire's performance is not an accident.

Buffett has also discussed the subject of the accidental as opposed to systematic nature of his investment success. In 1983, when calculations, had they been carried out, would have suggested that there was a minimal statistical chance that he had been simply flipping a coin, Buffett wrote "Superinvestors of Graham-and-Doddsville" [Buffett, 1984]. The paper was first presented at the Columbia Business School conference in honor of the fiftieth anniversary of Graham and Dodd's *Security Analysis*. The paper was then published as an article, and shortly afterward as an attachment to Benjamin Graham's *The Intelligent Investor* [Graham, 2003]. Buffett speaks ironically: Let us imagine that 225 million Americans play heads or tails every morning. Those who win earn $1 from those who lose. Only those who won the day before play in the next round, to gain $2. And so on. In 10 days, there will be only 220,000 people left, and each person will have slightly more than $10,000. In another 10 days, the number of participants will fall to 215 people, and each of those will have a million dollars. These people will lose their heads. They "will probably write books on 'How I Turned a Dollar into a Million in Twenty Days Working Thirty Seconds a Morning' and start jetting around the country attending seminars on efficient coin-flipping." But then business school professors will remark that a group of orangutans would have created the same outcome [Buffett, 1984].

When referring to business school professors, Buffett might have had in mind Michael Jensen, who spoke at the same conference and commented that if he had been studying the results of a group of "untalented" analysts throwing coins, he would have found that some of them obtained heads 2 times in a row and some 10 times. Or, Buffett might have been referring to William Sharpe, who popularized the coin-throwing analogy and compared Buffett to a five-sigma event. Buffett elaborates on why he finds the logic of coin flipping erroneous: if from among 225 million orangutans distributed roughly as the U.S. population, there emerged 215 winners after 20 days, and among those, 40 came from a particular zoo in Omaha, you would probably "ask the zoo-keeper about what he's feeding them, whether they had special exercises, what books they read. That is, if you found any really extraordinary concentrations of success, you might want to . . . identify concentrations of unusual characteristics that might be causal factors" [Buffett, 1984].

In Buffett's view, a disproportionately large number of successful coin flippers came from the intellectual village that he calls Graham-and-Doddsville. All inhabitants of this village had the same intellectual patriarch: Benjamin Graham. Graham's pupils joined different companies and invested in different stocks, but, according to Buffett, their results were such that they could not have been explained as an accident or a consequence of following signals from the patriarch. The patriarch simply created a system for how to throw coins, and each pupil developed his own method and manner of application. Also, the patriarch had died in 1976 and could no longer give investment signals to his pupils. When answering a question on whether there is commonality among Graham's apprentices, Walter Schloss, one of Graham's pupil's whose performance results Buffett refers to in his paper, remarked: "I think number one, none of us smoked. I think if I had to say it, I think we were all rational. I don't think that we got emotional when things went against us . . ." [Schloss, 1998]. Schloss describes a commonality that is of a far weaker degree than what is seen by Buffett.

Buffett lists seven people, including himself, who worked for Graham and two other followers of his theory. All of these associates and disciples delivered exceptional investment results. WJS Limited Partners, under the management of Walter J. Schloss, produced 6,679 percent overall gain for the limited partners of the fund over the period from 1956 to 1983, while the S&P 500 delivered 887 percent. Tweedy, Browne Inc., managed by Tom Knapp, delivered 936 percent for the period from 1968 to 1983, versus 238 percent. Sequoia Fund Inc., managed by William Ruane, delivered 775 percent for the period from 1970 to 1983, versus 270 percent. Pacific Partners Ltd., run by Rick Guerin, delivered 5,530 percent for the period from 1965 to 1983, versus 316 percent. Perlmeter Investments, managed by Stan Perlmeter, delivered 2,310 percent for the period from 1965 to 1983, versus 316 percent. In addition to these five investors, Buffett refers to Charlie Munger, his partner in Berkshire Hathaway, a lawyer by training, who, in Buffett's opinion, was also influenced by Graham. During the 1962–1975 period, Munger earned 500 percent, or 13.7 percent annually, when the Dow Jones rose by 97 percent (or 5 percent annually). His results were achieved despite colossal losses during 1973–1974. (Including Munger in the list of Graham's pupils is possibly far-fetched. Munger's biographer comments that "some of Graham's receipts did not impress him at all," and Munger thought that "a lot of them were just madness, they ignored relevant facts" [cited in Lowe, 2000, p. 77].) All these asset managers from the same "zoo" outperformed the market by notable margins over considerable periods of time (14 to 18 years).

As an explanation of his success, Buffett maintains that it is the result of applying the "right" investment theory. There are analysts and buffettologists who also focus on the "right" theory. However, most books on Buffett discuss only his investment principles. They simplify his approach, and the reader is assured that by following these principles, she will be as successful an investor as Buffett. An author of a book about Buffett and the value approach to investment writes: "Buffett has put together an extraordinary record by doing (in many cases) what the average investor could have done" [Boroson, 2008, p. 11]. The author of another book is confident that "investors with less-than-super investment powers can emulate his techniques and also create outstanding investment profits" [Ross, 2000, p. 3]. In this book, Buffett's investment techniques are reduced to acquiring companies with user-friendly products that capture mind share and market share, companies with high-quality management, and companies that are exceptional turn-around candidates. The author also recommends buying stocks in plummeting markets. Isn't this easier said than done?

Other interpreters of Buffett's strategy are enchanted by his idea that for successful investing, it is more important to be disciplined than to have an outstanding intellect. They conclude that since discipline is easy, anyone can achieve outstanding results.

Many authors have also written about the "secrets" of Warren Buffett's investment process. A former relation of Buffett's family coauthored *The New Buffettology*, in which the chapter titles include "Financial Information: Warren's Secrets for Using the Internet to Beat Wall Street," "Warren's Secret Formula for Getting Out at the Market Top, Stock Arbitrage," and "Warren's Best Kept Secret for Building Wealth" [Buffett and Clark, 2002].

Becoming a millionaire is not sufficient in modern times. The authors of *The New Buffettology* also wrote *The Tao of Warren Buffett: Warren Buffett's Words of Wisdom: Quotations and Interpretations to Help Guide You to Billionaire Wealth and Enlightened Business Management*" [Buffett and Clark, 2002].

Buffett may have instigated this fashion of simplifying his investment approach. He likes to highlight how easy it is to make decisions: "Stocks are simple. All you do is buy shares in a great business for less than the business is intrinsically worth, with management of the highest integrity and ability. Then you own those shares forever" [cited in Rowe, 1990]. One buffettologist argues that Buffett intentionally seeks to create an illusory impression of the investment game's ease. An example of this is one of Buffett's personal accounts of how he decided on an acquisition—the purchase, in 2005, of Forest River, a manufacturer of recreational vehicles: "On June 21, I received a two-page fax telling me—point by point—why Forest River met the acquisition criteria we set forth for . . . I have not before heard of the company, a recreational vehicular manufacturer with $1.6 billion of sales. . . . But the fax made sense, and I immediately asked for more figures. These came the next morning, and this afternoon I made . . . an offer" [cited in Janjigian, 2008, p. 109].

* * *

Intelligent selection of investment targets and skillful company valuation—the substance to which many reduce Buffett's approach—are only the part of the iceberg that is above water. This is the part of his philosophy that Buffett not only does not hide but also actively publicizes. Buffett would not have achieved his results without the "right" investment process and without his unique abilities as a business analyst. But icebergs always have much larger submerged parts. The true "secrets" may hide there, and for these, we need to enter an entirely different dimension of analysis. Importantly, the lasting duration of Buffett's success is his personal achievement. Supporting the investment process that he developed is the intellectual foundation beneath his accomplishment. Let us start by considering this intellectual core in detail.

1

Forefathers

How lucky I have been to have Phil [Fisher] and Ben
Graham write down their ideas when they had no
financial incentive to do so. I am leagues ahead
richer than I would be if I hadn't read Phil. I can't even
calculate the compound rate of return from the few
dollars spent buying his books 35 years ago.

—WARREN BUFFETT [BUFFETT, 1996]

BUFFETT OFTEN COMMENTS THAT HE HAD TWO TEACHERS. IN HIS
investment strategy, he is 85 percent a follower of Benjamin Graham
(1894–1976) and 15 percent a follower of Philip Fisher (1907–2004).
Both are famous theorists and practitioners of value investing. Graham
pioneered this approach and invented the term.

Buffett often refers to Graham's *The Intelligent Investor* [Graham,
2003],[1] which he considers to be by far the best book on investing
ever written [Buffett, 1977–2013, 1984]. In Buffett's view, the book,
originally published in 1949, explained for the first time in a way that
ordinary people could understand that the stock market does not

---

1 Buffett also recommends *Security Analysis*, which Graham coauthored with David Dodd.

operate through black magic [Schroeder, 2008, p. 126]. Buffett believes that the reason Graham's theory is rarely included in university programs is that it is not sufficiently difficult. "The business schools reward complex behavior more than simple behavior, but simple behavior is more effective" [cited in Lowe, 2007, p. 124].

Buffett also discusses two books by Fisher—the famous *Common Stocks and Uncommon Profits* [Fisher, 1996] and the less-known *Path to Wealth Through Common Stocks* [Fisher, 2007].

Benjamin Graham

> Investment is most intelligent when it is most businesslike.
>
> —BENJAMIN GRAHAM [GRAHAM, 2003, P. 523]

Buffett and Graham met when Buffett was studying at Columbia Business School, where Graham taught. Buffett turned out to be Graham's best pupil over the course of his 22-year teaching career and the only student who ever received an A+ in Graham's course [Schroeder, 2008, p. 135]. Later, Buffett worked at his teacher's fund for several years before the fund closed.

Graham had extraordinary intellectual abilities. Upon his graduation from Columbia University, he was offered teaching positions in three different departments: philosophy, English, and mathematics. His pupils were often impressed by Graham's "speed of thought": "Most people were puzzled at how he could resolve a complicated question directly after having heard it" [Kahn and Milne, 1977, p. 31]. Graham had been fascinated by the stock market from a very young age. In 1907, when he was only 11 years old, Graham started following the newspapers' financial pages in order to track the stock price of his mother's favorite company, U.S. Steel [Fridson, 1998, p. 6]. His mother, who had bought the shares on margin, lost her investment during the banking panic of that year.

As an academic career did not promise a large income, Graham joined a brokerage company on Wall Street after his graduation in 1914. At the time, the securities listed on securities markets were primarily bonds, which Graham initially focused on. Gradually his interest shifted toward stocks, which were in relatively limited supply, with most listed companies being railroads. Shares were regarded rather the way junk bonds are today: as low-grade securities with a high default risk, the potential for great return, and, as a result, high volatility. One of the primary ways of making money on stocks was to manipulate the market by spreading rumors. Manipulation was not outlawed until 1934, several years after the beginning of the Great Depression. Studies that analyzed relative returns on stocks, as opposed to bonds, over long periods of time had yet to be conducted—the first study of this kind is considered to be *Common Stocks as Long-Term Investments* by Edgar Lawrence Smith, who argued that stocks outperformed bonds over the long term.[2] This study was published in 1924, 5 years before the peak of the economic bubble of the 1920s.

Graham began by looking for shares that formally appeared to be cheap. He then made a misjudgment: he distributed a detailed statistical analysis of listed tire and rubber stocks, showing that the most underpriced shares appeared to be those of Ajax Tire. Shortly after the report's publication, the company declared bankruptcy [Kahn and Milne, 1977, p. 7]. Graham remembers: "Ajax Tire flourished only a little while and then declined into bankruptcy" [Graham, 1996]. Perhaps this was one of the experiences that pushed him to contemplate not only statistical but also qualitative analysis of stocks.

In 1927, Graham started teaching his pioneering course on security analysis at his alma mater. Such courses had never been offered before. By this time, Graham was a relatively well-known financial analyst. He had been managing clients' money for a number of years, and the stock market was booming. His course attracted 150 students. David Dodd, Graham's future coauthor, was among the students. The next year, even more students took the course, with many of them taking it for the second time. Graham used examples of real companies to illustrate his theory, and although he emphasized that he was not giving trading

2 Smith's book was positively reviewed by John Maynard Keynes. It became a bestseller. According to a Nobel Prize–winning economist Robert Shiller, Irving Fisher (a great economist and a contemporary of Smith's) thought that the bull market of the 1920s had been influenced by Smith's ideas, which had become popular among the wider investing public [Shiller, 2005, p. 196].

recommendations, many students bought the shares of the companies he discussed and earned considerable returns. History is silent on what eventually became of those recommendations or whether the positive market atmosphere prior to the crisis of 1929 contributed to those returns. Graham commented in his memoirs that, in his view, to a large degree it was the market that delivered the results.

Graham created his first fund in 1923. This fund, in Buffett's opinion, was the first hedge fund in the history of the United States [Tavakoli, 2009, p. 13]. The fund existed until 1925. Investors earned high returns against the background of strong market performance.

In 1926, Graham created a new fund, which remained in operation until 1936. From 1926 to 1935 Graham's fund outperformed the market only insignificantly: he achieved an average annual return of 6 percent when the S&P delivered 5.8 percent [Kahn and Milne, 1977, p. 42].

Graham's track record during the Great Depression is interesting. In 1929, he was invested in stocks, and his positions were riskier than those he had held a few years earlier. In 1929, his fund lost 20 percent. In 1930, the losses were an additional 50 percent; in 1931, they were 16 percent; and in 1932, they were 3 percent. Overall, the fund's holdings fell by 70 percent from their peak. During these years, all fund managers had comparable losses. Despite these huge declines, however, Graham was able to keep his fund alive at a time when few asset managers succeeded in remaining in operation. Most managers, working with borrowed capital, were forced to sell positions in falling markets to cover margin calls. Graham recouped his losses by 1935 [Kahn and Milne, 1977, pp. 18, 22, 42].

In 1936 Graham's fund was converted into a corporation (Graham-Newman Corporation) because of tax considerations. The corporation continued to function until 1956. When analysts discuss Graham's results, they are generally referring to the corporation's performance. During the 1930s to 1950s, Graham seemed to be regarded as one of the most famous and successful money managers. From 1936 to 1945 the annual percentage gain to stockholders averaged 17.6 percent as opposed to 10.1 percent for the S&P [Graham, 1946]. From 1945 to 1956 Graham delivered 17.4 percent on average, excluding GEICO. This return was slightly lower than that of the S&P at 18.4 percent [Kahn and

Milne, 1977, p. 43]. In the same source ([Kahn and Milne, 1977, p. 45]) we find the calculation of the returns of Graham-Newman Partnership with GEICO's[3] performance included for the period of 1948–1976. The partnership delivered 11.4 percent a year, when the S&P delivered 7.1 percent; Irvin Kahn assumed for this calculation that after the Graham-Newman partnership's liquidation in 1956 the funds were reinvested in S&P [Kahn and Milne, 1977, p. 46]. Probably, it is these data that are being referred to by some analysts, for instance Alice Schroeder, when they comment that Graham beat the market by at least 3 percentage points each year, despite having a portfolio with considerably lower risk than that of the market [Schroeder, 2008, p. 143]. Graham's accomplishment was repeated by other managers, as shown in Table 1.1, who achieved their returns over periods, occurring at various times, which means that Graham's performance over the 1930s to 1950s was repeated in different more contemporary economic climates. Buffett surpassed his guru very quickly.

Let us consider Graham's investment philosophy and its relationship to Buffett's in detail. Graham covers all aspects of the investment process, including the selection of an investment target and the management of acquired holdings. His philosophy comprises analytical and behavioral principles that aim to address comprehensively the full range of issues facing any investor.

First, it is important to note that Graham recommends a business-style approach to investment. He writes: "Investment is most intelligent when it is most businesslike" [Graham, 2003, p. 523]. In his view, a corporate security is an ownership interest in a business; if a person seeks to benefit from an investment in that security, she is entering into a business venture of her own, and if she is to have any chance of success, this venture must be run with accepted business principles in mind [Graham, 2003, p. 523].

---

3 Graham had to comply with the regulatory framework that prohibited high ownership concentration in the insurance industry. Therefore, he distributed some of the fund's holdings—shares in the insurance company GEICO—directly to his investors. The fund returned 17 percent, and those investors who did not sell their GEICO shares immediately after the distribution but continued to hold them eventually earned 28 percent.

TABLE 1.1 Returns of selected asset managers who invested in stocks (in alphabetic order).

Asset manager	Fund	Years (for the purpose of calculation)	Annualized return for the period	S&P annualized return (with dividends) for the period*	Difference
Phil Carret	Pioneer Fund	1928–1982[†]	12.9%	9%	2.9%
Mario Gabelli	GAMCO	1977–2011	16.3%[‡]	10.6%	5.7%
Peter Lynch	Magellan (Fidelity group)	1977–1990	29.2%	15.1%[§]	14.1%
John Neff	Windsor Fund	1964–1995	13.7%[**]	10.6%	3.1%
Walter Schloss	Walter and Edwin Schloss Associates	1956–2000	15.7%[††]	11.2%	4.5%
John Templeton	John Templeton Growth Fund (Class A shares)	1954–1992	14.5%[‡‡]	11.7%	2.8%

* Annual return on S&P, including dividends, calculated by the author for comparison with each investor's performance with the exception of Neff and Schloss. The calculator used: http://dqydj.net/sp-500-return-calculator/.
† Calculated by the author on the basis of the observation that $10,000 invested in Pioneer in 1928 grew to $8 million by 1982. This statistic is mentioned, for instance, in the description of a book by Carret.
‡ Wisner, 2012.
§ Calculated by the author on the basis of data provided by Lynch, according to whom $1,000 invested in May 1977 grew to $28,000 by May 1990 [Lynch. Interview on PBS].
** Neff, 1999, p. 247.
†† Schloss, 2003, p. 95.
‡‡ http://www.sirjohntempleton.org.

Graham contrasts stock in a business with a bond; the stock is a residual claim against the business, whereas the bond is geared toward the collection of interest payments. As we discussed, when Graham was developing his ideas, stocks were perceived as being equivalent to junk bonds. Graham's emphasis on seeing a share of stock as part of a business was, in a certain sense, conceptually novel. Buffett has viewed this idea of a businesslike approach to investing as the most important of all the principles that Graham laid out in *The Intelligent Investor* [Buffett, 1977–2013, 1984]. Well-known aphorisms from Buffett reflect a similar credo: "I am a better investor because I am a businessman, and a better businessman because I am an investor" [cited in Lenzner, 1993]; "When we invest in stocks, we invest in businesses" [cited in Lowe, 2007, p. 129]; and "If the business does well, the stock eventually follows" [cited in Mallory, 1994]. These sayings are very Grahamlike in style. Buffett considers himself first and foremost a business analyst: "When investing, we view ourselves as business analysts—not as market analysts, not as macroeconomic analysts, and not even as security analysts" [Buffett, 1977–2013, 1987].

Graham proposes a number of general investment principles. We could view "Know what you are doing, know your business" [Graham, 2003, p. 523] as the first of these principles. Graham advises that attaining this awareness is helped by distinguishing between speculation (a purchase with the expectation that the price of the asset will rise) and investment (a purchase based on an understanding of the business and its value). As another principle, Graham recommends a conservative approach. He suggests that it is advisable to purchase stock in an operation only if a reliable calculation demonstrates that the venture has a good chance of returning a reasonable profit. In Graham's words, it is better to keep away from ventures "in which you have little to gain and much to lose." Decisions must be based on sound calculations, not on optimistic feelings. Investors must seek reliable evidence that they are not risking a substantial part of their principal, particularly if their return is limited [Graham, 2003, p. 523]. The requirement of close personal supervision over the business could be regarded as yet another of these principles. Graham recommends that an investor not let anyone run his business unless he is able to monitor the manager's performance with adequate care and understanding, and unless he has specific reasons to trust the manager's integrity and ability [Graham, 2003, p. 523]. The last idea in this group emphasizes having an independent mindset and a strong character. Graham recommends trusting one's knowledge and experience and having the courage to act on one's judgment, even if others differ in their opinion. "You are neither right nor wrong because the crowd disagrees with you. You are right because your data and reasoning are right" [Graham, 2003, p. 524].

Buffett follows all these recommendations. He often comments that he never invests in businesses that he does not understand. One of his formal criteria is what he regards as the simplicity of the business. Buffett seeks to avoid risk and may, for instance, invest in convertible bonds rather than stock if certain risks are present. He maintains a consistent approach toward choosing managers for companies that he owns, and personal integrity is one of his prime considerations. Buffett's stance on personnel has attracted journalistic attention. The title of an article about him succinctly describes the substance of Buffett's views: "Warren Buffett's Idea of Heaven: 'I Don't Have to Work with People I Don't Like'" [Lenzner, 1993]. Trust in his own judgment is part of Buffett's approach— his "idea of a group decision is to look in the mirror" [cited in Lowe, 2007, p. 149].

In another set of principles, Graham focuses specifically on the process of selecting the investment target. Selection may be approached in two different ways: predictive and protective, or conservative [Graham, 2003, p. 364]. According to Graham: "Those who emphasize prediction will endeavor to anticipate fairly accurately just what the company will accomplish in future years—in particular whether earnings will show pronounced and persistent growth." Those who emphasize protection aim to make sure that the "indicated present value" is greater than the market price by a "substantial margin" that could absorb future negative developments [Graham, 2003, pp. 364–365]. The predictive approach may be viewed as qualitative, since it focuses on future prospects, management, and other nonmeasurable but nevertheless important factors. The protective approach may be described as quantitative or statistical, since it emphasizes the relationships between selling price and earnings, assets, dividends, and other measurable factors [Graham, 2003, p. 365].

Owing to his conservatism, in practice, Graham, when selecting companies for investment, preferred not to analyze potential targets qualitatively, or, as he thought, subjectively. He followed the quantitative approach and acted in a highly formalized manner. He always looked for quantitatively undervalued shares. In return for his investment, Graham wanted to receive "value in concrete, demonstrable terms" and did not consider "prospects and promises of the future as compensation for a lack of sufficient value in hand" [Graham, 2003, p. 365]. As Graham's intellectual heir, Buffett also does not invest in "a lemonade stand—with potential, of course, to grow into the next Microsoft" [Buffett, 1977–2013, 1995]. "If a company has a lousy track record, but a very bright future, we will miss the opportunity" [Berkshire Hathaway Annual Shareholders' Meeting, 1995].

In the 1934 edition of *Security Analysis* Graham and Dodd formulated the concept of the intrinsic value of a stock. They explain that the intrinsic value may be different from the "price," which, in their view, is influenced by "artificial manipulations" and "psychological excesses." Discounting had not been developed at that time, and the authors defined intrinsic value as "value justified by the facts, i.e. the assets, earnings, dividends, definite prospects" [Graham and Dodd, 2009, p. 64]. John Williams introduced the ideas of discounting and present value in 1938 [Williams, 1938]. In *The Intelligent Investor*, first published in 1949, Graham uses these concepts. Importantly, Graham's view of the present value is different from the conventional understanding of it that we are used to, and we discuss this later in the chapter.

The central component of Graham's protective quantitative approach to the selection of an investment target is the margin of safety by which the "indicated present value" must be higher than the market price. Only investments with this margin of safety will deliver the required returns, and an investment lacks an adequate margin of safety "when too large a portion of the price must depend on ever-increasing earnings in the future" [Graham, 2003, p. 349]. Let us examine the idea of the margin of safety in greater detail. In order to ensure a sufficient margin of safety, the earnings/price ratio should be at least as high as the current high-grade bond interest rate[4] [Graham, 2003, p. 350]. This would mean that the price/earnings ratio—the earnings/price ratio inverted—would be, at a minimum, 1 divided by the high-grade bond rate.[5] According to the Gordon model,[6] for a company whose annual profit growth is constant the share price can be expressed by the equation: $P = E/(r - g)$, where P — share price, E — net profit per share, r — discount rate, and g — expected profit growth rate. (We will set aside the dividend policy for the moment and assume that all profit is either paid out as dividends or reinvested at r percent—the rate of return required by the investor. In this case, the distinction between dividends and reinvestment has no impact on share valuation.) Therefore, $P/E = 1/(r - g)$ or $E/P = r - g$. Graham's requirement ($E/P > r_f$) may be expressed as $r - g > r_f$, where $r_f =$ the risk-free rate (return on short-term government bonds), or as $r > r_f + g$. The higher the expected growth rate, the greater the magnitude by which the discount rate (used to value the shares) must be higher than the risk-free rate. In practice, to value the future cash flow, Graham recommended using the risk-free rate r_f, setting the expected growth rate at nearly zero ($g = 0$)—a very conservative expectation (perhaps explained by long periods of low growth during Graham's lifetime)—and applying an additional deduction.

In modern literature, Graham's margin of safety is sometimes viewed as a purchase at a discount to fair value (for example, see *Margin of Safety: Risk-Averse Value Investing Strategies for the Thoughtful Investor* [Klarman, 1991] or *The Little Book of Value Investing* [Browne, 2006]). This reading reflects the spirit of Graham's theoretical and practical approach. At the same time it is possible to propose an alternative interpretation. Graham's margin of safety rule recommends purchasing shares at a price below the level achieved by discounting the company's cash flow at the risk-free rate (in Graham's low- or zero-growth world). Stocks are riskier instruments than bonds, and therefore the returns that they deliver must

4 This is a recommendation for an amateur investor. Graham sets his personal bar higher: E/P must be twice as good as the return on government bonds [Kahn and Milne, 1977, p. 45]. If the return on bonds is 5 percent, then Graham's coefficient must be 10 percent.
5 One divided by the high-grade bond rate would probably result in a P/E that is quite high. For instance, $1/0.05 = 20$. Graham's personal bar of E/P that is twice as good as the high-grade bond rate would result in a P/E of 10.
6 Although this framework already existed in Graham's time, he did not appear to discuss the margin of safety principle in this light.

be greater than the risk-free rate, and their fair price must be lower than the price calculated using the risk-free rate. Graham's price is not necessarily lower than fair value, but simply lower than a possibly optimistic valuation that results from using the risk-free rate.

A contemporary financial analyst is likely to regard Graham's approach as relatively simplistic. Graham did not formally evaluate the risk levels associated with assets. He applied a deduction intuitively. The author of *The Intelligent Investor* does not discuss the size of this deduction and whether it must be tied to the specifics of the asset. In addition to arguing that the earnings/price ratio must be higher than the high-grade bond rate (or the price/earnings ratio must be lower than 1 divided by the high-grade bond rate), Graham discusses reasonable share values in terms of multipliers. The P/E ratio that Graham viewed as satisfactory for investment was not as low as one might expect in light of the importance that Graham placed on a low cost of acquisition. Graham recommends paying no more than 15 times earnings for good companies. It is possible to satisfy this criterion, although not necessarily in any given year. According to Robert Shiller, the average P/E throughout the history of the U.S. stock market since 1871 equals 14.5. In addition, Graham recommends to calculate the P/E ratio as based on average profits over the last three years.[7] Shares also must have a moderate price/book value (P/BV) ratio (not exceeding 1.5;[8] or, alternatively, P/E multiplied by P/BV should not exceed 22.5) [Graham, 2003, pp. 348–349].

---

7   Later behavioral economists observed that investors, when evaluating company financial results (in particular, the rate of growth), assign greater weights to the more recent years than to the earlier years. In addition, Graham invites investors to treat the current profits of cyclical companies particularly carefully. He believed that investors suffered their chief losses when buying "low-quality securities at times of favorable business conditions"—they "view the current good earnings as equivalent to 'earning power' and assume that prosperity is synonymous with safety" [Graham, 2003, p. 516].

8   This indicates that Graham does not like companies whose business model is based on intangible assets. When Graham was very young, during the 1910s, he worked at a brokerage firm on Wall Street, and Computing-Tabulating-Recording Company attracted his attention. The company produced a tabulating machine, developed by Herman Hollerith, that allowed mass processing of statistical data. Graham believed that the company was unrecognized by the market and that its shares were undervalued as a result. When he brought the investment idea to his management's attention, it was turned down. Graham's superiors examined the company's balance sheet and concluded that the assets lacked substance, as the company did not have many tangible assets. Graham was advised not to bring forward proposals of this kind in future. He followed this advice and never bought shares of the company. The company later became known as International Business Machines (IBM), and many investors who owned its shares eventually prospered [Fridson, 1998, p. 64].

When valuing shares, Buffett prefers being old-fashioned and uses Graham's approach. He often admits that he uses the bond rate—the risk-free rate—as his discount rate, although he argues that his investments, such as Coca-Cola, are not too different from risk-free,[9] particularly, over the long term. Like Graham, Buffett never discusses the precise levels of his margin of safety or his growth-rate assumptions. He also defines his margin of safety indirectly. For a long time, Buffett set a requirement that the annual return must be no less than 15 percent; subsequently, the requirement was lowered to 10 percent, and it is now set at 9 percent a year or beating the market by five percentage points a year, whichever is less [Schroeder, 2008, p. 306]. These benchmarks are far tougher than the levels achieved by discounting with the risk-free rate.

Buffett does not use the popular capital asset pricing model (CAPM). This model did not exist during Graham's times. It is a relatively modern development in risk assessment methodology that attempts to evaluate the risk premium required for a stock investment mathematically. The higher the risk, the higher the discount rate. The CAPM defines the return required for an investment as the sum of the risk-free rate and, multiplied by the beta coefficient, the difference between the return on the market as a whole and the risk-free rate, where the beta coefficient reflects the volatility of the stock: $r = r_f + \beta(r_m - r_f)$. Discounting cashflows with this rate is different in methodology from obtaining the present value by discounting with the risk-free rate and applying an intuitive deduction in Graham's universe.

Buffett has no interest in the CAPM, but possibly not because of its complexity. It is likely that Buffett disagrees with the model's assumptions. The CAPM describes the risk level associated with an asset as a function of its price fluctuation (through the beta coefficient). In Buffett's view, for an investor who is purchasing shares for a very long holding period or "forever," the risk does not lie in the market price volatility. Buffett believes that investment risks and, therefore, investment mistakes are driven by lack of knowledge about the specific company or the industry as a whole. He does not trust market valuations, and short-term views of the market are of no concern to him.

9 We will discuss the company and to what extent it is risk-free in Chapter 2.

Another critical test of share value validity for Graham is what this share would be worth to a private owner—would a private investor pay the same price as the market? (Buffett voiced this idea in his letters to investors throughout the 1960s.) This framework is fully in agreement with the idea that buying stocks must be viewed as acquiring a share in the underlying business. Finding the right answer to this question (the value of a business to a private buyer) is not easy; it will be necessary to perform a valuation, and a heuristic approach will be unavoidable. Current statistics on acquisitions indicate that, on average, companies are purchased at a premium to their market price, so it is arguable that the value of a company to a private owner is higher than the company's market capitalization.

In addition to margin of safety and a share's worth to a private owner, Graham discusses other specific parameters that make a company an attractive investment target. The company must be relatively large (have a present-day value of more than $2 billion in revenue, as calculated by the author). It must have a sufficiently strong financial position (current assets must be at least twice as large as current liabilities, and long-term debt must not exceed the net current assets or working capital). The company must have been profitable during the previous 10 years and have been paying dividends for 20 years.[10] Profit must have risen by at least a third over the previous last 10-year period (this is slightly less than 3 percent annually).[11] These criteria indicate that although Graham preferred a quantitative approach, nevertheless, he did not reduce it to locating just *any* undervalued company.

Perhaps Graham's method was a natural response to the economic circumstances of the day. The general inexpensiveness of stocks during the 1930s to 1950s was sustained by the memories of the Great Depression and the humongous losses that stock prices had suffered in 1929–1932, when stock indexes fell by approximately 90 percent

---

10 It seems to be contradictory to set the profitability history requirement at 10 years, when the dividend history must be 20 years. It is difficult, although far from impossible, to pay dividends from negative profits.
11 Graham formulated this principle in a period when there was practically no inflation. He talks about the profit growth in real terms.

(and those who had invested using high leverage lost everything).[12] The capital markets were also relatively young. Inefficiencies in the dissemination of financial information resulted in opportunities being overlooked by investors. However, even though undervalued companies, to some of which Graham and his students referred as "cigar butts," were in ample supply, trawling for them systematically was not a trivial task. Accessing information and analyzing it demanded greater resources in the predigital era.

Gradually it began to seem that the opportunities for application of Graham's strict approach were growing more limited. This may have been driven by several factors. First, on average the stocks were no longer as cheap. The transition from one generation of investors to another led to a growth in stock market values. Second, Graham's theory was becoming more popular, and its followers were searching for and buying undervalued shares—"Graham-Doddsville" was becoming overpopulated. Buffett pointed out that the "disadvantage" of Ben Graham's approach was that it was such a well-known method that investors had already picked up most of the things that met the criteria [Buffett and Jaffe, 1987]. (Probably the same can be said about Warren Buffett's method today.) Third, continual tightening of the information disclosure requirements for public companies has also helped in making undervalued stocks more apparent to investors. Graham remembers an example of investing in a spin-off of Standard Oil, Northern Pipeline, whose balance sheet contained bonds that were 12 times greater in value than the annual revenue of the company. These data were withheld from investors. Graham found out about the value of the bonds only after he had visited Washington and researched the files of the Interstate Commerce Commission. Nobody had thought of doing this before him [Graham, 1996, Chapter 11]. In modern times, computers, analyzing financial databases and information on the securities exchanges, leave practically no opportunities for a mechanical search for "cheap" stocks. Information about stocks is available to many investors almost immediately. Today, if a stock

---

12 One of the reasons for Graham's conservatism was that he regarded the stock market as a zero-sum game; however, a small, innovative company that delivered great growth would add value to the market as a whole.

seems undervalued in terms of multipliers, it is likely that the price is a reflection of the market's view of the company's prospects. The market may be mistaken, of course, or there may be liquidity difficulties.

Joel Greenblatt[13] found that by the middle of the 1990s, strongly undervalued stocks had simply disappeared [Greenblatt, 1997, p. 82], although he made this assessment at a time when the market had already been diagnosed as being in a state of a bubble, which subsequently crashed in 2000. In the opinion of a buffettologist, the era of cigar butt–style investing in the United States came to an end in the 1970s [Calandro, 2009, p. 4] or even earlier. A pupil of Graham, Walter Schloss, who regarded as "cigar butts" working capital stocks, or shares that trade at a price below the working capital a share, remarked that these stocks vanished by the end of the 1950s ["The Money Man," 1973].

In the last edition of *The Intelligent Investor* published during his lifetime, in 1973, Graham acknowledged that locating undervalued shares had become extremely difficult: "The investor would do well to recognize . . . that the old package of good profit possibilities combined with small ultimate risk is no longer available to him" [Graham, 2003, p. 516]. Toward the end of his life, Graham argued that even a genius would not be able to make money by studying company financial reports better and more deeply than his competitors. All analysts study reports.[14] Possibly this position was extreme. After all, it was a Wall Street analyst who examined the Enron reports and noticed irregularities. This analyst's comments during a conference call on Enron's financial results triggered the collapse of the company.

Despite the disappearance of volumes of unjustifiably cheap stocks, interestingly, the scholars of finance observed that investing in *relatively*

---

13 Joel Greenblatt (born 1957) is a value investor and a theorist of value investing. Practically occupying Graham's chair, he teaches value investing at Columbia Business School. His book *You Can Be a Stock Market Genius* [1997] is a brilliant work and a must-read on value investing. Greenblatt shows that in modern times, value investing cannot be reduced to the relatively simple ideas discussed by Buffett. Delivering great returns through value investing is not as simple as it seems.

14 Martin Fridson finds that Graham was the pioneer of this approach. He was one of the first to study reports of U.S. Steel (his mother's favorite company, which he had followed as a child), even before the start of his career on Wall Street. He "uncovered idle assets that could be distributed to shareholders. He uncovered the level of subsidiaries unconsolidated earnings which were the subject of speculation to other investors" [Fridson, 1998, p. 185].

cheaper shares still remains a strategy that can earn excess returns. There is a notable body of research showing that investing in stocks with lower P/BV (price to book value), P/E (price to earnings), P/C (price to cash flow) multipliers, and higher DIV/P (dividend yield), the so-called value stocks, delivers higher return than investing in stocks with high P/BV, P/E, P/C multipliers and low-dividend yield, otherwise known as the glamour stocks. The earlier studies of this kind were conducted over the 1970s and 1980s ([Basu, 1977], [Oppenheimer, 1984], and [Oppenheimer, 1986]); they examined the stock returns from the end of the 1950s to the first half of the 1980s.

Later research, covering the second half of the 1980s and the 1990s, produced similar results. For example, Lakonishok and colleagues provide evidence that market value strategies yield higher returns on the American market because these strategies exploit the mistakes of the typical investor and not because these strategies are fundamentally riskier [Lakonishok, Shleifer, and Vyshny, 1994]. Lakonishok in the article coauthored with other scholars finds that investing in value stocks defined as shares with low P/BV multipliers generates abnormal returns compared to investing in glamour stocks, or shares with high P/BV [Chan, Jegadeesh, and Lakonishok, 1995]. The authors of "Good News for Value Stocks" find that a significant portion of the return difference between value and glamour stocks is attributable to earnings surprises that are systematically more positive for value stocks [LaPorta, Lakonishok, Shleifer, and Vyshny, 1997].

This effect has been observed on other markets also. Michael Keppler found it present for 18 countries included in the Morgan Stanley Capital International National Equity Indexes (Australia, Austria, Belgium, Canada, Denmark, France, Germany, Hong Kong, Italy, Japan, The Netherlands, Norway, Singapore/Malaysia, Spain, Sweden, Switzerland, the United Kindom, the United States) [Keppler, 1991a and 1991b]. Jun Caj finds that in general on the Tokyo exchange value stocks listed outperformed glamour stocks by between 6 and 12 percent a year for the five years after portfolio formation [Caj, 1997]. Comprehensive studies covering 1961 to 1998 ([Levis, 1989a and 1989b], [Gregory, Harris, and Michou, 2001]) confirm that value stocks listed on the British market also outperform glamour stocks. The authors of "International Value and

Growth Stocks Returns" find excess returns when investing in value shares in France, Germany, Switzerland, the United Kingdom, Japan, and the United States [Capaul, Rowley, and Sharpe, 1993]. It is interesting to note that some explorations found that the best return is achieved not through investing in shares in the cheapest decile, but in the second-cheapest decile [Fluck, Malkiel, and Quant, 1997]. Perhaps the cheapest decile contains shares that are nearing bankruptcy and are not just undervalued shares.

Further details on multipliers and time periods in these studies are discussed in the Appendix. In more recent years the methodology of this area of research has grown considerably more advanced. Scholars study more specific effects.

Faithful to his teacher, Buffett started his career as an independent investor and money manager by looking for cigar butts. Over a lengthy period, he followed the price criteria set out by Graham in his investment decisions. Eventually, however, Buffett began to contemplate the handicaps associated with the method. At some point he commented: "You see this cigar butt down there, it's soggy and terrible, but there's one puff left, and it's free." That's what Berkshire was when Buffett, paying less than the working capital, bought it, "but it was a terrible, terrible mistake" [Schlender, Buffett, and Gates, 1998]. Although he may have moved away from buying the cigar butts, and his experience has shown that cherry-picking from more expensive stocks produces the best results, Buffett continues to maintain that the purchase price must be so low that the acquisition will remain profitable even if the sales prospects are poor.

In the early 1970s, Buffett moved toward a more qualitative approach to investing. He acquired experience through discussing ideas and investing jointly with Charlie Munger, who has never been as devoted an admirer of Graham as Buffett. This approach was conceptually new. Its essence is expressed in one of Buffett's succinct aphorisms: "It's far better to buy a wonderful company at a fair price than a fair company at a wonderful price" [Buffett, 1977–2013, 1989]. This is different from Graham's ideas; for Graham, shares are either cheap or expensive, not good or bad, and buying a good business may be a bad investment if it is acquired at a high price. Walter Schloss explained that Graham advised to buy stocks as if they were groceries, not perfume. Buffett's later investments in Coca-Cola or Gillette were purchases of perfume stocks [Schloss, 1998].

The breakthrough was Buffett's acquisition in 1972 of See's Candies, a company producing premium chocolate and running a chain of stores in California. Munger reminisces that See's Candies was purchased at a premium to book value and the acquisition was successful, while the department store Hochschild, Kohn & Co.[15] was bought at a discount to both book and liquidation values and the purchase failed. "Those two things together helped shift our thinking to the idea of paying higher prices for better businesses" [cited in Lowe, 2000, p. 132]. See's Candies was purchased at a price that was three times greater than the book value of net assets, but at only six times annual profits—in today's terms, a very modest price. However, it is important to take into account the unfavorable macroeconomic situation of the time.

Robert Miles, author of *The Warren Buffett CEO: Secrets from the Berkshire Hathaway Managers*, evaluated See's financial performance in 1999 (at the time Miles was writing his book). The company earned pretax profit of $75 million a year. This was three times its purchase price. Sales rose from $31 million in 1972 to $306 million in 1999. In 1999, See's valuation, at 5 times sales and 30 times earnings (comparable to the multiples for a publicly traded peer), would have amounted to a conservative market capitalization of $1.5 billion. This represents nearly an 18 percent annual return on investment. See's Candies delivered more than $900 million in pretax earnings over the 28 years after the purchase. This return was made on an original capital base of $7 million. The business retained only $71 million for capital investment. The company was earning 100 percent on capital each year [Miles, 2002, p. 258]. When we are valuing a business, it is possible to assess the value with respect to the capital base. Miles is probably referring to the net book value of assets. If we are considering the value of a business from the point of view of shareholders, then it is more insightful to value the business with respect to the purchase price. It was more than three times higher than the capital base.

Valuing a company at 30 times the annual profit and 5 times sales is not necessarily conservative, even for a growing company. For comparison, according to well-known valuation theorist Aswat Damodaran, at

15 We briefly discuss this purchase in Chapter 3.

the start of 2014, the P/E of the American specialty retail sector equaled 25 and the price/sales ratio (P/S) was 0.83 [www.damodaran.com]. The peer valuations that Miles used were current for 1999, while that year the stock market reached a peak. According to Robert Shiller, in that year, the P/E of the S&P 500 fluctuated between 40 and 44,[16] while the historical average is only about 14.5, as we discussed. The market was overvalued by three times (the old economy companies were not overvalued by as much, but they were also overvalued). As a result of inflation from 1972 to 1999, money had been devalued by approximately four times. By 1999, See's annual revenue had grown to only $124 million in 1972 dollars. Taking inflation into account and applying a more conservative (Graham's) P/E multiplier of 15 leads to a valuation of $187 million—still a very impressive result, given the acquisition price of $25 million.

Graham also started moving toward investing in shares with growth potential. He felt that this style of investing was not entirely in contradiction with his margin of safety principle. When calculating the margin of safety, the growth stock buyer relies on an expected earning power that is greater than the average shown in the past. At some point, Graham made the observation that diligent evaluation of the future was becoming a trend in security analysis. He remarked that there was no reason to think that carefully estimated future earnings should be a less reliable basis than the record of the past. Thus, the growth stock approach may supply a reasonable margin of safety "provided the calculation of the future is conservatively made, and provided it shows a satisfactory margin in relation to the price paid" [Graham, 2003, p. 517].

Discussing factors that may result in a share price rise, Graham mentions "investor expectations" with regard to profit growth. The idea of expectations is important, as it allows a positive gap between share prices and fair valuations: "A considerable momentum is attached to those companies that combine the virtues of great size, an excellent past record of earnings, the public's expectation of continued earnings growth in the future, and strong market action over many past years" [Graham, 2003, p. 390].

16 Shiller calculates P/E for profits averaged over 20 years. See monthly data on http://www. multpl.com.

Nevertheless, Graham is not entirely a supporter of growth investing. First, he focuses his attention on undervalued shares. Second, Graham believes that the core investment principles of a conservative investor must concentrate on the past and present position of the company. He only touches upon the idea that a company that has been growing and showing good financial results may also continue growing in the future. Graham never formulates requirements for valuing growth potential. Also, he discusses a relatively moderate rate of historical growth, not the rates looked for by the followers of growth investing. The ideal target for investment, in Graham's view, remains a large, stable, and slowly growing company, not a small, agile rising star.

According to Walter Schloss, Graham focused on doubling the money; he emphasized making money but not a lot of money [Rabinovich, 2003]. Exiting investments once they have doubled in value is a sign that the investor avoids growth shares. Approximately in 1947 one of the analysts, working in Graham's fund, proposed to invest in The Haloid Photographic Company—the future Xerox, which was already nearing its first copying machine. Even though the stock traded at a price only a little higher than what it was during the time of the Great Depression, Graham turned down the idea: "It is not our kind of stock" [cited in Schloss, 1998]. Graham did not have a time horizon in mind when investing but preferred to sell his stocks once they reached a certain level. Buffett differs from his teacher in this respect and seeks to own companies "forever," while Graham buys low and sells high. We discuss Buffett's views on the investment horizon in greater detail in Chapter 3.

The pioneer of growth investing philosophy, Philip Fisher, is regarded as the second "intellectual parent" of Warren Buffett. Let us discuss the companies that he considers attractive.

Philip Fisher

> The growth stocks . . . seem to show gains in value in the hundreds of per cent each decade.
>
> —PHILIP FISHER [FISHER, 1996, P. 52]

Like Graham, Philip Fisher was a well-known fund manager. Born in 1907, he began his investment career as an analyst in 1928, without completing his studies at Stanford University. Although Fisher started his own investment business in 1931, he made the transition to large-scale investing only in the 1950s. He remained active until 1999. There are many accounts of the great returns he delivered for his investors throughout his 70-year career, but formal public information about his performance is limited to reports of specific successful investments. Fisher, like Graham, was interested in writing. His bestselling book *Common Stocks and Uncommon Profits*, first published in 1958, has not lost its relevance today. Like Graham, he taught at his alma mater—in his case, Stanford University.

Buffett tells us that he started contemplating Fisher's ideas in the beginning of the 1960s, when he was reading Fisher's books. In Buffett's view, Fisher was "one of the first, if not the first, to develop the thesis that growth stocks have identifiable characteristics that make them different from ordinary stocks" [Buffett and Jaffe, 1987]. Investment in growth stocks was Fisher's solution to the circumstances in which Graham's approach had been exhausted. Interestingly, Fisher also argued that his method, aside from being a natural progression from the older investment techniques, would have delivered better returns even in the earlier days, when older systems still generated successful investments. For instance, in the nineteenth century and the early part of the twentieth century, when the inherent instability of financial systems caused recurring booms and busts,[17] one of the common investment policies was betting on the business cycle, or buying stocks during bad times and selling them during good ones. As Fisher observed, this method created fortunes. However, he maintained that those who used a different approach made far more money and took far less risk. "Even in those earlier times, finding the really outstanding companies and staying with them through all the fluctuations of a gyrating market proved far more profitable to far more people than did the more colourful practice of trying to buy them cheap and sell them dear" [Fisher, 1996, p. 7].

Fisher explains the advantage of investing in high-quality growth companies. He finds that over a sufficient time, for example, five years,

---

17 Discussions about the causes of recurring booms and busts and about the role of the regulatory framework in mitigating them are ongoing; however, the frequency of financial crises fell considerably during Fisher's lifetime—the creation of the Federal Reserve in the early twentieth century was an important factor that altered the landscape of the financial system.

the profit that even the most skilled statistical bargain hunter will create will be only a small proportion of the profit generated by an investor who is reasonably evaluating well-managed growth companies. Fisher believes that this notion holds true even when losses sustained by the growth stock investor on ventures that did not turn out as expected and losses sustained by the bargain hunter on bargains that did not deliver are taken into account. "The reason why the growth stocks do so much better is that they seem to show gains in value in the hundreds of per cent each decade. In contrast, it is an unusual bargain that is as much as 50 per cent undervalued" [Fisher, 1996, p. 52].

Fisher cites another reason why he finds growth companies attractive: growth stocks are superior not only in terms of capital appreciation, but also, given a reasonable time, in terms of dividend yield [Fisher, 1996, p. 60].

As we know, the highest-growth companies often are very young companies. However, investing in extremely young companies is not what Fisher proposes, even though young growth stocks offer by far the greatest possibility of gain, sometimes as much as several thousand percent in a decade. Fisher suggests investing in more established companies while following his recommended principles (we examine these later in the chapter). Any losses that might occur in the older growth companies should be temporary, the result of a period of unforeseeable declines in the general market [Fisher, 1996, p. 57].

Like Fisher, Buffett recommends exercising great care when considering investing in very young growth companies. He reminds investors that growth can destroy value if monetary injections are required in the early years of the project or company, and these exceed the future cash flow. Growth is just one of the components of company value. It can affect value both negatively and positively [Buffett and Loomis, 1999]. While Fisher finds that technology is an investor's friend, Buffett views investment in technology companies as too risky.

Since Graham adheres to tough formal restrictions on investment, the use of his method automatically leads investors to refrain from investing when markets are at high levels and investing actively when markets are low. Fisher, who primarily considers the quality of shares and not their price levels, discusses the timing of buying as a separate issue. Certainly, buying at low levels is the best option: "If the right stocks are bought and held long enough they will always produce some profit. . . . However, to produce close to the maximum profit, the kind of spectacular profit . . . some consideration must be given to timing" [Fisher, 1996, p. 61]. What should an investor do if she finds a company that is ideally suited for investment, but the timing is wrong? In Fisher's view: "Since a decline of 40 to 50 per cent from its peak is not at all uncommon for even the best stock in a normal business depression, is not completely ignoring the business cycle rather a risky policy?" [Fisher, 1996, p. 74]. According to Fisher, it is reasonable to take on the risk associated with investing at high market levels if this is a relatively small purchase, and if the large majority of the portfolio was acquired when market conditions were beneficial.

On the other hand, it is important to keep in mind that macroeconomic and financial indicators, including market dynamics, are difficult to forecast, and it is preferable to avoid any guesswork concerning the general market trend unless speculative buying is dominant and economic storm warnings are very clearly present [Fisher, 1996, p. 74]. "Postponing an attractive purchase because of fear of what the general market might do will, over the years, prove very costly. This is because the investor is ignoring a powerful influence about which he has positive knowledge through fear of a less powerful force about which . . . he and everyone else is largely guessing" [Fisher, 1996, p. 81]. The balance of Fisher's advice shifts between deliberate market timing and away from it. Buffett agrees with this position in principle: "We try to price, rather than time, purchases" [Buffett, 1977–2013, 1994].

Fisher also does not share the widely held view that an asset must be sold if it has had a huge advance, or if there is an expectation of a market fall. Fisher cites as an example shares that he had once bought for a profit-sharing trust where he served as an advisor. The shares grew in price, and the pressure to sell was colossal. One of the trust owners strongly felt that this was a good opportunity to sell some of the stock so that it could be repurchased later when the markets fell. "That is a totally ridiculous argument. Either this is a better investment than another one or a worse one. Getting your bait back is just a question of psychological comfort. It doesn't have anything to do with whether it is the right move or not," comments Fisher [Buffett and Jaffe, 1987].

Fisher finds that investors often feel that "just because it has gone up, it has probably used most of its potential" [Fisher, 1996, p. 83]. He disagrees with this view, as he believes that exceptional companies are the only ones that an investor should buy and that these companies simply function differently [Fisher, 1996, p. 83]. In Fisher's opinion, it is the long-term investor who wins, as over the long term, the profits are substantially greater [Buffett and Jaffe, 1987]. Fisher assesses: "If the job has been correctly done when a common stock is purchased, the time to sell it is—almost never" [Fisher, 1996, p. 85]. He is echoed by Buffett almost verbatim, who also buys shares to hold them "forever."

Fisher does not believe in the rationality of the markets. There are fashions of the day in the stock market, just as there are in the clothing industry. In Fisher's view, an investor should be particularly careful with the market's obsessions of the moment to make sure that these purchases are adequately priced and that the investor, owing to an unjustifiably positive interpretation of facts, is not paying for a fleeting infatuation [Fisher, 1996, p. 134]. Like Graham, Fisher strongly advises investors not to follow the crowds. In his opinion, refraining from comparing one's decisions with those of the majority is a very important investment principle that is difficult for an inexperienced investor to master. He comments that his book *Path to Wealth Through Common Stocks* "is dedicated to all investors, large and small, who do not adhere to the philosophy: 'Everyone seems to believe it, so it must be so'" [Fisher, 2007, p. x]. Effectively, Fisher was one of the very early critics of the efficient market hypothesis.

What are the requirements for the right investment opportunities? In his book *Common Stocks, and Uncommon Profits*, Fisher formulates 15 principles that he uses in choosing his investments. These principles are well known. Let us briefly review the main ones. The company must have products or services with sufficient market potential to provide a sizable increase in sales for at least several years; a product development pipeline that will further increase total sales when the growth potential of currently attractive products has been largely exploited; an effective research and development arm; a well-functioning sales department;

worthwhile profit margins (in Fisher's experience, the highest long-term investment profits are acquired not by investing in companies with low profit margins but by investing in companies with strong profitability [Fisher, 1996, p. 35]); profit margins that are maintained and improved; a long-range outlook with regard to profits ("the investor wanting maximum results should favor companies with a truly long-range outlook concerning profits" [Fisher, 1996, p. 46]); outstanding labor and personnel relations (Fisher comments that when ordinary employees are not made to feel valued, then managers often do not create companies that are suitable for investment [Fisher, 1996, p. 40]); and the ability to finance growth with good judgment (if raising equity financing is likely to occur within a few years of stock purchase and if this financing will result in only a small rise in the following common stock earnings, then the company's management does not have the quality of judgment that would make this company a good investment [Fisher, 1996, pp. 47–48]). When describing an attractive business, Buffett does not go as deeply into detail—after all, he is not writing a textbook, or perhaps he views a sustainable competitive advantage, which we discuss in the next chapter, as a considerably more important concept. Nevertheless, as we have seen, his statements are similar to Fisher's when it comes to profitability, attitude toward personnel, the importance of a long-term investment horizon, and financing growth through stock issues.[18]

Fisher spoke about inflation as a constant threat to profit margins, though his thoughts on the subject are also applicable to noninflationary situations. Companies that can maintain their profit margins simply by raising prices, either because demand for their products is unusually high or because prices for similar products have risen even more strongly, appear to be in a fortunate position. However, the ability to maintain or improve profit margins in this way often ends up being temporary. New competitive production capacity is built. This new capacity eventually makes it impossible to pass on cost increases, and profit margins fall [Fisher, 1996, p. 36]. This is particularly detrimental if the undistributed profit is "consumed." Either inflation destroys the accumulated amortization to such an extent that it is eventually

18 We discuss Buffett's views on stock share issues in Chapter 5.

insufficient to replace equipment, or a change in customer habits compels companies to spend money on types of assets that do not themselves increase the turnover, but that may lead to a turnover reduction if the expenditure is not incurred. An air-conditioning system in a retail store is a good illustration of such an asset [Fisher, 1996, p. 88]. Buffett elaborates on these concepts when he contemplates the nature of good and bad fundamentals and competitive advantage, which we discuss in the next chapter.

In Fisher's view, all of a company's profit may be used to finance its growth only at early stages of company development. More mature companies, unless they are under pressure because of inflation or change-of-habits-related expenditures, must pay out 25 to 40 percent of their profit as dividends [Fisher, 1996, p. 92]. Fisher thought that dividends are a signal that a company can sustain and develop its business without consuming all its profit. Buffett argues against dividend payouts in cases when profit reinvestment brings a better return. We discuss Buffett's views on dividend policy in detail in Chapter 5.

Both Graham and Fisher, and consequently Buffett, are cautious about diversification as a risk reduction tool. Graham admits that on the one hand, diversification is an old principle of conservative investing, but on the other hand, it is dangerous to make diversification a goal in itself, as the quality of the investment portfolio and buying at moderate prices are more important: "If one could select the best stocks unerringly, one would only lose by diversifying" [Graham, 2003, p. 365], and, "If the average market level . . . is too high to provide an adequate margin of safety for the buyer, then a simple technique of diversified buying . . . may not work out satisfactorily" [Graham, 2003, p. 517]. This attitude toward diversification logically follows from Graham's philosophy: requirements for the investment target are tough, and finding satisfactory targets is difficult. Fisher states that investors eventually discover that their problem is finding good investments, not choosing among a large number of suitable opportunities. "Usually a very long list of securities is not a sign of the brilliant investor, but of one who is unsure of himself" [Fisher, 1996, p. 117]. Fisher also writes that it is better to improve one's understanding of companies than to reduce the risks that result from lack of knowledge by diversification. He advises that investing in companies without sufficient grasp of their business practices is likely to be even more pernicious than lacking adequate diversification [Fisher, 1996, pp. 108–109]. Later Buffett continued to develop similar ideas with great and sustained passion. We pursue the discussion about his thoughts on diversification in Chapters 4 and 5.

* * *

A purchase of undervalued shares is based on having confidence that, sooner or later, those shares will be valued fairly by the market. Once, at a congressional hearing devoted to stock market conditions, when asked to explain what compels undervalued shares to grow in price, Graham remarked: "This is one of the mysteries of our business, and it is a mystery to me as well as to everybody else. [But] we know from experience that eventually the market catches up with value" [Graham, 1955]. Fisher shares Graham's opinion. In Fisher's view, patience is required if considerable profits are to be made from an investment. "It is often easier to tell what will happen to the price of a stock than how much time will elapse before it happens" [Fisher, 1996, p. 4]. There is no doubt that Graham and Fisher's approaches are potentially successful. However, how would one carry them out in practice? Are there many investment targets that satisfy Graham and Fisher's criteria, including the purchase price? Ideally, it would be best to buy Phil Fisher stocks at Ben Graham prices, but that is even more difficult. In Buffett's view, these circumstances occur (or have occurred) in financial markets. In Chapter 3, we talk about the price levels that Buffett views as appropriate for investment and the times when these levels appear. Now, let us examine the fundamental attributes of companies that help Warren Buffett generate his returns.

2

What Kind of Business Does Warren Buffett Like?

The really big money tends to be made by investors
who are right on qualitative decisions.
—WARREN BUFFETT [CITED IN SCHROEDER, 2008, P. 265]

BUFFETT TALKS ABOUT THE IMPORTANCE OF QUALITATIVE DECISIONS.
We will begin by examining in detail what qualitative decisions are.

A Business That Warren Buffett Views as Problematic

In a business selling a commodity-type product, it's impossible
to be a lot smarter than your dumbest competitor.
—WARREN BUFFETT [BUFFETT, 1977–2013, 1990]

In order to understand what businesses Buffett would find attractive,
or, more generally, what businesses he would consider good businesses,
it may be helpful to draw an inspiration from the logic of proof by
contradiction and consider the subject from the opposite point of view.
What kind of business is not a good investment? These companies are

in the majority. Buffett once remarked: "There aren't that many wonderful businesses in the world" [cited in Lowe, 2007, p. 187].

The worst type of business to own is one that must "consistently employ ever-greater amounts of capital at very low rates of return" [Buffett, 1977–2013, 1992]. Most businesses fit this description. Often it is necessary to invest capital continuously, as without doing so, the business will have limited upside potential [Buffett, 1977–2013, 1982].

Buffett also comments that companies in industries with both substantial overcapacity and a uniform product are prime candidates for profit troubles. If costs and prices are determined by full-scale competition, if there is a large amount of excess capacity, and if the buyer cares little about whose product or services he uses, then the industry economics are almost certain to be unexciting, if not outright disastrous [Buffett, 1977–2013, 1982].

As examples of businesses with challenging fundamentals, Buffett cites the textile and insurance industries. He comments that insurance is a classic example of an industry that has excess capacity and a uniform product [Buffett, 1977–2013, 1980]. Nevertheless, Berkshire has substantial exposure to the insurance industry; we discuss Berkshire's insurance businesses in some detail throughout the book. The textile industry also "illustrates in textbook style how producers of relatively undifferentiated goods in capital intensive businesses must earn inadequate returns except under conditions of tight supply or real shortage. As long as excess productive capacity exists, prices tend to reflect direct operating costs rather than capital employed" [Buffett, 1977–2013, 1978]. This means that the prices of finished goods are lower than the full production cost, which should include amortization. The capital employed not only does not earn a return, but also does not reinstate itself.

The story of Berkshire itself provides a "textbook-style" illustration of this process. The company was formed in 1955 as the result of a merger between two textile manufacturers in New England, Hathaway Manufacturing and Berkshire. Textile manufacturing in the area had begun to decline in the 1920s, far earlier than the emergence of low-cost Chinese production. First, the industry in the north was challenged by that in the south, where the labor force was cheaper. As manufacturing became less and less profitable or even created losses, the majority of the factory owners in New England ceased to invest locally—they either moved their production facilities to the south or stopped operating altogether. Perhaps the only regional company whose owners continued to invest capital into production was Hathaway Manufacturing. The company managed to be the first to organize the production of artificial silk and became the largest U.S. manufacturer of lining for suits. The company survived the 1940s and even accumulated reserves with the help of military orders for parachute material. Unfortunately, in 1954, the factory building suffered severely during a storm. This forced the company to merge with another New England producer: Berkshire Fine Spinning Associates, Inc. During the war, Berkshire had also been profitable and had also amassed a considerable amount of funds; however, it operated with old equipment and was able to process only cotton. As a result, in the 1950s, the company began to encounter economic difficulties. In 1955, Berkshire Hathaway shares cost $14 a share. By 1962, the price had fallen to less than $8 a share, while the company's working capital amounted to $16.50 a share. When the share price of a business is less than 50 percent of its working capital, this indicates that the market believes that the company will "consume" its current assets.

After Berkshire Hathaway's textile business closed in 1985, Buffett commented that over the years, there had always been the possibility of making a large capital investment in the textile business that would have resulted in a reduction of variable costs. Those investment opportunities, if viewed through the prism of standard return on investment tests, would have brought greater economic gains than if similar investments had been made in other Berkshire businesses (candy and newspapers). However, the potential benefits from investing in the textile industry were imaginary. Berkshire's competitors were implementing the same types of capital expenditures, and once a certain proportion of the industry participants had made these investments, the reduced cost base in the industry would have resulted in a reduction in prices. Considered individually, each company's investment appeared to be justified, but viewed collectively, these decisions affected every company and did not benefit the individual players ("just as happens when each person watching a parade decides he can see a little better if he stands on tiptoes"). After each cycle of capital investment, all the companies had more money tied up in the business, but their returns did not improve [Buffett, 1977–2013, 1985].

In light of this, Buffett's analysis of Burlington Industries, a leading American textile manufacturer that had followed the modernization strategy over the course of many years, is poignant. Buffett talked about the company in connection with the closing of Berkshire's own textile business. By 1985, Burlington had sales of about $2.8 billion—seemingly, a vast sum of money. Between 1964 and 1985, the company had made capital expenditures of about $3 billion, or more than $200 per share on that $60 stock. A very large part of this spending was devoted to cost improvement and expansion. Nevertheless, Burlington lost sales volume in real dollars and had far lower returns on sales and equity in 1985 than it had had 20 years earlier. Split 2-for-1 in 1965, the stock sold at $34 in 1985, just a little over its 1964 price of $60. Over this period, the Consumer Price Index had more than tripled. Regular dividends were paid, but they, too, had shrunk significantly in terms of purchasing power. "This devastating outcome for the shareholders indicates what can happen when much brain power and energy are applied to a faulty premise" [Buffett, 1977–2013, 1985]. In 2003, Burlington went bankrupt.

As Buffett's parade revelers rising on tiptoes demonstrate, the managerial decisions of individual participants in uniform industries are intertwined. Poor judgment by a single manager may lead to further losses for all involved. "In a business selling a commodity-type product, it's impossible to be a lot smarter than your dumbest competitor," commented Buffett in relation to his investment in convertible bonds of USAir [Buffett, 1977–2013, 1990]. If your competitors set prices at a level that is lower than your production costs, then you also must set prices at that level and suffer the losses if you are to remain in business.

"The trick is to have no competitors. That means having something that distinguishes itself" [Buffett, 1991a]. As a result, every vendor struggles continuously to establish and bring to the attention of her customers the special qualities of her product or service. "This works with candy bars (customers buy by brand name, they do not ask for a 'two-ounce candy bar') but doesn't work with sugar (how often do you

hear, 'I'll have a cup of coffee with cream and C & H sugar, please')"
[Buffett, 1977–2013, 1983]. Buffett gives another example: "a Cadillac
with steel that came from the South Works of US Steel" [Buffett,
1991c].

While the degree to which it is possible to introduce product differentiation within an industry may change because of technology developments or the evolution of consumer preferences,[1] in many industries
differentiation among products may be simply impossible to implement. A few producers in such industries may consistently do well if
they have a wide sustainable cost advantage, but such exceptions are
rare or, in many industries, nonexistent. For the great majority of companies selling "commodity-type" products, persistent overcapacity without regulated prices (or costs) results in poor profitability. Overcapacity
may eventually self-correct as capacity shrinks or demand expands, but
such corrections are often long delayed, and "when they finally occur,
the rebound to prosperity frequently produces a pervasive enthusiasm
for expansion that, within a few years, again creates overcapacity and a
new profitless environment" [Buffett, 1977–2013, 1983]. Buffett voices
Fisher's ideas that we discussed in Chapter 1.

Businesses with Good Fundamentals

> One of the lessons . . . is the importance of being in
> businesses where tailwinds prevail rather than headwinds.
>
> —WARREN BUFFETT [BUFFETT, 1977–2013, 1977]

Keeping in mind Buffett's definition of a business with no potential,
we will contemplate the attributes of a business with strong prospects.
The best type of business to own is "one that over an extended period
can employ large amounts of incremental capital at very high rates of
return" [Buffett, 1977–2013, 1992]. This is, of course, common sense.
However, even though it is very desirable to employ endless capital at
the best rate of return imaginable, in practice, this is only possible in a

---

1 For instance, a discerning consumer may wish to differentiate between a Hershey bar and a
   single-estate cocoa-bean chocolate or organic fair-trade chocolate.

fantasy, for "most high-return businesses need relatively little capital" [Buffett, 1977–2013, 1992]. At the same time, while the highest return attainable as a criterion is understandable, how capital intensive is a business is a very important consideration. Buffett opines that between two "wonderful" businesses one should choose the least capital intensive. He admits that it took Charlie (Munger) and him 25 years to figure this out [Buffett, 1991b].

This rationale is something akin to a cornerstone in its relation to other factors contributing to the overall success of the business. Buffett stresses that "with few exceptions, when a management with a reputation for brilliance tackles a business with a reputation for poor fundamental economics, it is the reputation of the business that remains intact" [Buffett, 1977–2013, 1980]. Situations in which the quality of management has limited influence over the operational results are an indication of a "commodity-type" business, whose other potentially problematic aspects we discussed in the preceding section. Buffett sold his investments in Kaiser Aluminum and Alcoa in 1980 and explained his decision by saying that the long-term performance of these companies would be more affected by the future economics of the aluminum industry than it would be by the direct operating decisions that management makes [Buffett, 1977–2013, 1980].

Nevertheless, the role of management in a business and the relationship between the economic fundamentals and management, despite the latter's somewhat secondary status, require a more detailed consideration. On the one hand, Buffett finds that the fundamentals will always prevail over management. On the other hand, a highly qualified management is necessary for a good business. "Buying a retailer without good management is like buying the Eiffel Tower without an elevator" [Buffett, 1977–2013, 1995]. Since interpersonal relationships always involve an element of subjectivity, Buffett, who is known to have said, "I do not have to work with people I don't like," admits that in some cases he has turned down otherwise acceptable deals because he did not like the people with whom he would have had to work [Buffett, 1999]. Another remark illustrates Buffett's attitude toward the quality of management: "A horse that can count to ten is a remarkable horse—not a remarkable mathematician" [Buffett, 1977–2013, 1985]. A later

Buffett comment was: "I go out on the street and look for seven-footers. If some guy comes up to me and says, 'I'm five-six, but you ought to see me handle the ball,' I'm not interested" [cited in Pare, 1995]. However, it has been observed that Buffett did not always operate like "a basketball coach," but at some point arrived at this philosophy. At the same time, according to Bill Gates who is a close friend of Buffett, Buffett does not believe in buying businesses in which success is possible only if all the employees involved are excellent [Gates, 1996].

There is another side to the issue of management. Buffett uses the example of Jack Welch, chairman and CEO of General Electric from 1981 to 2001. If it had been possible to create 499 clones of Jack Welch, put them in charge of the remaining 499 companies in the Fortune 500, and leave the original Welch in charge of General Electric, then in five years the return on equity in the Fortune 500 would have probably fallen, not risen, as the 500 Jack Welchs would have been doing things in a competitive way that might well have produced lower returns for American business as a whole. Great variation in the quality of management considerably improves the chances that some number of managers will obtain terrific returns [Schlender, Buffett, and Gates, 1998]. The current state of science does not permit the cloning of people, and it may still be a long time before excellent managers can be manufactured at a production facility. Until this becomes reality, Buffett's observation about the significance of good management in circumstances in which there is great variability in the quality of managers will remain insightful. We are reminded of the interconnectedness of managerial decisions, but in this case, to the upside. To paraphrase Buffett, it may be as difficult "to be a lot smarter than your" smartest, as opposed to "dumbest competitor."

Buffett's views on management and business fundamentals underwent a certain evolution. He once thought that certain star managers were able to "recognize that rare prince who is disguised as a toad, and who [the star managers] have managerial abilities that enable them to peel away the [prince's] disguise" [Buffett, 1977–2013, 1981], although he also commented that most managers overestimated their abilities in this area. Eventually Buffett admitted that he too was ultimately unsuccessful in his investments in this category of company. He tried to look for princes disguised as toads, but all the princes that he invested in had been princes prior to the acquisition, while those that were toads at the time of his investment did not become princes regardless of how much he kissed them. As he put it, he kissed and they croaked. Thereafter he revised his strategy and made the transition to looking for high-quality businesses at the right prices[2] [Buffett, 1977–2013, 1992]. It may be that this was one of the experiences that helped Buffett arrive at an understanding that between the poor fundamentals and the strong management, it is the fundamentals that will prevail.

In light of the framework that we have been discussing, it may be interesting to review Buffett's investment in the insurance company GEICO. It is a successful company that nevertheless operates in a fundamentally bad industry. It has been through periods when it masqueraded as a toad. Buffett's introduction to the company happened in a rather unusual way, which later compelled him to retell the story numerous times. He heard about the company from Graham, who admired it and owned its shares. On a January Saturday in 1951, Buffett traveled to Washington and arrived at GEICO's head office. The entrance was locked, but when Buffett rang the doorbell, a security guard answered. Buffett enquired whether any members of the staff were present in the building, and the guard explained that indeed there was one person, who was working on the sixth floor. This person turned out to be the assistant to the president of the company, and later GEICO's general director, Lorimer Davidson. Buffett's position as an apprentice of Graham proved to be the entrance ticket to Davidson's office, and the two ended up talking for four hours. Davidson told Buffett about GEICO and about the insurance business in general. According to Buffett, that meeting turned out to be the best introduction to the insurance business that could have been possible over a day and a half. The encounter made such a strong impression on Buffett that he rushed to buy the company's shares, which he subsequently sold at a 30 percent profit earned over less than a year. Later he deeply regretted the sale, as the stock price kept rising. During the following 25 years, Buffett followed the stock closely. In 1976, he began acquiring the shares again.

2 Buffett made these comments in reference to investing in "cigar butts" early in his career, when he was following the framework of his mentor, Benjamin Graham.

By 1980, Buffett had acquired 33 percent of the shares. He continued his acquisition process until he obtained a controlling stake. In 1995, he bought out the minority shareholders, and Berkshire became the sole owner of the company.

Although GEICO operates in an industry that Buffett regards as unattractive, the company has, in his view, "the coupling of a very important and very hard to duplicate competitive advantage with an extraordinary management who have skills both in operations and in capital allocation" [Buffett, 1977–2013, 1980]. GEICO's competitive advantage is its direct marketing of its products. Other insurers sell their policies through agency networks—according to Buffett, this form of distribution is so ingrained in the business of these insurers that it is impossible for them to give it up[3] [Buffett, 1977–2013, 1995]. About half of GEICO's sales come from existing customer referrals [Miles, 2002, p. 37]. GEICO's business model turned out to be particularly suitable to the Internet age, as opposed to that of companies using insurance agents. This, of course, could not have been foreseen in the 1950s.

How did this prince find itself in a toad's attire? In the middle of the 1970s, the company was experiencing serious problems. Established in 1936, GEICO had originally sold automobile insurance only to the military and federal government employees.[4] The risks associated with members of this kind of clientele were relatively low, as they were generally careful and reliable drivers. In 1952 the company started to sell insurance to state and municipal government employees, and in 1958 to those employed in the private sector. This latter customer group turned out to be considerably riskier clients, as they were not all such careful drivers. As a result, insurance payouts rose dramatically. The situation was compounded by the oil shock–driven high inflation, which had not been taken into account in pricing the policies. The premiums that the company had been collecting simply became insufficient. This premium shortage, combined with the growth of its office network, brought

---

3 This means that during tough years, when the sale of policies results in losses, the companies feel it is necessary to reduce their agency networks.
4 The abbreviation GEICO stands for Government Employees Insurance Company.

GEICO to near bankruptcy. Aside from double-digit inflation, the rise of competition in the industry was another factor that negatively affected the company's deteriorating financial position. In 1975, net assets fell from $144 million at the start of the year to $35 million at the end. However, by 1977, having replaced its CEO and reorganized its policy sales, GEICO had returned to profitability. The company's competitive advantage—direct sales—was retained. Buffett's long-term investment horizon, which enabled him to provide the needed financing during the difficult years, saved the firm. Today, GEICO is rather profitable.

The current director of GEICO, Tony Nicely, has aimed to achieve a leading position in terms of brand recognition, as, in his view, eventually only two or three brands will survive: "My ultimate objective is for GEICO to be like Coke or McDonald's. If I say 'Soft drink,' you say 'Coke.' If I say 'hamburger,' you may say 'McDonald's.' When I say 'automobile insurance,' I want you to say 'GEICO'" [cited in Miles, 2002, p. 41]. It seems that the company has been working toward this goal. Its market share has been growing consistently. As of May 2014, GEICO has 12 million clients. It is the second-largest private passenger auto insurer in the United States. However, even a strong position may deteriorate under pressure from an external challenge. At the shareholders' meeting in May 2014, it was suggested that such a challenge for GEICO may arrive in the form of a self-driving car. The accident rate is likely to fall considerably, and therefore the premiums collected will fall as well. The market as a whole will possibly shrink by orders of magnitude ["Recap: The 2014 Berkshire Hathaway Annual Meeting," 2014].

Constructing common-sense definitions of good and bad fundamentals is simplistic, although it is helpful in creating discipline in one's approach to investing. The importance of great management is common sense. GEICO's evolution illustrates the complex interplay of these issues. Despite the definitions, GEICO has remained a successful business in what we define as a fundamentally bad industry. However, even though one might legitimately label the insurance industry as bad in terms of the framework chosen, the industry also has good aspects in that it is one of the few industries in which large lump sums are received up front, of which most, with good management, are retained; this is one of the reasons why Berkshire has such a substantial footprint in this particular bad industry. It plays a crucial role in Berkshire's cost of financing, which is fundamental to the success of any business. We discuss Berkshire's insurance business in detail in Chapter 6.

Finally, we will review Buffett's comments on how business fundamentals are affected by inflation. In 1981, when the U.S. economy was experiencing double-digit inflation, Buffett, echoing Fisher's views, commented that certain of his investments had delivered excellent results in the inflationary environment. These were the companies that, either by design or by accident, were able to meet two conditions. First, these companies had the ability to raise prices relatively easily, even when demand was stable and production capacity was not fully utilized. These companies could do so without risking considerable market share or sales reduction in real terms. As a result, they delivered significant sales growth in dollar terms (often driven by inflation and not by real increasing demand) with only insignificant additional capital infusions [Buffett, 1977–2013, 1981].

In short, it is Buffett's recommendation that one should buy tickets only for good shows: "The funny thing is, better shows don't cost that much more then lousy shows" [cited in Lowe, 2007, p. 170].

In Search of a "Money Printing Press"

> We are trying to widen at all times the moat that
> protects our business from invading hordes.
>
> —WARREN BUFFETT [BUFFETT, 2000]

"All animals are equal, but some animals are more equal than others"—among businesses with good fundamentals, Buffett looks for those that are ideal. A perfect investment is a business that functions like a money printing press. However, Buffett's search for a money printing press is not quite the same as the search for a perpetual motion machine. Businesses that generate stable cash flows exist. Buffett calls such a business an economic franchise. He finds that a franchise arises from a product or service that is needed or desired and that is thought by its customers to have no close substitute, when this product's price is not regulated. The existence of these three conditions allows a company to price its product or service aggressively and thereby earn high rates of return on capital.

"Moreover, franchises can tolerate mismanagement. Inept managers may diminish a franchise's profitability, but they cannot inflict mortal damage" [Buffett, 1977–2013, 1991]. A good business is one that earns a lot of money even when this business is not managed. In this case, we see the role of management in yet a different light from those which we discussed in the previous sections.

It is important to differentiate between an economic franchise and a well-known brand, for a key attribute of a well-known brand is that it is recognizable, but not all recognizable brands are able to generate strong cash flow. In 1993, as examples of brands that seemed strong but whose ability to make money turned out to be weak, Buffett cited Polaroid and Texas Instruments [Lenzner, 1993]. Charlie Munger thought that it was quite possible to negatively affect the profitability of Kellogg [Munger, 2007a, p. 186].

The simplest analogy for an economic franchise that Buffett finds insightful is a toll bridge over a river when there are no other bridges in the vicinity. Interestingly, Buffett once owned such an enterprise. He was the main shareholder of Blue Chip Stamps,[5] which in 1977 bought 24.9 percent of shares of Detroit International Bridge Co. This company owned the concession to manage the Ambassador Bridge over the Detroit River between Detroit in the United States and Windsor in Canada. This was the only toll bridge in the United States that belonged to private shareholders. It was highly profitable. In 1976, the concession owner earned 31 cents of net profit from every dollar of revenue. Charlie Munger could not imagine a more secure investment than that bridge.

Buffett and Munger tried to gain full control over Detroit International Bridge. In 1977, they made a tender offer to acquire 100 percent of the company's stock at $20 a share. They lost to a transport

---

5 At the present time, this company is owned by Berkshire. We discuss Blue Chip Stamps in greater detail in Chapter 6.

company from Michigan that had also accumulated a position in the stock. Buffett and Munger sold their holding at $24 a share with a good profit on the purchase price. Subsequently, the business environment changed. The company was unable to increase toll rates. The Canadian government either did not wish to allow an increase in toll prices or wanted a reduction in the concession's profits. A toll bridge with no other bridges in the vicinity to offer competition is a rarity. Even when a business like this exists, it is regulated, and nowadays regulators would not be inclined to allow a 30 percent net profit margin.

Buffett uses another metaphor to illustrate the concept of the economic franchise: a castle with a moat. (The castle is the business, and the moat is the competitive advantage that this business possesses.) It is desirable for the owners that the moat widen with time. Buffett writes to his managers: "We are trying to widen at all times the moat that protects our business from invading hordes" [Buffett, 2000]. It is even better when the moat is inhabited by piranhas and other dangerous fish. How would moats form around castles? One of the pathways is through certain economies of scale. Munger explains: "In some businesses, the very nature of things is a sort of cascade toward the overwhelming dominance of one firm. It tends to cascade to the winner-takes-all outcome. And these advantages of scale are so great, for example, that when Jack Welch came into General Electric, he just said, 'To hell with it. We're either going to be number one or number two in every field we're in or we're going to be out'" [Munger, 2007a].

Examples of industries in which economies of scale lead to the formation of a castle with a moat are, in Buffett's view, supermarket chains and newspapers. In 1987, Buffett commented that the economic law that governs the business environment in these industries is the "survival of the fattest" [Buffett, 1977–2013, 1987]. This is a variation of "the winner-takes-all" outcome in my view. In retail, the "fattest," where Berkshire is a shareholder, is undoubtedly the largest American hypermarket chain—Walmart, which Munger classified, in one of his lectures, as a first-class business [Munger, 2007a, pp. 182–185]. We discuss the newspaper industry in the next section of this chapter and in Chapter 3.

Following the law of the survival of the fattest, Buffett has invested in furniture distribution. He acquired several independent stores—leaders in their respective local markets—and in 1999 he commented that each of Berkshire's furniture operations was number one in its territory and that Berkshire now sold more furniture than anyone else in Massachusetts, New Hampshire, Texas, Nebraska, Utah, and Idaho [Buffett, 1977–2013, 1999].

A franchise does not always arise from economies of scale, and the mechanism of the survival of the fattest does not operate in all industries. Munger cites an example: a travel magazine targeted at a narrow audience, for instance, managers of corporations who organize trips for their staff—this magazine may become more successful than a general travel publication [Munger, 2007a, pp. 179–180]. This would be an example of a relatively small demand niche that requires only one or a few players.

Buffett also observes that companies that have competitive advantages creating a franchiselike position often appear to have certain attributes. They "possess large amounts of enduring goodwill" and "utilize a minimum of tangible assets" [Buffett, 1977–2013, 1983]. In addition to the travel magazine dominating a narrow segment of a broader market in Munger's earlier example, classic illustrations of companies with this type of competitive advantage are Gillette and Coca-Cola. Buffett has said that he regarded Gillette and Coca-Cola as the strongest franchises in the world[6] [Buffett, 1977–2013, 1993]. He has been a shareholder in both of these companies. Buffett remains a shareholder in Coca-Cola, but he converted his shares in Gillette into those in Procter & Gamble when the former was acquired by the latter in 2005.

In 1995, Buffett commented that in volume terms Gillette had 30 percent of the global razor blade market of 20 billion razor blades; in value terms, it had 60 percent of the market, and it had 90 percent of the market in some countries (Scandinavia and Mexico). He described Gillette's competitive advantage this way: "When something has been around as long as shaving and you find a company that has both that kind of innovation, in terms of developing better razors all the time, plus the distribution power, and the position in people's minds . . . for 20 bucks [per year] you get a terrific shaving experience. Now men are

---

6 Buffett also included Wrigley's into this list. In 2013, Coca-Cola's brand held the third position in the rating of the most valuable brands in the world, after Apple and Google.

not inclined to shift around when they get that kind of situation" [cited in Lowe, 2007, p. 199]. We discuss Coca-Cola later in this section.

Another example of a franchiselike position arising through "enduring goodwill" is Hershey's. It is franchise value if you go into a store to buy a chocolate bar, but if the store does not have Hershey's, you walk across the street to buy a Hershey's bar at another store instead of taking the manager at the first store's suggestion that you try "this unmarked chocolate bar that the owner of the place recommends" [cited in Lowe, 2007, p. 200]. Buffett described Oreo cookies, Jell-O, Kool-Aid, and See's Candies, which are often given on Valentine's Day, in similar terms to Hershey's [Buffett, 1991d].

> The test of a franchise is what a smart guy with a lot of money could do to it if he tried. If you gave me a billion dollars, and you gave me first draft pick of fifty business managers throughout the United States, I could absolutely cream both the business world and the journalistic world. If you said, 'Go take *The Wall Street Journal* apart,' I would hand you back the billion dollars. Reluctantly, but I would hand it back to you.
>
> Now, incidentally, if you gave me a similar amount of money and you told me to make a dent in the profitability or change the market position of the Omaha National Bank . . . or the leading department store in Omaha, I could give them a hard time. I might not do much for you in the process, but I could cause them a lot of trouble. The real test of a business is how much damage a competitor can do, even if he is stupid about returns [cited in Train, 1987, p. 98].

Buffett's franchise test is a very helpful tool; however, for the franchise to stop making money, it is not necessary for it to be attacked by competitors. Let us remember that Buffett believes that true franchises cannot be destroyed by poor management, as we discussed at the start of this section. What would destroy a franchise? A change in the macro environment? A combination of poor management and negative changes in the macro conditions? From this standpoint, the evolution of Coca-Cola is particularly interesting. In 1991, Buffett told us that Coca-Cola sells its products in 150 countries and that in each country, the consumption of the company's products is growing annually. Had the Candler family, which bought the company from the Pemberton family in 1904 or 1906, been sending the Pembertons royalties of one penny a serving, this royalty would have amounted to $2 billion a year, but this sum would have had no impact on Coca-Cola's bottom line [Buffett, 1991b]. In Buffett's opinion, in 1993, when Coca-Cola's shares grew rapidly, Coca-Cola was stronger than a "franchise." In order to dismantle the brand, even a far larger sum would have been insufficient: "If you gave me $100 billion and said take away the soft drink leadership of Coca-Cola in the world, I'd give it back to you and say it can't be done" [cited in Huey, 1993]. However, in the 1960s and 1970s, the company was not in the best shape. The share price had hardly changed over the period from 1960 to 1980. As an example of management's helplessness and lack of strategic thinking, analysts often cited investments in shrimp farms in Mexico. The situation was remedied by Roberto Goizueta, who was appointed CEO and chairman of the board of directors in 1980. He proved to be a very talented manager, during whose tenure (until 1997) the company's capitalization grew from $4 billion to $150 billion.

Buffett accumulated a stake in Coca-Cola during two periods. The majority of the stake was acquired in 1988–1989, and the rest in 1994. The total cost basis of the stake amounted to approximately $1.3 billion, of which around $1 billion was invested in 1988–1989. The shares grew rapidly until April of 1998. At the end of that year, the value of Berkshire's stake amounted to $13.4 billion. Since that time, the company has not been performing particularly well.

In 1997, Roberto Goizueta died. He was replaced by Douglas Ivester. The company's affairs took a turn for the worse. In many markets, sales began to flounder as a result of market saturation and consumer preferences shifting toward mineral water. In Europe, large amounts of product had to be withdrawn because of quality problems. Ivester did not manage to win the battle to acquire the French brand Orangina, a drink similar to Fanta. In the United States, Coca-Cola became the target of an investigation into racial discrimination charges. Profit reductions resulted in the need to fire approximately 6,000 employees. Investment write-offs took place in Russia, India, and Vietnam.

Fortune magazine published an in-depth article about the CEO and blamed the company's problems on him [Sellers and Tarpley, 1999]. In 1999, Buffett compelled Ivester to resign (we discuss the details of Ivester's resignation further in Chapter 8). Nevertheless, his resignation did not provide a respite. The shares continued to fall until 2005. (In 2004, the company was found to have manipulated its accounts, and the stock sank [Schroeder, 2008, p. 777].) As of February 2015, the value of Berkshire's stake has not returned to its 1998 highs, if the share price is adjusted for splits.

Despite relatively poor recent performance some asset managers continue to praise Coca-Cola—perhaps, merely because it is an investment of Buffett's. "Coca-Cola benefits from the advantage of high switching costs. As you drink more Cokes, you begin to develop a habit that is hard to break. . . . I can't think of anyone who will give up Coke for another brand or save a dime per can. If you're traveling in a foreign country, I'd be willing to bet that you will grab a Coke, not a local brand. Coke has an amazing moat that will likely stay strong for a very long time" [Gad, 2009, p. 105]. By 2009, when this opinion was expressed, the shares of the company had been falling for 11 years.

The company is facing serious challenges. From a purely geographical standpoint, expansion has reached its limits. The company has recently entered Myanmar. Few markets, if any, remain unexplored (barring, perhaps, North Korea). The global population is expected to grow, but so is public awareness of the health issues associated with processed foods, and concerted government action to implement regulation is not impossible even in the emerging markets.[7] This pushes the company to enter local drink markets and supply traditional local

---

7 After their sharp decline in the developed economies, the tobacco companies were able to expand very aggressively in the developing countries, as those lack the health culture and government regulation that are prevalent in the West. Coca-Cola is not a tobacco company by any means, but the health issues related to the consumption of processed foods exist. The company is facing the effects of growing public understanding of medical reality. On government action, including in emerging markets, against junk food, please see, for instance [Boseley, 2013] or [Bottermiller Evich, 2014]. Coca-Cola, of course, has zero-calorie products made with artificial sweeteners, but the tide may turn against those products also, if it has not yet done so already.

drinks that are popular in a particular region (for instance, kvass[8]—in Russia), or flavored or mineral waters. The company is becoming the holder of a portfolio of local beverages, flavored waters, and juices, but this is a very different business from that of selling the same highly recognizable product in every area.[9] Finally, climate change is putting pressure on the potable water supply and agricultural resources. There is a possibility, however small, that consumption of carbonated drinks or flavored waters may simply become nonviable, or come to be perceived as unethical, should drinking water come to be in short supply globally or in some geographical areas. The company is already involved in water purification technologies to counter this trend. There is no guarantee that Coca-Cola will be able to continue growing or even to sustain its customer base.[10]

In this light, and with the hindsight knowledge of what happened to the tobacco industry, it is interesting to recall Buffett's comments, made in 1993, about Marlboro. A pack of Marlboro, which in 1993 cost $2, was twice as expensive as generic cigarettes. A smoker who consumed two packs a day paid an extra $500 a year if he smoked Marlboro. The consumer would need to think that the product was considerably better in order to overpay to this extent. Competing with generic producers, Philip Morris, which owned Marlboro, decided to reduce prices in 1993. As a result, the company's market capitalization fell by $16 billion. Buffett explained that Gillette, whom we have discussed, was far better protected against generic competition than Marlboro was because using Gillette razor blades and not buying the cheapest blades to avoid "an uncomfortable experience" would cost only $11 more a year [Berkshire Hathaway Annual Shareholders' Meeting, 1993]. The damage to Marlboro was inflicted by generic

---

8 A traditional nonalcoholic drink made through the fermentation of rye or other grains.

9 Here the company would be competing with, for instance, Nestlé. Let us remember that the mighty Walmart did not find it at all easy to compete with the European value supermarkets.

10 Buffett and Munger do not consider the possible effects of climate change when they make their investment decisions. Munger says that people who imagine that they know exactly how the climate change will evolve are "talking out of their hats" ["Recap: The 2014 Berkshire Hathaway Annual Meeting"]. The current scientific consensus on climate change, of course, does not speak in terms of absolute certainty. It is not impossible that technology will allow us to deal with the challenge of climate change.

competition when the industry as a whole was yet to acquire the pariah status, relating to healthcare concerns.

This susceptibility to generic competition is an illustration of the difference between a well-known brand and an economic franchise. We discussed the significance of this difference earlier. The "well-known" status may be achieved through, for instance, an expenditure on an advertising campaign and subsequent maintenance of the brand name's "presence" in the minds of consumers through PR, while the franchise-like position requires a foundation of a more solid nature.

In his book *Margin of Safety: Risk-Averse Value Investing Strategies for the Thoughtful Investor*, Seth Klarman lists an interesting set of companies that were considered to be strong franchises in the 1980s but that turned to be investment fads [Klarman, 1991]. He cites Silk Greenhouse (a silk flower store that went bankrupt in 1990 after eight years of operation); TCBY (The Country's Best Yogurt is a chain of frozen yogurt stores that was created in 1981 and went public in 1984; its shares reached a peak of popularity at the end of the 1980s, but the company entered into a crisis in the early 1990s); Eastern, Pan Am, Continental, and TWA (airlines among which the first two were dissolved in 1991, the third applied for bankruptcy protection in 1990, and the last filed for bankruptcy in 1992 and 1995—all of these companies suffered because of deregulation of the airline industry in the middle of the 1980s); Crazy Eddie (a consumer electronics retailer specializing in telephone sales, founded in 1971; it went through a highly publicized bankruptcy in 1989); B. Altman (a New York City–based department store on Fifth Avenue; it was founded in 1865 and purchased in 1987 by Australian investors, who attempted to expand the franchise across the country; the store went bankrupt in 1989); Bank of New England (seized by the Federal Deposit Insurance Corporation in 1991); and Home Shopping Network (a home-shopping television network that was created in 1982; in 1988, its share price fell from $47 to $3.50). Klarman also mentions the franchises of Eastman Kodak and American Express,[11]

---

11 Berkshire holds shares in American Express; Buffett regards this holding as permanent. We discuss this company later in the book.

which turned out to be not very permanent and not particularly resilient—competitors or new technologies made significant inroads into their businesses or destroyed them. Kodak filed for bankruptcy in 2012.

As examples of castles that were surrounded by moats, in 1991, Buffett cited Kirby and World Book, Inc. [Buffett, 1991b]. Today, World Book would probably not be included in the ranks of moat-surrounded castles—resources available for free over the Internet took away most of the company's competitive advantage. In 2004, Buffett referred to Microsoft and eBay [Buffett, 2004b] as such examples.

In 2014, Buffett admitted that See's profits have not been growing in the last few years. He feels that this is explained by the lack of growth in the boxed chocolate market. See's "can't do much about increasing the size of the market." The company tried to move outside its home market in the western United States, but was unable to do so ["Recap: The 2014 Berkshire Hathaway Annual Meeting," 2014].

Finding an indestructible franchise, if such a thing exists, is only the first step. Even excellent companies go through lengthy periods of underperformance. This was the case with Coca-Cola. Analysts have also found that Buffett has stumbled on occasion when he invested in well-established economic franchises. It has been suggested, although Buffett has never commented on the subject, that he sustained losses of around 15 percent on his investment in Guinness, a company that owns one of the most famous brands in the world.

The question of whether a sustainable competitive advantage exists in principle (and whether it is possible to find a business that is akin to a money printing press) is contemplated not only by investors, but also by economists. In the opinion of Robert Wiggins and Timothy Ruefli, who wrote "Sustained Competitive Advantage: Temporal Dynamics and the Incidence and Persistence of Superior Economic Performance" [Wiggins and Ruefli, 2002], such an advantage may be possible. They researched the economic performance of 6,772 companies from 42 industries over a period of 25 years—from 1972 to 1997. As criteria for success, they chose two measures: an accounting one (return on assets, or ROA) and a market one (Tobin's q, the ratio of the firm's market value to the replacement cost of its assets). Superior economic performance was defined as statistically significant above-average economic performance (relative to the industry or reference set) over a five-year period. Sustained superior economic performance was defined as superior economic performance that lasted for six or more consecutive rolling five-year windows (10 years).

Among those reviewed, there were four industries in which there was at least one company that demonstrated sustained superior economic performance, as measured by Tobin's q, during 16 out of 20 windows, or over 20 years. These four companies were Tambrands, Inc. (paper and paperboard), CCH Inc. (periodicals publishing), Worthington Industries (steelworks and blast furnaces), and Food Lion Inc. (grocery stores). Tambrands, Inc., was acquired by Procter & Gamble in 1997; the other three companies still operate as independent entities.

By the ROA measure, such industries and such companies are more numerous—18 out of 40 industries, and 32 companies. As far as I am aware, Buffett did not invest in any of those companies. However, only independent companies were analyzed, whereas Buffett typically buys out companies fully and consolidates the shares, so assets that Buffett acquired would not have been reviewed.

Over a 10-year period, 5.17 percent of the sample showed sustained superior economic performance as measured by ROA, and such companies were present in every industry; 2.16 percent showed sustained superior economic performance as measured by Tobin's q, and these were found in 35 industries. Among the five industries that were not represented were airlines, the economics of which Buffett viewed negatively, and broadcasting corporations, in which Buffett had invested. These observations are, of course, distorted, as the best companies are often acquired. Nevertheless, it is arguable that sustained superior economic performance exists. Since so few of these companies are found ex post, this may mean that locating them ex ante is practically impossible.

We have tried to define the economic franchise. We have examined how it may form and what may undermine it. We have also looked at some of the evidence discussed by economists on whether such things exist at all or whether it is just a figment of imagination of a wishful investor.

We will now look at NetJets, an interesting example of a castle with a moat among companies acquired by Buffett. The company was created in 1984 by Rich Santulli, who sold it to Buffett in 1998. Until the mid-1990s, this company remained one of a kind—Santulli was the inventor of time-sharing in private air travel. Robert Miles recounts the history of Rich Santulli and NetJets. The moat around NetJets seemed to be immense. It was almost impossible to buy new business aircraft at any price, as the waiting list was several years long. (NetJets had purchased most of the airplanes of suitable capacity.) Pilots with 6,000 hours of flying experience—the required qualification—were not available. The company had an excellent client base that included partners and clients of Goldman Sachs (Santulli had worked for the bank previously) and many large shareholders of Berkshire Hathaway, including Warren Buffett. NetJets could offer a wide variety of airplanes, as it was not affiliated with any of the producers in the aviation industry. Finally, the larger fleet resulted in a lower operating cost for supplying the service and a higher quality of service, as the greater number of planes reduced the average distance that any aircraft would fly, lowered the use of fuel by empty airplanes, and shortened the length of time needed to make aircraft available to clients [Miles, 2002, pp. 125–127].

NetJets' model allowed for relatively low capital intensity. Although it was possible to lease the aircraft, a substantial proportion of the customers preferred to own shares in the airplanes. A considerable part of the fleet was owned by the company's clients. NetJets bought aircraft from producers and then sold fractional shares in those aircraft to its customers at a markup. The scheme provided an avenue for achieving a good return on shareholders' equity even if the operating margin was relatively low, as the structure made it possible to reduce the capital needs. It may be that this is why Buffett considered this business attractive, as a high return on capital was possible in conditions of low operational profitability.

Although the creation of NetJets demonstrated that the idea was potentially lucrative, the first competitor emerged only in 1995—11 years after NetJets had appeared on the market. Jet Solutions was a joint venture between the Canadian aircraft producer Bombardier and a charter flight subsidiary of American Airlines. In the same year, Bombardier created a subsidiary, Flexjet. Later still more competitors joined the marketplace: Raytheon Travel Air, Flight Options, and Avolar, a subsidiary of United, appeared in 1997, 1998, and 2001, respectively. The emergence of a great number of these companies coincided with the stock market bubble.

At the end of the 1990s, Buffett still had complete faith in the competitive advantages of NetJets—the widening of its moat and its continuing commercial success. In 1998 he commented that NetJets had the best operations and the best managerial team. Buffett felt that the company was ahead of its competitors and that its lead was only going to continue growing over time. In Buffett's view, the company with the most airplanes in operation would be able to deliver the best service and remain a winner [Miles, 2002, p. 128]. At the annual shareholders' meeting in 2001, Buffett again remarked that competitors were unlikely ever to close NetJets' lead. Charlie Munger spoke about a pilot culture at United that was unsuitable for the fractional jet business and about United's high cost structure. He felt that this NetJets' competitor did not have a justifiable rationale for remaining in the business [Kilpatrick, 2005, p. 632].

Buffett and Munger proved to be right. In 2002, after failing to raise sufficient capital, United Airlines shut down its fractional jet business, which had existed for less than a year. On March 22, 2002, United released a statement saying that the economic slowdown and the deterioration of demand following the attacks of September 11, 2001, had rendered the timeshare venture unprofitable. The reduction in demand was possibly caused not only by a change in sentiment because of the attacks, but also by the collapse of the securities market when the bubble of the late-1990s deflated. In the same year, Raytheon Travel Air merged with Flight Options. The other competitor, Jet Solutions, announced the termination of its plans to expand in Europe.[12]

---

12 Jet Solutions, Flight Options, and Flexjet still exist. In 2013, Bombardier left the timeshare aviation market. The company sold Flexjet to the parent company of Flight Options. Bombardier's share in Jet Solutions was sold to the firm's other shareholders.

In a young, rapidly growing industry, all companies are likely to be successful. When weaker companies enter into a crisis state, this may mean that the industry leader is also experiencing difficulties. At some point, analysts began to notice that NetJets' operations appeared to be taking a turn for the worse. The business model was no longer as perfect as it had seemed. In 2008, Vahan Janjigian noted that not being affiliated with an aircraft manufacturer made a negative contribution to the company's performance. Using the airplanes of a single manufacturer would have made it easier to train pilots and control the costs of service delivery. Another problem lay in the inherent instability of demand—it spiked on Friday night and Monday morning. That forced the company to carry excess capacity through the rest of the week. In addition, guaranteeing service within four hours of a request at any location in the United States led to considerable expenses arising from shuttling around empty airplanes.

In 2005, when the business was expanding rapidly, the company ended up showing an $80 million loss as a result of aircraft shortages and the need to sublet planes from others.[13] Entrance into the European market was unsuccessful, as costs turned out to be considerably higher than anticipated [Janjigian, 2008, pp. 136–138]. The company had also showed losses in not only 2005, but also 2001–2003, when the losses were sustained in the European market. During the first five years of its presence in Europe (2000–2004), NetJets accumulated only 80 clients [Buffett, 1977–2013, 2000–2007]. Independent analysts found that the company's difficulties in Europe arose because most local airports closed for the night and because clients were not allowed to be late for their flights, as takeoff and landing slots needed to be requested in advance.[14] Nevertheless, the clientele began to expand. During 2005–2006, the number of clients grew by 589.

---

13 Janjigian also talks about high capital expenditures driven primarily by aircraft purchases. It is important to remember that the fleet should have been paying for itself at an accelerated rate, as a result of arising from fractional ownership. As discussed, most planes were owned by customers. In principle, this ownership structure can reduce capital use, as the company has the ability to charge its customers a markup, effectively as if buying the aircraft "wholesale" and selling it "retail."

14 See Motley Fool: http://boards.fool.com/executive-jet-my-notes-12588152.aspx.

In his annual letter to shareholders in 2007, Buffett admitted that over the 10 years that Berkshire had owned NetJets, the company on the whole had generated losses, and the total loss amounted to $212 million [Buffett, 1977–2013, 2007]. In 2008, he did not comment on the company's performance. In 2009, he reported that over the course of the 11 years that the business was under Berkshire's ownership, the company had showed an aggregate pretax loss of $157 million. This loss was lower than it should have been, as the company's borrowing costs had been reduced by the practically free credit available from Berkshire. In 2009 alone, the losses amounted to a record $711 million. The later losses resulted from a sharp fall in demand, as interest in status goods and services contracted during the recent financial crisis. At its highest level (during Berkshire's ownership up to 2009), the debt burden reached $1.9 billion [Buffett, 1977–2013, 2009, 2010]. Finally, Buffett admitted that NetJets would have ended up in bankruptcy had it not been for Berkshire's deep pockets [Berkshire Hathaway, March 30, 2011].

In 2009, the CEO was replaced. This was a very rare case of management change implemented by Buffett. The new CEO, David Sokol, reduced the debt burden[15] and returned the company to profitability in a very short time. In 2010, the profit reached $207 million; in 2011, it was $227 million. Buffett again began to discuss the concept of a moat as it applied to the company. He felt that the moat could be widened by expansion into China [Buffett, 1977–2013, 2010, 2011]. In 2012, NetJets announced the largest order for airplanes in the history of private aviation: 425 aircraft that would cost the company $9.6 billion.

The story of NetJets illustrates that it is not particularly easy to pin down exactly what the nature of a moat is. Factors such as a lack of new aircraft or appropriately trained pilots may add to the depth and width of the moat if the company has locked out the potential competitors from development opportunities by securing the entire supply of these resources. Aircraft manufacturing, given entry barriers, is not

---

15 I was unable to find information on how this debt reduction was achieved, and I am nearly certain that the company did not disclose this.

dissimilar to a monopolistic industry, so it may be difficult to increase the supply of this resource. Alternatively, the moat-creating influence of any resource-related factor may prove temporary should the landscape of the industries supplying the resources change. More pilots or more airplanes may become available for various reasons, although this would take some years. The part of the moat that is created through more efficient operations may also prove transitory. Managing the operating costs is probably not all that straightforward,[16] even if the capital costs of buying the aircraft are successfully passed on to the customers. Of course, there has to be demand for the "castle's" products, as otherwise the most impenetrable "moat" will prove ineffective. In the case of NetJets, the demand rests on the habits and preferences of a specific, limited social segment. Should those preferences change, the business may be adversely affected. The fur industry, for instance, went through a period of slump driven by animal rights campaigners until demand reappeared in the emerging markets.[17] Should environmental campaigners effect, hypothetically speaking, a change of mindset in the users of civil aviation, the demand may fall globally.[18] In more general terms, the moat may be something akin to the reality of working in a very specific demand niche where the sophisticated logistics of entry are tough to overcome, and where once the niche is occupied by one or a few players, they are able to satisfy all the demand, so that it is not worthwhile for other competitors to attempt to enter. Also, a moat may be something that helps a particular company incur fewer losses when the whole industry is suffering. NetJets' story highlights that a castle with a moat is exposed to risks. It may fall victim to changing economic circumstances—for instance, when the castle's rapid expansion is undermined by a deep crisis.

16 In principle, although it is generally true that the larger the fleet, the better, for any geography and demand distribution, there will be a specific optimal quantity of aircraft that would maximize the quality of service while minimizing the operating costs. Sophisticated dynamic probabilistic modelling is continually needed to manage the operational costs.

17 For a good update on the recent evolution of the fur industry, please refer to the book by Frances Corner, head of London College of Fashion, [Corner, 2014, pp. 127–130].

18 The likelihood of this eventuality is probably not very high. Besides, technology may develop that will make aviation more environmentally friendly.

The Newspaper Business as a Franchise

Newspapers are "constantly losing ground in a battle for eyeballs."

—WARREN BUFFETT [BUFFETT, 1977–2013, 1993]

Since 1987, when Buffett talked about the survival of the fattest, the onset of the Internet age has altered the economic circumstances for newspapers, in particular, considerably. The industry could once have been described as fundamentally good, but because of technological changes, a deep structural transformation has begun in recent years, the outcome of which remains to be seen. This again points to the fleeting nature of competitive advantage. Buffett nevertheless continues to expand his presence in news publishing (he talks about his rationale in his recent letters to shareholders) and his forays into the newspaper industry present an interesting story. Let us start by exploring Buffett's earlier acquisitions in this industry, when it was still in its original form, which had probably been largely the same since newspapers were first invented. Clear economic franchises could still arise.

Buffett's first investment in the newsprint industry was probably his acquisition in 1969 of the *Omaha Sun*, a group of weekly papers in the Omaha area, which turned out to be a bad business: when the newspaper raised its prices, its circulation fell considerably. We already know that the *Omaha Sun* eventually met a sad end. Buffett held the paper until 1980, when it was sold to a publisher in Chicago, Bruce Sagan. By 1983, the paper had ceased to exist. As a result, the other Omaha paper, the *Omaha World-Herald*, became the only local paper. Buffett acquired the *Omaha World-Herald* in 2011.

After his unsuccessful investment in the *Omaha Sun*, Buffett began to research the economics of newsprint and media companies in depth. He arrived at the conclusion that if a paper had the second position in some area, then it was practically bound to fail. The view of many newspaper owners that in a large city a number of papers could coexist did not prove true in reality [Lowenstein, 1996, p. 223]. In a letter to one of his colleagues, Buffett argues with great conviction that in the early twentieth century in about 1,200 cities with daily newspapers almost 60 percent had two or more papers. By the 1970s, in about 1,500 cities with daily papers only 2.5 percent had two or more papers. The proprietors of those papers that were viewed as secondary in their respective markets realized that being second led to constant losses that could not be remedied by either monetary infusions or by diligent management [Lowenstein, 1996, p. 147]. Achieving this understanding brought optimism. It was simply necessary to find a paper that was or could become the only paper in its market. This pursuit of the surviving fattest ended up with the 1977 purchase of the *Buffalo Evening News*.

When Buffett bought the *Buffalo Evening News*, there was another paper in the local market: the *Buffalo Courier-Express*. The former had a larger circulation during the business week, while the latter had a Sunday edition. Sunday issues usually published more advertising—information about sales in department stores and the like—that targeted consumers. For this reason, many readers subscribed to the Sunday edition only. After the acquisition, the manager appointed by Buffett also introduced a Sunday edition to the *Buffalo Evening News*. During the promotional period, the price of the Sunday edition was set at 30 cents, while the price of the competitor's Sunday paper was 50 cents. For a time, the newspapers openly battled each other, with both understanding that in the end, only one of them would survive. During the local recession, the price war led to losses for both companies, but the position of the *Buffalo Evening News* was nevertheless stronger. Buffett stood behind the paper, and his pockets were deeper than those of the owners of the *Courier-Express*. He was able to continue covering his paper's losses for a longer period of time.

In the end, Buffett's competitors shut down their paper. Having acquired the local monopoly position, Buffett raised the prices for advertisers. He recouped the money that he had invested in approximately seven years, even though at the beginning he had been carrying substantial losses. According to independent estimates made in the late 1990s, Buffett was earning a nearly astronomical return on his investment in the *Buffalo Evening News*: around 90 percent annually (as estimated based on the original acquisition price; however, it is important to remember that there would also have been an impact from inflation) [Lowe, 2000, p. 145]. The *Buffalo Evening News* turned out to be one of the most profitable of Buffett's acquisitions.

There might have been, however, another significant element in the story of the *Buffalo Evening News*. According to some unconfirmed indications, which have not been discussed widely in public, the *Buffalo Evening News* did not publish a Sunday edition prior to its acquisition by Warren Buffett because of an informal agreement about the division of the market between the families that owned the two papers. If so, the original owners may have felt uncomfortable about breaking the agreement, but Buffett probably did not share their feelings. The value of the business may have been higher for him than for the old owners. The parties to the transaction could reach a mutually satisfactory sale price. The sale of the paper may have been a way to restructure the business and abandon personal obligations that could have been construed as unprofitable.

Buffett recommended a similar strategy to his friend Katharine Graham, the owner of the *Washington Post*, and the namesake of Buffett's mentor Ben Graham, with respect to her direct competitor on the local market—the *Washington Star*, which at one point belonged to the holding company Time Inc. The *Star* was losing its market share to the *Post*, which at the end of the 1970s controlled nearly two-thirds of their market. The *Star* proposed an agreement that would have lowered the costs and allowed both papers to stay in operation. The agreement stipulated that each paper would have retained a certain proportion of the market share and therefore the profit. Largely based on Buffett's advice, Graham made a much tougher counteroffer, which the *Star* rejected. Soon after that, the *Star* went out of business, creating a windfall for the *Post* [Lowenstein, 1996, p. 186].

In her memoirs, whose style at times is similar to that of Buffett's writings, Katharine Graham later talked about why the *Star* did not survive. Her reminiscences illustrate the idea of the winner-takes-all principle. In the case of the *Star*, there were no issues with the management or shortages of funding—the management was first-rate, and the owners were rather well off. She explains that social changes in the country, such as the growth of television network news, population flight from the inner cities to the suburbs, and urban problems that affected afternoon home deliveries, had strengthened morning newspapers and weakened the traditionally strong afternoon and evening papers. "Possibly most important of all was the economy. As prices rose, particularly for labor and newsprint, newspapers raised rates, forcing advertisers to choose between papers—not divide their advertising, as many had previously done. If a newspaper rose to a certain dominance, there was often a snowball effect: advertisers realized that more people could be reached through the larger newspaper, so in an effort to cut costs they eliminated the weaker one. Once the momentum got going, there was not much that could be done. In some ways, this is what happened to the *Star*" [Graham, 1998, p. 585].

While focusing on the acquisitions of the earlier years allows us to witness the process by which the winner takes it all, Buffett's investment in the Washington Post Company highlights how the "fattest winner that has taken all" can succumb to the technological changes affecting its industry.

The company went through an initial public offering (IPO) in 1971. Buffett began buying up the shares as early as 1973 during a period when the share price slumped. He fairly quickly built up a large stake, approximately 12 percent of the outstanding equity, at a cost of $10.6 million. The main media assets of the company were the newspaper the *Washington Post* and the magazine *Newsweek*. The company also owned five radio and television broadcasting stations, printing shops, and some other assets such as timberland in Canada.

We will focus on the media parts of the company. Adam Smith—the famous American journalist George Goodman, who wrote under this pen name—comments that neither during the IPO, which took place in June 1971, nor in the following years did the market see the value in the Washington Post Company. Professional investors did not seem to understand the Washington Post Company's business. Adam Smith tried out this idea on his Wall Street friends. "They could not see it. 'Big cities newspapers are dead,' they said. 'The trucks can't get through the streets. Labor problems are terrible. People get their news from television'" [Smith, 2006, p. xxxi]. The market had its own reasons for giving the Washington Post Company a low valuation. In 1971, the turnover amounted to $85 million and the profit to $4 million. In spirit, the *Post* still remained a local paper. In 1972, the paper got involved in the Watergate scandal by publishing scathing revelatory material about the wiretapping practices in the Nixon administration. Throughout the scandal, the company was under severe political pressure to stop publishing scandal-related information. Specifically, two of the company's broadcasting stations in Florida were at risk of losing their licenses.

The times were not particularly easy for the free press. Only a short while earlier, a federal district court had issued an injunction against the publication of the Pentagon Papers—archival material related to the decisions about the start of the war in Vietnam—by the *New York Times*. These archives were also published by the *Post*, and the paper was involved in a lawsuit with the government[19] [Schroeder, 2008, pp. 372, 373]. Then, in 1973, the paper's printers went on strike. In 1974 and 1975, the paper had to deal with another two serious strikes.

Graham's memoirs describe these events in detail [Graham, 1998]. They show that from the point of view of an outside observer, Buffett's investment in the *Post* would have appeared to be very risky. A many-month-long strike by the unions that started after Buffett's purchase of the stock could have resulted in the company's bankruptcy. If the paper was not published for several days, then its advertisers could migrate to competitors, and it might be difficult to get them to return. The strikers disabled the printing presses and set up a fence around the offices and the printing facility; the most active among the strikers were the printers, who worked in the same building as the journalists. Mrs. Graham was forced to look to small nonunionized printing shops for help. The printing plates were sent over by helicopters, which took off from the roof of the building. Permission for helicopter flights had to be obtained from the White House. The journalists worked in the building without leaving the premises at night. Once the printing presses had been repaired, they were operated by people who were loyal to the owners of the paper and had been specially trained to operate them. They worked 15 hours a day. In the end, the owners of the paper won the battle.

According to some sources, throughout the confrontation, Buffett was steadfast and confident that the conflict would be resolved. He believed in Mrs. Graham's ability to handle the pressure and prevail, eventually, in the fight.

In 1984, Buffett commented that in 1973, when the Washington Post Company was selling for $80 million on the market, he valued the company's assets, that is, its liquidation value, at a minimum of

---

19 The *Post* eventually won the lawsuit: http://www.washingtonpost.com/wp-srv/inatl/long term/flash/july/pent71.htm.

$400 million, or "probably appreciably more" [Buffett, 1984]. In 1991, Buffett again remarked that the "fair value" of the company at the time of his buying its shares amounted to between $400 and $600 million [Buffett, 1991b]. If we analyze the Washington Post Company as a going concern, then such a valuation is possible only if the model assumes taking over the business of competitors and growing market share and the business aggressively. By 1973, the *Post* had achieved the leading position in Washington—it accounted for 66 percent of the advertising space, 57 percent of the daily circulation, and 67 percent of the Sunday circulation. The paper competed with only one other paper, the *Star*. The company's role in Watergate and the publication of the Pentagon Papers brought the *Washington Post* nationwide fame.

Max Olson, an investment manager, attempted an ex post valuation reconstruction of the Washington Post Company for 1973. He valued the company on the basis of the information that would have been available in 1973, without taking any later data into account. In his model, he used a slowing growth rate assumption for the revenue (12 percent in the next five years, 8 percent in the five years after that, and 4 percent in perpetuity, whereas in 1971 and 1972, the company's growth rate had amounted to 13 percent a year) and a growth rate of 2 percentage points a year for the net profit margin. Olson viewed this as an adequate assumption, as it was lower than the industry average. This calculation resulted in a valuation of $380 million as a going concern [Olson, 2006]. This valuation, however plausible, would not have meant anything if the company had not prevailed against the strikers. The stock reached its peak level in 2004. In the annual report for that year, Buffett's stake was valued at $1.7 billion as of the year-end. This was an increase of 21 times or 18 percent a year, excluding dividends, which the company paid regularly.

After reaching these levels, the stock began to fall. At the end of 2005, Buffett's stake was valued at $1.4 billion, and in 2008, it was valued at $678 million. From 2009 on, Buffett no longer disclosed the value of the stake, as it was too low in comparison with Berkshire's other assets. It is possible to estimate the value of the stake through the market prices of the shares, however. The share price remained more or less stable until the end of 2012, although the problems within the

TABLE 2.1   The Washington Post Company's newspaper publishing division revenue and operating profit in 2005–2012.

	2005	2006	2007	2008	2009	2010	2011	2012
Revenue, million dollars	957	962	890	801	679	676	623	582
Revenue, year-over-year growth, percent	1%	0.5%	−7.5%	−10.0%	−15.2%	−0.4%	−7.8%	−6.6%
Operating profit, million dollars	125	36	66	−193	−164	−10	−21	−54

Source: The Washington Post Company 2005–2012.

company grew. As shown in Table 2.1 the Washington Post Company's publishing division revenue started to fall in 2007, and the profitability moved into the red in 2008. Buffett did not sell his shares, perhaps because of his loyalty to the Graham family.

For a considerable period of time, the loss-making business was subsidized by what is still the firm's cash cow, the Kaplan Company, which was acquired in 1984. This was a test-prep company that later moved aggressively into for-profit higher education. However, problems began to emerge even within the Kaplan Company.[20] The Washington Post Company started selling its media assets in 2010. *Newsweek* was sold for a symbolical price of $1. The buyer, the billionaire Sidney Harman, assumed $40 million in liabilities. *Newsweek*'s circulation peaked (at 3.3 million, according to the Alliance for Audited Media) in 1991. Later, the magazine suffered many of the problems facing the print media industry in general as more and more readers migrated to the Web for news. In 2011, Harman died. In the autumn of 2012, *Newsweek* announced that it would stop publishing a

---

20 The analysis of the Kaplan's problems is outside the scope of this book. For a good review of the issue, see for instance, the article on Kaplan in the *New York Times* [Lewin, 2010].

print edition at the end of the year. In August of 2013, *Newsweek* was bought by the digital news company International Business Times for an undisclosed amount [Haughney, 2013].

In August of 2013, the Washington Post Company reported the sale of the *Washington Post* newspaper and a number of other papers and assets for $250 million. The buyer was Nash Holdings, the investment company of Jeff Bezos, the founder of Amazon.com. His deep pockets allowed him to afford this purchase privately. Don Graham, the CEO, chairman, and a major shareholder of the Washington Post Company, convinced Bezos that Amazon.com's initiative in technologically driven delivery could create a robust future for the *Post* [Brandom, 2013]. Analysts concluded that the price tag was hefty. Bezos paid about 17 times 2012 EBITDA (earnings before interest, taxes, depreciation, and amortization), which was estimated to be $15 million, while the average sale of a metro U.S. newspaper has recently commanded a valuation of 3.5 to 4.5 times EBITDA [Saba, 2013]. Most likely, Bezos purchased the *Post* as a trophy asset.

Despite Buffett has continued with investment in newspapers, as we mentioned, he walked away from this acquisition. When he was asked to explain why, he jokingly remarked that "for him to have bought it for Berkshire would have saddled the next CEO with a metro newspaper that he or she possibly wouldn't want and to buy it personally would have at his death burdened his three children with the same kind of complex considerations" [Loomis, 2013]. In March of 2014, the final separation of Berkshire and Graham Holdings, as the Washington Post Company was renamed after the sale of the *Post*, took place. In the deal, which could be described as a cash-rich split-off, Berkshire will exchange its shares in Graham Holdings, with a market value of $1.1 billion,[21] for some of the holding's operating assets, a Miami television station, the shares of Berkshire owned by Graham, and about $328 million in cash. (We will not discuss the terms in depth, as they have been covered in detail in the press only recently.) If we assume that in exchange for his shares, Buffett receives assets that amount to around $1.1 billion, the market value of his stake, this implies that his return on a $10.6 million investment in 1973 equals 12 percent a year, not including dividends.

---

21 Owing to the performance of other assets held by the company, the market value of the stake had recovered from the levels seen in 2008.

Importantly, it is possible that Buffett remained a shareholder because of nonmaterial factors, and it may be that without these, he would have exited this investment at an earlier stage.

Buffett's expedition into the newspaper industry does not end here, and we continue the discussion of his investments in the industry in the next chapter. The story so far demonstrates how nontrivial is the task of finding first-class investment targets even within the "right" industries—one may have to take considerable risk, bet against the market, and invest in companies that are being besieged by strikers—and how complicated it is to find industries or companies with sustainable competitive advantage when technological shifts may change the economics of business entirely at any time.

Simple, Understandable, and Predictable Business; Conservative Attitude to Investment

> In investing, there is no score multiplier for making
> difficult investments.
> —WARREN BUFFETT [BUFFETT, 2003]

Buffett's other requirements for a business are easiness to understand: simplicity[22] and predictability of results. Investing in such a business is a reflection of an *investor's conservative position*. According to Buffett, it is the conservatism that separates true investing from speculation.

"Investment must be rational; if you can't understand it, don't do it," recommends Buffett [cited in Lowe, 2007, p. 152]. He prefers to be able to explain his mistakes. This means that he buys only things that he completely understands [Lowe, 2007, p. 152]. The ability to understand a business is a function of not only its relative simplicity or complexity, but also the investor's experience and her capacity to appreciate the mechanics of any particular business.[23] Thus, Buffett's next

---

22 Buffett discusses his requirements for the acquisitions' targets in his letters to shareholders. In the section Miscellaneous, from 1982 to 1989, he mentions that a business must be "simple" [Buffett, 1977–2013, 1982–1989].

23 Derivatives are not a simple business; however, Buffett uses derivatives extensively. We will discuss this in Chapters 5 and 6.

well-known principle is investing within one's circle of competence. We will discuss this concept in detail in the next chapter.

Buffett points out that when purchasing and managing businesses, he aims to follow a straightforward rationale. If the results are influenced by one factor and there is a 90 percent probability that this factor will have a positive effect, then the probability of success is 90 percent. If the situation is controlled by 10 factors and each will also have a positive effect with a 90 percent probability, then the probability of success is only 35 percent. "Since the chain is no stronger than its weakest link, it makes sense to look for—if you will excuse an oxymoron—mono-linked chains" [Buffett, 1977–2013, 2004]. Although in practice, Buffett invests in businesses with varying degrees of complexity, this framework can be used as a helpful analytical tool.

Buffett cites another motivation to invest in a "simple" business. He remarks, probably jokingly, that he invests only in companies that can be managed by "idiots" as the management of any company is bound to eventually stumble, show weakness, or find itself out of its depth. This complements Buffett's ideas on management that we discussed in the earlier sections of this chapter.

Buffett looks for businesses for which he believes he will be able to predict what the business will look like in 10 or 20 years. That means businesses that will be more or less the same as they are today, but will be larger and more internationalized [Schlender, Buffett, and Gates, 1998]. His definition of a great company is a company that will be great for 25 or 30 years [Lowe, 2007, p. 195]. Therefore, Buffett looks for the predictability of the results. Munger, who was instrumental in Buffett's making the transition from buying businesses inexpensively to paying higher prices for high-quality businesses, suggests another test: If you were stranded on a desert island for 10 years, in what stock would you invest? [Schroeder, 2008, p. 331]. Brad Kinstler, the current CEO of See's Candies, told Buffett that he once received a letter from a customer who was 100 years old. In the letter, she praised the company: the world has changed, but the taste of See's has remained the same [Chan, 2010, p. 103].

Predictability of how a business will look is significant for a number of reasons. First, the requirement for predictability over a specific time period ties in with the long-term investment horizon, which, in turn, frees the investor from focusing on short-term market movements that cannot be anticipated. The market is not always rational and may underestimate the value of assets, but sooner or later it will value the assets fairly, as was discussed by Graham.

Second, when the business is unpredictable, it is too easy to make strategic mistakes. "If something isn't very predictable, you should forget it because you don't have to be right about every company," advised Buffett in 1998 at the Berkshire shareholders' meeting ["Questions Concerning Warren Buffett and Investing"].

Unpredictable businesses are difficult to value, as the predictability and accuracy of valuation are connected: "Indeed, the formula for valuing all assets that are purchased for financial gain has been unchanged since it was first laid out by Aesop in about 600 B.C. His enduring investment insight was that 'a bird in the hand is worth two in the bush.' To apply this principle, one must answer only three questions. How certain is the investor that there are indeed birds in the bush? When will they emerge and how many will there be? What is the risk-free rate? If one can answer these three questions, the investor will know the maximum value of the bush—and the maximum number of the birds in the hand that should be offered for it" [Buffett, 1977–2013, 2000]. "If every financial asset were valued properly, they would all sell at a price that reflected all of the cash that would be received from them forever until Judgment Day, discounted back to the present at the same interest rate. There wouldn't be any risk premium, because you'd know what coupons were printed on this 'bond' between now and eternity. . . . If I can't do that, then I don't buy. So I'll wait" [Schlender, Buffett, and Gates, 1998].

It is the principle of predictability that guided Buffett to avoid investing in Internet companies.[24] "A business that must deal with fast-moving technology is not going to lend itself to reliable evaluations of its long-term economics,"—insisted Buffett already in 1993, when Internet

---

24 In the 1960s, Buffett also missed the boom in the so-called Nifty-Fifty stocks—fashionable shares of fast-growing companies with innovative products or marketing strategies. Companies in this group that remain well known today are Polaroid, IBM, Xerox, and Avon Products.

shares did not yet exist [Buffett, 1977–2013, 1993]. Later, when the fashion for Internet shares was at its peak, Buffett proposed including the valuation of Internet companies in final exams in business schools and marking the responses as follows: if a student gives a valuation, he fails the exam. Buffett was not referring to the prospects of the Internet as an industry as a whole. He simply felt that all Internet companies were simply too young and at such an early stage that it was impossible to judge which of them would succeed and which would fail.

Successful investing is not about assessing the extent to which a certain industry will affect society, or how much it will grow, but about understanding the competitive advantage of any given company and correctly evaluating the durability of that advantage. "The auto industry transformed the world, but many hundreds of car makers became road kill" [Buffett and Loomis, 1999]. "There is a lot of difference between making money and spotting a wonderful industry" [cited in Klott, 1999].

It was important to avoid investing not only in the Internet companies but also in those businesses that could be affected negatively by the Internet. The majority of the retail companies that Buffett owns specialize in products that are more difficult to sell over the Internet. He owns jewelry and furniture stores and the Dairy Queen chain of ice cream cafés. One of the shareholders of Berkshire remarked: "Since you can't download calories from cyberspace, it'll be difficult for captains of technology to eat much into Dairy Queen's profits" [Kilpatrick, 2005, p. 617].

If it is not possible to "muster conviction" about the value of a business because the possible estimates of its future cash flows are too widely dispersed, and such circumstances occur frequently when it is a new business or when the industry is changing rapidly, then any investment in this business must be regarded as speculative [Buffett, 1977–2013, 2000]. "The focus is not on what an asset will produce but rather on what the next fellow will pay for it." Speculation "is neither illegal, immoral nor un-American. But it is not a game in which Charlie and I wish to play" [Buffett, 1977–2013, 2000]. Munger expresses a similar view when he argues that Wesco—one of the companies in Berkshire's portfolio that Munger supervised over a long period of time—"continues to try more to profit from always remembering the obvious than from grasping the esoteric." "It is remarkable how much long-term advantage people like us have gotten by trying to be consistently not stupid, instead of trying to be very intelligent. There must be some wisdom in the folk saying, 'It's the strongest swimmers who drown'" [cited in Bevelin, 2003, p. 58].

In conservative investment strategy, compound interest assists capital growth over the long-term horizon: "Compound interest is a little bit like rolling a snowball down a hill. You can start with a small snowball and if it rolls down a hill long enough . . . and the snow is mildly sticky, you'll have a real snowball at the end" [Buffett, 1994a].

* * *

Successful investing requires finding a business with excellent fundamentals or, better still, a business that is also an economic franchise. It is also desirable that this business be simple, understandable, and predictable, and that it does not depend on fast-changing technologies. It is also important that the business is run by an excellent management team (even though the business must be idiot-proof). It is critical to not only have clarity as to what constitutes a great business and know how to value it, but also adhere to other principles, which we discuss in the next chapter, that must guide the investor's behavior, while the investor must remain consistent in his approach.

3

Warren Buffett's Investment Principles

Areas do not make opportunities.
Brains make opportunities.

—WARREN BUFFETT [CITED IN MATTHEWS, 2009, P. 104]

INVESTMENT IS DIFFERENT FROM SPECULATION. CONSERVATISM IS ONE of the prerequisites for the correct investor mindset. It follows naturally from this requirement that an investor must act only on things that she knows and understands. The investor must always remain strictly within her circle of competence. Conservatism also means that the investor must absolutely avoid speculation, and that, since the market will possibly delay valuing a business fairly, but will do so eventually, the investor must have a long-term horizon. If, when assessing a business, we rely on its internal value, not on its market valuation, then this means that we make decisions independently, rather than following others. In-depth study of the investment target, investing only within one's circle of competence, having a long-term investment horizon, and having an independent opinion are the four behavioral principles that Buffett follows and recommends to others. Conservatism also implies acquiring businesses inexpensively. This idea may perhaps be the most important of all Buffett's principles; however, he discusses it very little.

In-Depth Study of the Question

> There are no gains without pains.
>
> **—PROVERB**

Buffett studies any business thoroughly before making an investment in it, even though he is often able to make offers very quickly and seemingly without due diligence. To the seller, this process of deep study often remains invisible.

It is well known that, while he was at Columbia Business School, Buffett would spend hours in the library. He read old newspapers in order to reconstruct the past. "I would get these papers from 1929. I couldn't get enough of it. I read everything—not just the business and stock-market stories. History is interesting, and there is something about history in a newspaper, just seeing a place, the stories, even the ads, everything. It takes you into a different world, told by somebody who was an eyewitness, and you are really living in that time," remembers Buffett [cited in Schroeder, 2008, p. 148].

Bill Gates comments that when Buffett "invests in a company, he likes to read all of its annual reports going back as far as he can" [Gates, 1996]. Buffett indeed attempts to go back as far as possible. For instance, in 1996, Buffett admitted that he had been studying Coca-Cola's annual report for 1896 [Buffett, 1977–2013, 1996]. (In one of his essays, Charlie Munger reviews Coca-Cola's development since the nineteenth century [Munger, 2007b, pp. 181–197].) Buffett explains his fascination with hundred-year-old financial reports: he collects antique financial reports the way some people collect vintage cars. "As with geography or humans, it is interesting to take a snapshot of a business at widely different points in time—and reflect on what factors produced change as well as what differentiates the specific pattern of development from others also observed" [cited in Graham, 1998, p. 534]. In addition to annual reports and newspapers, Buffett reads specialist and trade publications, such as *Progressive Grocer*, which teaches how to stock a meat department in a supermarket [Schroeder, 2008,

p. 828]. He also reads *Broadcasting, Property Casualty Review,* and Jeffrey Meyer's *Beverage Digest* [Buffett, 2003]. Buffett owns 100 of almost every stock he can think of just to be sure he gets annual reports [Buffett, 2003].

It is not just a matter of broad research, however, extreme attentiveness to detail is also unerring. A characteristic example is Buffett's purchase of the Texas company Star Furniture. Buffett asked for the past three years' financial reports. Once he had examined them, he made additional inquiries. Melvyn Wolff, the then-owner of the company, recalls that one of these questions was about minor comments that the auditor had made concerning the statements for some of the years. Although the comments for each year were fundamentally the same, in one year the auditor had used a slightly different wording. Buffett noticed the difference and wanted to understand why the phrasing had been changed. Wolff remembers that he "almost fell off his chair" when he heard the question. He felt that, first, nobody would read that kind of footnote, but that even if someone did, it would be nearly impossible for that person to remember that the same footnote was phrased differently a couple of years earlier, and only a rather "incredible mind" would notice something of this kind [cited in Miles, 2002, p. 205].

Not everything about a company can be glimpsed by reading its whole history of financial reports. Katharine Graham tells a story about Buffett's devotion to studying the business of the *Washington Post* after he had bought shares in the company. Observing the production process, he spent several Saturday evenings in the mailroom. The individual papers were rolled up in brown wrappers, then addresses were pasted on them, and the wrappers were sealed shut. Later Buffett remarked that this experience "made him rethink the price of the Sunday paper" [cited in Graham, 1998, p. 550].

Adam Smith talks about one of Buffett's deals of the 1960s: "Warren noticed that bonds of the Indiana Turnpike were selling in the 70s, while the nearly identical bonds of the Illinois Turnpike sold in the 90s. The casual word among the bond crowd was that the maintenance allowance wasn't high enough behind the Indiana bonds. Warren got into his car and drove the length of the Indiana Turnpike. Then he went to Indianapolis and turned the pages of the maintenance reports of the highway department. He thought the Indiana Turnpike didn't need that much work and bought the bonds. They closed the gap with the bond of the Illinois Turnpike" [Smith, 2006].

There are plenty of similar examples. Prior to investing in the Walt Disney Company, Buffett went to see *Mary Poppins*—and was the only adult in the audience who was not accompanying a child [Boroson, 2008, p. 75; Lowe, 2007, p. 162]. He almost felt as if he had "to rent a kid" [Buffett, 1991c].

Investing Within One's Circle of Competence

> If you try to predict the future of everything,
> you attempt too much.
>
> **—WARREN BUFFETT [CITED IN LOWE, 2007, P. 158]**

Once at a shareholders' meeting, responding to a question from the audience about how one could learn to invest correctly, Munger remarked: "Ask, 'What do you own and why do you own it?' And if you can't answer that, you aren't an investor." Buffett added: "If you can't write an essay describing 'why I'm going to buy the entire company at the current valuation,' you have no business buying 100 shares of stock" [Matthews, 2009, p. 77]. "We don't bring anything to that game, so we don't play it"—this is how Buffett at one point explained why he had no interest in investing in nonferrous metals and precious stones[1] [Berkshire Hathaway Annual Shareholders' Meeting, 1988].

One should search for companies that are suitable for investment not within the whole economy, but only within one's circle of competence. This notion is a key principle of Buffett's investment philosophy. Charlie Munger points out, that "The game of investing is one of making better predictions about the future than other people. How are you going to do that? One way is to limit your tries to areas of competence. If you try to predict the future of everything, you attempt too much. You're going to fail through lack of specialization" [cited in Lowe, 2000, p. 176]. Buffett agrees: "Anybody who tells you they can value . . . all the stocks

---

1 Only a short time later, Buffett purchased a jewelry store, Borsheim's. We discuss the acquisition in this chapter and in Chapter 7.

in Value Line . . . must have a very inflated idea of their ability because it's not that easy. But if you spend your time focusing on some industries, you will learn a lot about valuation" [cited in Lowe, 2007, p. 158].

Perhaps, as far as your circle of competence is concerned, it is important that you have a clear awareness of its scale and limitations: "The most important thing in terms of your circle of competence is not how large the area of it is, but how well you've defined the perimeter" [Buffett, 1996b], and, "It's no sin to miss a great opportunity outside one's area of competence" [Buffett, 1977–2013, 1989].

Expanding one's circle of competence, even if one has Buffett's affection for the investment business, is a slow process. In an interview, Buffett was once asked to advise a beginner investor on how to start investing. Buffett recommended that the investor "learn about every company in the United States that has publicly traded securities," as he himself had done when he was young. "That bank of knowledge will do [an investor] terrific good over time." The journalist objected to the suggestion on the grounds that there were 27,000 public companies in the United States. This did not put Buffett out of countenance: "Well, start with the A's" [cited in Hagstrom, 2005, p. 26]. Buffett advises researching everything personally, without taking anything for granted. He recommends that an investor study one industry at a time, develop a level of expertise in half a dozen industries, and not accept the conventional wisdom about any industry as meaning anything at all until this wisdom has been thought through [Lowe, 2007, p. 157]. Once, in 2003, Buffett remarked that he is "generally familiar" with 1,700 or 1,800 American companies [Buffett, 2003].

This indeed was Buffett's starting point. As his biographers discuss, already by 1957, Buffett had deep understanding of practically every listed security, stock, or bond. He had been absorbing the details from the financial sections of newspapers and Moody's publications; "day after day, he had built up a mental portrait of Wall Street" [Lowenstein, 1996, p. 61]. As a young man, he read about "a couple of thousand" financial statements a year [Lowenstein, 1996, p. 130]. In later years, he studied approximately 20 annual reports a week, or around 1,000 a year.

In his letters to the shareholders, in the section that outlines his requirements for acquisition candidates, Buffett used to emphasize that he typically responds to all offers to buy companies within five minutes. If this is, indeed, the case, this is undoubtedly a reflection of Buffett's great erudition and professionalism, developed through reading many thousands of financial reports.

By examining Buffett's investments, we are able to contemplate the natural expansion of the circle of competence in practice.

He made investments in relatively unfamiliar industries, but at very low prices and involving noncritical sums relative to the size of his total capital. A good example of this is the acquisition of the furniture store Nebraska Furniture Mart (NFM) in Omaha. Buffett had never before invested in furniture stores, and his experience of investing in the retail sector generally had probably been negative.

In 1966, before the Berkshire Hathaway holding company was created, Buffett had acquired control of Diversified Retailing Company, a holding company that had been created to invest in retail. The holding company invested in Hochschild, Kohn & Co., which owned a department store in central Baltimore, and in Associated Retail Stores, a chain of women's apparel stores. Shortly after making these investments, Buffett realized that competition among department stores in Baltimore was very strong. He sold his stake in Hochschild in 1969. The new owners closed the flag-ship store in 1977, and the company went out of business in 1983. Buffett's investment in Associated Retail Stores turned out to be more successful, but it was sold in 1987 because of the declining econom-ics of the business. When the opportunity to acquire NFM arose in 1983—Buffett had been contemplating buying the company for some time; we cover this purchase in detail in Chapter 7—he took the risk. Arguably, he acquired NFM at such a discount that finan-cially the investment was probably perfectly safe.

Gaining a small foothold in a new area of interest before making a larger investment moderates the risks. Buying convertible bonds limits the downside[2] and allows the investor to study the company

---

2 The risk is limited to a degree, as, should the shares fall, the investor may be able to retain the bond component of his investment and earn fixed interest.

more deeply by having greater access to information about it. Some of Buffett's well-known acquisitions did not go beyond the purchase of the convertibles (for USAir and Williams, conversion did not occur).

Buffett also invested in diversified companies where he knew the main business well, but not the lateral ones. He studied this new (for him) business area, then made acquisitions in the industry, but through a company for which this business area was primary. We review examples of this later in the chapter.

Another avenue is acquiring a business that is adjacent to something that he already owned. For instance, Buffett invested first in a furniture store and then in a jewelry store. Both businesses are retail. Alternatively, buying a shoe store may serve as an introduction to the acquisition of a shoe brand and/or manufacturer. It is quite possible that the idea of buying the ice cream chain Dairy Queen in Nebraska emerged from the experience of successfully buying See's Candies, a California chain of stores selling premium chocolate.

Finally, it is possible to build up a position in a company gradually—first acquire a small stake, hold it for a period of time, study the business, and prepare for a larger acquisition should the opportunity arise.

Buffett's acquisition of a stake in Capital Cities, a large media holding company that included a publishing business (newspapers and magazines), broadcasting stations, and cable channels, presents an interesting case study from the point of view of the expansion of the circle of competence to include the whole of the newspaper and media industries. We will try to cast a wide net and contemplate the relevant circle of competence in the broadest sense by revisiting the story of Buffett's involvement in the newspaper industry. Newsprint and broadcasting are adjacent and interconnected aspects of news publishing and media. Both industries are being affected by the technological changes that are fundamentally reshaping them.

In 1985, Capital Cities' management approached Buffett with an offer to sell him a considerable number of newly issued shares in order to finance the acquisition of ABC, a well-known media company that was considerably larger than Capital Cities. This deal (the purchase of ABC by Capital Cities) was closed in early 1986. Buffett's share in the merged business amounted to 18 percent. The size of the original investment was around $518 million. This amount exceeded the size of Buffett's preceding transaction (the acquisition of the furniture store NFM) by 8 times and the size of Buffett's first transaction in this industry by 50 times, as observed by Roger Lowenstein[3] [Lowenstein, 1996, p. 261]. Despite the relative size of the deal, Buffett agreed to it immediately and offered a price that was appropriate in light of the market valuations. The speed with which he was able to make the decision was startling. He made his offer in the evening of the day of his meeting with the management of Capital Cities in New York, after a flight home to Omaha. It may be that Buffett had performed due diligence on all these companies in his mind as part of his continuous market research well before he was offered the opportunity to invest in them.

What specific *practical* experience stood behind Buffett's decision-making in this transaction?

First, Buffett's family history may have been of assistance. His grandfather on his mother's side had owned a paper. His father at one time was the editor of the *Daily Nebraskan*, the paper of the University of Nebraska. As a boy, Buffett delivered the *Washington Post*. He also managed distribution for the *Lincoln Journal* in Omaha. Charlie Munger, when he was living in California, was acquainted with the managers of the *Los Angeles Times*.

In 1966, Buffett bought shares in Disney, paying $4 million for 5 percent of the company. The company was valued by the market at $80 million. *Mary Poppins* alone earned $30 million in that year and would remain popular among children. "It's like having an oil well where all the oil seeps back in," commented Buffett. At the time, the company was still managed by the founder. Buffett went to see Walt Disney, who had not heard of him, as Buffett was still only 35 years old. Disney was extremely nice to Buffett, who concluded that the company could not have been more mispriced: "It was a joke." If Disney had

---

3 Roger Lowenstein refers to Buffett's investment in the Washington Post Company. Although this was not his first transaction in the industry, this acquisition is nevertheless a meaningful illustration of the magnitude of important preceding deals.

reached out to a large venture capital firm and asked it to buy into the business, the investment would have been made on the basis of a $300 or $400 million valuation, whereas the market was "convinced" that $80 million was the appropriate price. The market "ignored" the company because it was so "familiar," summarized Buffett. Nevertheless, Buffett sold his shares in the company the same year, but earned nearly 54 percent on his investment. He later admitted that selling Disney in 1966 was the greatest mistake of his career [Buffett, 1991c]. An extensive personal encounter with Walt Disney would undoubtedly have added to anyone's circle of competence.

At approximately the same time, as we discussed briefly in the previous chapter, Buffett was considering expanding into news publishing. Probably his first investment in the industry was the acquisition of the *Sun* in 1969. In 1971, he made an offer to buy the *Cincinnati Enquirer*, but it was not accepted. In 1973, he acquired a 4 percent stake in Affiliated Publications, the parent company of the *Boston Globe* (later he made a rule not to invest in IPOs). Buffett also became a minority stockholder in Booth Newspapers, Scripps Howard, and Harte-Hanks Communications—companies that owned newspapers and information sheets.

In the previous chapter, we talked in detail about Buffett's investments in the Washington Post Company in 1973 and the *Buffalo Evening News* in 1977. The Washington Post Company was a holding company that owned not only the famous newspaper, but also a minority stake in Capital Cities. Buffett obtained control over the *Buffalo Evening News* after the *Post* had declined to buy the company. Although the *Buffalo Evening News* had a direct competitor, Buffett must have felt that in the fight for the local market, his paper would win. Buffett also managed to accumulate a 4 percent stake in Time, Inc. which he later sold. At the end of the 1980s, Buffett approached the board of directors of Time to obtain permission to buy a large stake in the company, but his request was denied.

In 1977, Buffett briefly held a small stake in Capital Cities. He liquidated his position as a result of, as he put it, temporary insanity after a sharp rise in the company's share price. Capital Cities was also known to Buffett through another channel. In 1972, Charlie Munger, together with Rick Guerin, his Los Angeles partner and one of the early shareholders in Berkshire, bought the controlling stake in the Fund of Letters,[4] among whose investments were shares of Capital Cities and Daily Journal Corporation, which published one of the Los Angeles–based law newspapers. In 1986, Buffett was also a 2.5 percent shareholder in ABC. With this experience of investing into newspaper publishing and media under his belt, Buffett moved to commit to Capital Cities what for him at that moment was a considerable sum.

One year after the deal the shares of Cap Cities fell from $630 to $360, but by the end of 1992 the market value of Berkshire's stake in Capital Cities had risen by approximately three times. This growth implies a 17 percent annual return, excluding dividends. In 1993, Buffett sold a third of his stake in Capital Cities/ABC Inc. The rest of the stake was exchanged for shares of Walt Disney Company and some cash in 1996, when Disney acquired Capital Cities.[5] At the time of the exchange, Berkshire's residual stake in Capital Cities had a market value of $2.5 billion, where the whole stake had been acquired for $345 million originally. Berkshire had held the Capital Cities shares for about 10 years. The annual return amounted to 22 percent, excluding dividends. Most of the return was made up of unrealized gains. The newly acquired stake in Disney was sold in the late 1990s. This time Buffett's judgment served him better, as the company started going through a difficult period. In 1995, Disney's return on equity (ROE) amounted to 25 percent (this is a very high level for ROE). By 2000, the ROE had fallen to 3 percent, and in 2001 it was equal to 0; over the

---

4 Fund of Letters invested in the so-called letter stocks. Only qualified investors can buy these securities, and their liquidity is lower than that of the regular stocks. This fund was managed by Fred Carr. He was extremely successful early on, but he then brought the fund into such dire straits that it had to be closed by the SEC in 1970. It was reopened again in 1972. At the moment of its acquisition by Munger, the fund's shares traded at less than the balance sheet value of the stocks that the fund owned.
5 Buffett might have welcomed the acquisition. Michael Eisner remembers in his book *Work in Progress: Risking Failures, Surviving Success*, that when he mentioned to Buffett, who was a large Capital Cities shareholder, of his intent to acquire the company, Buffett replied: "Sounds good to me." Consequently, Buffett assisted the deal [Eisner and Schwartz, 1999, p. 378].

2002–2003 period, the indicator returned to the low level of 3 percent. Disney's share price again reached its 1998 peak only in 2010.

Buffett's circle of competence in this family of industries has continued to expand. In 1994, for instance, a large newspaper holding company, Gannett, announced that Buffett had bought 4.9 percent of its shares [Kilpatrick, 2005, p. 1151]. These shares were sold shortly after the purchase. In 2011, Buffett acquired a local paper, the *Omaha World-Herald*. In 2012, he announced the purchase of a stake in Media General newspaper group, which owned 63 local newspapers across the southeastern United States. According to Berkshire's annual report for 2012, Berkshire owns 28 newspapers in nine states. These are the *Buffalo Evening News*, the *Omaha World-Herald*, and the newspapers of the Media General Newspaper Group.[6] Buffett also moved into buying companies that supply investor information. In 1999, he began buying shares of Dun & Bradstreet. In 2000, he received shares of Moody's as a result of its spin-off from Dun & Bradstreet and has held this stake in the rating agency since that time.[7] In 2006, he acquired the information service Business Wire. Finally, as a result of Buffett's sale of his shares in the Washington Post Company, recently, Buffett is receiving other media assets.

There is another important component of the "circle of competence" principle. The managers of the acquired company are the carriers of

---

6 Buffett's most recent annual report does not discuss the performance of these new acquisitions.

7 During the spin-off, Buffett received 24 million shares of Moody's with a cost basis of $499 million, or $20.80 a share. As a result of a 2-for-1 split, Buffett ended up with 48 million shares at $10.40 a share. In 2007, Berkshire held 19.1 percent shares of Moody's. Perhaps owing to tactical considerations, Buffett did not reduce his stake in the company during the peak of the crisis, when the share price was at its lowest and when the attacks on the agency were at their strongest, but he began selling the shares gradually in the third quarter of 2009. By that time, the prices of Moody's shares had somewhat recovered their levels (at their 2007 peak, the shares cost $74 a share, and at their lowest level in March 2009, they cost $16 a share) By the end of 2010, Buffett had sold around 20 million shares, or 40 percent of his stake. The shares were sold at approximately $25 a share [LaFon, 2011]. Selling even at these low levels resulted in an annual return of around 10 percent, if we do not include dividends. Over the 2001–2009 period, the company paid dividends of $0.10–$0.40 a share annually. In 2013, when Moody's share price moved above $60, Buffett continued to reduce his stake. As of the time of this writing in May 2014, Moody's shares cost around $83 a share. Buffett still holds 24 million shares.

valuable information about which companies in their industry they consider as having good prospects. Many successful conglomerates have relied on insider information in making successful acquisitions in particular industries. Successful conglomerates often do not seek broad diversification; instead, they construct chains of acquisitions in only a few industries. In an interesting case study on this subject, focusing on the conglomerate Beatrice [Baker, 1992], it was shown that the company was creating value when its acquisitions were based on the industry knowledge of the managers of its subsidiaries, and the company was losing value when the acquisitions were made outside of the areas of managers' expertise.

The sequence of Buffett's acquisitions in the furniture industry is an insightful example of a construction of such a chain of purchases. After Buffett acquired Nebraska Furniture Mart at an extremely low price, Irv Blumkin, one of the managers and the son of the founder of the business, recommended that Buffett have a look at the chain of furniture stores R.C. Willey Home Furnishings in the state of Utah, the acquisition of which became possible in 1995. In turn, the owner of this chain, Bill Child, recommended that Buffett buy Star Furniture from the Texas entrepreneur Melvyn Wolff. This transaction took place in 1997. Finally, all three—Blumkin, Child, and Wolff—advised Buffett to buy Jordan's—a chain of furniture stores in New England owned by the Tetelman brothers. This purchase was made in 1999. In 2000, NFM bought Homemakers Furniture. This was the largest furniture retailer in Iowa. The company also had its own furniture production facilities. This acquisition was not done directly by Buffett. The decision was made at the level of NFM's management. In this group of acquisitions of furniture businesses, it is also possible to include the purchase of CORT, a company specializing in furniture leasing.

The sequence of deals in the jewelry industry is somewhat shorter. Buffett's first purchase—Borsheim's, a large jewelry store in Omaha—was suggested by the Blumkins, the owners of NFM. Borsheim's was owned by the Fridman family, relatives of the Blumkins. Their recommendation of the Fridman family to Buffett as decent and honest people was a very important factor in his acquisition of such a nontransparent business as dealing in jewelry and precious stones [Buffett, 1977–2013, 1988]. In 1995, following the advice of the new management of Borsheim's (the management had been changed after the death of the founder of the business), Buffett acquired Helzberg Diamond Shops. In 2000, he bought the Ben Bridge Jeweler chain.

Sometimes adhering to the principle of investing within one's circle of competence compels Buffett to sell shares. For instance, he sold his stake in the publishing business Affiliated Publications because he did not understand the value of a large stake in McCaw Cellular which Affiliated Publications held. Buffett admitted that he missed the play in cellular because it was outside his circle of competence [Kilpatrick, 2005, p. 881].

Expanding the circle of competence with great care does not fully ensure against mistakes in investment judgment. For instance, Buffett's purchase of the Dexter Shoe Company, which specialized in shoe manufacturing, in 1993 was not successful. Dexter could not withstand the competition from cheap Chinese imports and had to be restructured in 2001. In letters to Berkshire shareholders, Buffett noted that the purchase of Dexter was a mistake from two points of view: first, the acquisition itself was a mistake, and second, Buffett had paid for the acquisition not with cash, but with shares of Berkshire. He paid for Dexter with about 2 percent of Berkshire, which cost around $420 million at the time of purchase. In 2002 Robert Miles calculated that since the time of Buffett's purchase of the company, it had returned only $100 million in estimated pretax earnings, while its annual sales amounted to $200 million. According to Miles, the total value of Dexter could be estimated at $100 million (if using a price/sales multiplier of 0.5). The value of the Berkshire stake that had been paid for the company had risen to $2 billion, of which Dexter Shoe made up only 5 percent. Dexter may prove to have been Buffett's worst investment, commented Miles [Miles, 2002, p. 175]. In 2008, Buffett admitted the mistake and also called the deal the worst he had ever made [Buffett, 1977–2013, 2008].

Buffett may have had sufficient experience to avoid this investment. First, when he was acquiring Dexter Shoe, Berkshire's textile business had been already suspended for reasons similar to those that would eventually lead to the restructuring of Dexter. Second, Buffett and Munger had had some experience in the shoe industry. The family of Charlie Munger's first wife had owned a shoe store, and Berkshire had invested in shoe businesses previously. In 1990, Buffett acquired H.H. Brown Shoe, a Connecticut company specializing in the manufacturing, import, and retail sale of everyday footwear and footwear for active recreation. The company sold shoes through its own distribution network and through the footwear departments of large department stores. The company also manufactured shoes for specialized market segments—for example, shoes for mineworkers, repairers of telephone lines, and other workers. H.H. Brown Shoe remained successful largely because the manufacturing had been moved to China. In 1986, Buffett bought Fechheimer, a manufacturer of work clothes and uniforms (mostly for prison guards). This manufacturer also had a division that produced shoes for specialized uses. This investment was successful.[8] Therefore, strangely, the Dexter Shoe must have been within Buffett's circle of competence.

Long-Term Horizon

> My favorite time frame for holding a stock is forever.
>
> **—WARREN BUFFETT [BUFFETT, 1977–2013, 1988]**

"We don't sell. We have an entrance strategy, but we have no exit strategy," assures Buffett [cited in Kilpatrick, 2005, p. 770]. "Whenever Charlie and I buy common stocks . . . we do not have in mind any time or price for sale. Indeed, we are willing to hold a stock indefinitely so long as we expect the business to increase in intrinsic value at a satisfactory rate" [Buffett, 1977–2013, 1987]. "If you aren't willing to own a stock for ten years, don't even think about owning it for ten minutes" [Buffett, 1977–2013, 1996].

---

8 This acquisition must have been very successful indeed. The United States has the largest prison population in the world, both in absolute terms and in relative terms, as a proportion of the population. Prisons are often privately run but publicly funded; see http://news.bbc.co.uk/1/shared/spl/hi/uk/06/prisons/html/nn2page1.stm; http://www.economist.com/blogs/economist-explains/2013/08/economist-explains-8.

Indeed, Buffett's preferred investment horizon is not simply long-term, but forever. In his letters to shareholders, Buffett describes some of his investments as permanent holdings. Once in 1990, at a meeting at Harvard Business School, a student asked Buffett when he plans to retire; Buffett responded, "About five to ten years after I die" [Buffett, 1977–2013, 1991]. Perhaps Buffett is keen to make sure that the positive effects of his decisions are self-sustaining even after he is gone.

A long-term horizon is the logical consequence of the investment principles we discussed earlier. If we accept the idea that markets are irrational, and if we invest based on the fundamental attractiveness of industries and companies, then we will be successful only if we have the ability to wait for a time when the market will value our investment assets fairly. We need time, which is "the friend of the wonderful business, the enemy of the mediocre" [Buffett, 1977–2013, 1989]. "Many shall be restored that now are fallen and many shall fall that are now in honor." These words of Horace, quoted by Ben Graham and David Dodd at the start of their *Security Analysis*, were first read by Buffett in 1949. He remarks that he has come to appreciate these words more and more over the years [Buffett, 1977–2013, 2001].

Buffett's example of investing in the shares of Coca-Cola, which we discussed in the preceding chapter, is again poignant. In 1992, he told the following story: "You could have bought a share of Coca-Cola in 1919 for $40 a share. A year later it was $19.50. Sugar prices went up and you lost half your money. Today that $40, if you had reinvested all dividends, is worth $1.8 million and that's with depressions and wars. How much more fruitful it is to invest in a wonderful business" [Berkshire Hathaway Annual Shareholders' Meeting, 1992]. This observation was made in 1992. It would be interesting to know what Buffett would say about the company now, after a period of stagnation in the stock price that has lasted from the late 1990s until the present time.

Buffett speaks ironically about those who try to make money on short-term price movements. Already in 1968, he discussed some remarks made by a money manager: "The complexities of national and international economics make money management a full-time job. A good money manager cannot maintain a study of securities on a week-by-week or even a day-by-day basis. Securities must be studied in a minute-by-minute program." "Wow!" reacted Buffett. "This sort of stuff makes me feel guilty when I go out for a Pepsi"[9] [Buffett, 1957–1970, January 22, 1969]. This brings to mind the definition of a long-term investment by Nick Leeson, who bankrupted Barings Bank. He regarded a position as long-term if it was not closed out overnight [Leeson, 2007, p. 50]. Buffett insists that he never attempts "to make money on the stock market." He buys "on the assumption that they could close the market the next day and not reopen it for five years" [cited in Goodman, 2013]. In his view, one "could be somewhere where the mail was delayed three weeks and do just fine investing" [Grant, 1994, p. 58].

Buffett's stay-put behavior reflects his view that the stock market serves "as a relocation center at which money is moved from the active to the patient" [Buffett, 1977–2013, 1991]. He disapproves of speculation with Berkshire shares and does not advertise Berkshire's short-term results. The company does not talk about quarterly earnings, does not have an investor relations department, and does not do conference calls with Wall Street analysts. Buffett does not want to have people who are focusing on what's going to happen in the next quarter or even the next year among Berkshire's shareholders. "We want people to join us because they want to be with us until they die" [Schlender, Buffett, and Gates, 1998].

Having a long-term investment horizon allows investors to save significantly on transaction costs, such as brokers' commissions, and on taxes, which are levied on actual income and not on paper profits. Indeed, a considerable part of investors' profit is distributed among fund managers, financial consultants, and traders executing transactions. In 2001, Buffett estimated that these sums were approximately $130 billion a year, of which around $100 billion were related to the Fortune 500 companies. In other words, investors were dissipating almost a third of the profits that the Fortune 500 companies were earning for them—$334 billion in 1998—by handing it over to various types of "helpers." Investors would have preserved their $130 billion if things in reality were as they were described in a cartoon in which a news commentator says: "There was no trading on the New York Stock Exchange today. Everyone was happy with what they owned" [Loomis, 2001].

9 Evidently, Buffett was yet to transition to Coca-Cola.

Internet trading has reduced investors' costs somewhat, but in substance, Buffett's views remain topical.

Buffett does not liquidate his investments even when, in his view, they are considerably overpriced. This buy-and-hold approach is one of the contentious aspects of his strategy. Various disagreements exist among the supporters of value investing. Scholars of finance argue that even Buffett's teacher, Benjamin Graham, insisted in the 1940s that a simple market timing strategy (entering the market when the shares were inexpensive relative to long-term average profits and selling the shares when they were relatively expensive) delivered better results than a buy-and-hold strategy [Barsky and DeLong, 1990, p. 276]. Fisher cited arguments in favor of market timing. Marc Faber is another famous value investor who does not agree with the buy-and-hold approach.

In Chapter 8, we discuss other aspects of the buy-and-hold strategy. It is a critical part of Buffett's professional image. It aids in negotiations with family business owners. This may be one of the reasons why the strategy is advertised. In practice, this principle is not something that Buffett follows dogmatically. The reasons for this, some of which we mentioned already, may be varied. A researcher compiled a list of companies whose shares Buffett bought after 2000 that did not remain in the portfolio for a long time: Citigroup, Walt Disney, Best Buy, Gap Inc., Duke Energy, Cadbury Schweppes, Liz Claiborne, and Level 3 Communications, among others [Janjigian, 2008, p. 120]. Another buffettologist found 29 stocks that Buffett had held for less than five years. Among these stocks are those of companies that Buffett regards as being in strategically suitable industries. For instance, Buffett held the shares of the newspaper holding company Times Mirror, bought in 1980, and Gannett, purchased in 1994, for only a year. The shares of the publishing holding company Time Inc., purchased in 1982, he kept for four years [Altucher, 2005, p. 4].

Buffett warns against calling long term those investments that were meant to be short-term but became long-term because the investors could not achieve the desired results quickly. Buffett recommends being suspicious of those managers who fail to deliver in the short term and blame it on their long-term focus. "Even Alice, after listening to the

Queen lecture her about 'jam tomorrow,' finally insisted, 'It must come sometimes to jam today'" [Buffett, 1977–2013, 1992].

Independence of Opinion

> You can't buy what is popular and do well."
>
> **—WARREN BUFFETT [CITED IN HUGHEY, 1985]**

"It always amazes me how high-IQ people mindlessly imitate. I never get good ideas talking to other people," Buffett tells us [cited in Grant, 1994]. If this is not always true, then it is almost always true.

Following the majority is not the best way to earn large amounts of money. "I give you the one piece of advice that I got at Columbia from Ben Graham that I've never forgotten, which is: You're neither right nor wrong because other people agree with you. You're right because your facts are right and your reasoning is right—and that's the only thing that makes you right" [Buffett, 1991a]; we discussed this in Chapter 1 when we analyzed Graham's investment principles.

Buffett comments that people are interested in stocks when their prices are high or too high, but prices are too high because human psychology makes them so. The mechanics of bubble formation in the securities markets is simple: during a bull market, there comes a point when all participants have made money, regardless of what system each of them subscribes to; then more people are drawn into the market, and they are influenced not by interest rates and company profits, but by the idea that it simply appears to be beneficial to be invested in stocks. "These people superimpose an I-can't-miss-the-party factor on top of the fundamental factors. . . . Like Pavlov's dog, these 'investors' learn that when the bell rings—the one that opens the New York Stock Exchange at 9:30 a.m.— they get fed. Through this daily reinforcement, they become convinced that there is a God and that He wants them to get rich" [cited in Loomis 2001]. In reality and not in one's imagination, this process will end with losses. A bubble market allows the creation of bubble companies that are designed to make money from investors rather than for them, but "a pin lies in wait for every bubble. And when the two eventually meet, a new wave of investors learns some very old lessons: First, many in Wall

Street . . . will sell investors anything they will buy. Second, speculation is most dangerous when it looks easiest" [Buffett, 1977–2013, 2000].

As Buffett observes, the line separating investment and speculation becomes blurred when most market participants have recently enjoyed triumphs. "Nothing sedates rationality like large doses of effortless money" [Buffett, 1977–2013, 2000]. "Many people get interested in stocks when everyone else is. The time to get interested is when no one else is. You can't buy what is popular and do well" [Hughey, 1985]. "I will tell you how to become rich. Close the doors. Be fearful when others are greedy. Be greedy when others are fearful."[10] Buffett appreciates pessimism because of the prices it produces: pessimism, "sometimes pervasive, sometimes specific to a company or industry," is the most common cause of low prices. "It's optimism that is the enemy of the rational buyer" [Buffett, 1977–2013, 1990]. "Fear is the foe of the faddist, but the friend of the fundamentalist"—remember that sooner or later, the market will price securities at their fair value [Buffett, 1977–2013, 1994].

In Buffett's view, to be a successful investor, it is not sufficient to have an appropriate education. To be able to distinguish between a good and a bad business, it is necessary to have an intuition. One must also have self-control and self-confidence to be courageous enough to hold an opinion that is independent of that of the crowd, to act conservatively and without leaving the framework of the boundaries that one has set for oneself. An independent opinion is a key component of Buffett's investment doctrine. Buffett, as Munger comments, "believes successful investment is intrinsically independent in nature" [Grant, 1991].

The Purchase Price

> We try to price, rather than time, purchases.
>
> —WARREN BUFFETT [BUFFETT, 1977–2013, 1990]

Early in his career, Buffett spoke openly about the importance of a low acquisition price. In 1963, he wrote to the partners in his fund: "Never

---

10 Most sources suggest that Buffett spoke these words at a lecture at Columbia Business School in 1951, when he was 21. Perhaps he borrowed these words from Graham.

count on making a good sale. Have the purchase price be so attractive that even a mediocre sale gives good results" [Buffett, 1957–1970, January 18, 1963]. In 1977, he wrote to his shareholders that Berkshire was ready to buy other companies that were things that "we can understand, with favorable long-term prospects, operated by honest and competent people, and available at a very attractive price" [Buffett, 1977–2013, 1977]. In 1978, he published advertising that repeated his earlier words: he was looking for businesses that were "priced very attractively" [Buffett, 1977–2013, 1978]. In 1992, in his letter to shareholders, he quoted his own advertising from 1977. He was looking to buy at low prices. "All intelligent investing is value investing—to acquire more than you are paying for" [Questions Concerning Warren Buffett and Investing]. In more recent times, a low acquisition price has no longer been included in the formal requirements for acquisition targets. In my view, such a requirement has the ability to deter sellers.

Buffett appears to feel that the market is excessively high when investments that he would consider suitable are not available at a price that he considers reasonable and vice versa. In 1973, during a period of inflated markets, when share prices were very high and Buffett could not find anything to buy, he remarked that he felt "like an oversexed guy on a desert island" [cited in Lenzner, 1993]. In 1974, the market corrected. It fell 50 percent from its peak in November 1972; shares were relatively inexpensive, and, in Buffett's opinion, the time to start investing had arrived—this time, he felt like an "oversexed man in a harem" [cited in Davis, 1990]. In 1984, Buffett noted that it had been a considerable time since it was as difficult to find equity investments that met his standards of quality and value versus price.[11]

Pricing of purchases automatically leads to market timing. When Buffett is unable to locate investment targets that suit his requirements, he may avoid investing, sometimes for over the course of several years in a row. This demonstrates his independence of opinion in practice.

11 What would be Buffett's opinion today? In 1974, the S&P fluctuated between 83 and 94 points; by 1984, the index rose to 150 to 160 points; consequently it grew almost without interruption until its peak of around 1,500 points in March of 2000. (As of the time of this writing, in January of 2015, the S&P was around 2,000 points.)

He seeks not to compromise his investment standards, although he finds that doing nothing is the most difficult task of all: "One English statesman attributed his country's greatness in the nineteenth century to a policy of 'masterly inactivity.' This is a strategy that is far easier for historians to commend than for participants to follow" [Buffett, 1977–2013, 1984]. Nevertheless, Buffett appears to be able to cope with the challenge.

During peaking markets Buffett either fully suspends or reduces portfolio investments, for it is possible to buy shares in a company at any time. He left the market as a portfolio investor when the market bubble was inflated—as it was, for instance, in the 1960s, when he closed his fund, or in the late 1990s (between 1997 and 2000). At the same time, Buffett disregards market conditions when it is a matter of buying a company as a whole, as there is a risk of losing the investment opportunity forever.

Buffett avoids talking about what he considers inexpensive. He does not "get specific on [particular] stocks" [Buffett, 1994a]. In my view, he does not elaborate on whether any share price is cheap or expensive because such information is actually of little use. His assessment of whether a specific company is under- or overvalued is not directly transferable to other companies; and such an assessment is not easily transferable in time, either. A general understanding of business valuation principles is necessary. However, Buffett offers valuation guidance that relates to the market as a whole. Estimates of whether general market levels are high or low, are informative, because in a stable economy, aggregated indicators ought to be more stable. GDP is less volatile than the profits of individual companies. The growth rate of GDP also does not fluctuate as widely as the growth rate of a company or an industry might. Historical average aggregate indicators are likely to provide better guidance.

The general level of the market may be assessed through a number of indicators. P/E (price/earnings ratio), Tobin's q, DIV/P (dividend yield—dividend/price), and MC/GDP (market capitalization/GDP). Buffett prefers MC/GDP. He finds that "if the percentage relationship falls to the 70% or 80% area, buying stocks is likely to work very well for you. If the ratio approaches 200%—as it did in 1999 and a part of 2000—you are playing with fire"[12] [Buffett and Loomis, 2001]. Starting from the 1950s, MC/GDP remained at an acceptable level in all years until 1996, if we exclude a short period during the 1960s. From 1996 onward, this indicator hovered at dangerous levels, except for 2003 (the market low when the bubble of the late 1990s corrected) and during the crisis of 2008–2009.

In my view, the P/E multiplier also works. In the second section of Chapter 1, we discussed the benchmarks of P/E and Shiller's P/E ratios. The average historical P/E indicators for the American market from 1871 are 14 and 14.5, respectively. We do not know what levels Buffett considers to be as reasonable value, and we will not attempt to guess, as the dynamics of MC/GDP and P/E do not quite coincide. I would suggest using as guidance the P/E levels examined by Robert Shiller. He showed that the higher the market multiplier when the investment is made, the lower will be the return on the investment in the long term.

* * *

The conversation about Buffett's investment principles does not end here. His investment philosophy is based on his beliefs about how the capital markets work and what drives the behavior of managers of public companies. Buffett's understanding of these issues is different from that of the traditional views. We discuss Buffett's position on modern financial theory in Chapters 5 and 6. In the next chapter, we talk about his approach to investment as opposed to that of two other investors and financial theorists who played significant roles in the securities markets at the end of the twentieth century.

---

12 Following Buffett's advice, investors must also remember that MC/GDP depends strongly on the institutional organization of an economy and the share of GDP, generated by public companies. Thus, this indicator does not have a target level and is not directly transferable to other markets. For example, this indicator is much higher for Switzerland, a country with a relatively small market but with large corporations that operate globally.

4

Comparing Buffett with Other Investors

It is better to be approximately right than precisely wrong.
—WARREN BUFFETT [BUFFETT, 1977–2013, 1993]

IN THIS CHAPTER, WE WILL COMPARE BUFFETT'S INVESTMENT STRATEGY to those of two other investors. The first is Robert Merton, a famous financial theorist, a critical contributor to the Black-Scholes paradigm, a Harvard Business School professor, a Nobel Prize winner, and one of the founders of the notorious Long-Term Capital Management (LTCM) hedge fund. Based on the efficient market hypothesis, which we briefly discussed in the Introduction (and continue to discuss in Chapter 5), a new approach to investment and risk management began to emerge during the 1970s and 1980s. It was founded on the premise that it was possible to model the behavior of the stock market and the individual prices of securities through the prism of a statistical distribution. The average return and the return's variation around its mean would be used to describe that distribution.

Probabilistic assessment of the likelihood of any return occurring was one of the central ideas that defined this new school of thought. Roger

Lowenstein reports that by the 1990s this mentality was absorbed from academia by most on Wall Street: "Every investment bank . . . on Wall Street was stuffed by young, intelligent PhDs who had studied under Merton, Scholes, or their disciples" [Lowenstein, 2002, p. 64]. Robert Merton could be viewed as the philosophical parent of this new paradigm[1] and LTCM as the ultimate expression of this philosophy based on broad statistical assessment and probabilistic modeling.[2]

The second investor is Peter Lynch, a celebrated financial manager who ran the Magellan mutual fund at Fidelity Investments from 1977 to 1990. Peter Lynch, although active at a slightly earlier time, was a follower of a more traditional approach. I will show that the first of these two investors was practically the direct opposite of Buffett, and the second a near perfect clone.

Warren Buffett and Robert Merton

Underneath the mathematical elegance . . . there was quicksand.

—WARREN BUFFETT [CITED IN LOOMIS, 1998]

Robert Merton, like Warren Buffett, is not just a theorist of finance and investing or portfolio management. Merton has tested his models and theories in practice. While Merton made the transition from theory to practice, Buffett's system emerged naturally from his work.

I once studied in Merton's class. I was left with a very strong impression. He is probably one of the most intelligent people I have ever encountered, and most certainly the best teacher I have ever had. People often say the same thing about Buffett: "He is the most intelligent

---

1 Although other scientists could be described as cocreators of the paradigm, it was Merton who finalized the most advanced version of the model that relied on the concept of continuous time and prices.

2 While Robert Merton and another famous academician, Myron Scholes, were the intellectual backbone of the fund's activities, the investment strategies were driven by the fund's traders, who were often Merton's former students. We will be comparing Buffett's approach to that of an aggregate persona as Merton's ideas blended with the personalities of his colleagues. In my analysis I draw inspiration from the excellent books by Nicholas Dunbar [Dunbar, 2000] and Roger Lowenstein [Lowenstein, 2002]. The authors thoroughly review the LTCM story and offer a portrait of the contemporary intellectual climate.

person among everyone I know." The first comparison between Merton and Buffett is called for here. Whereas Buffett thinks, or at least declares that he thinks, that for successful investing, it is not necessary to be particularly clever, as self-discipline is more important, Merton and his colleagues, on the contrary, when creating their fund, LTCM, believed that they would be more successful than others because their models were better, more sophisticated, more advanced, and therefore more capable of predicting the future accurately than those of everyone else.

The managing company of the fund was created by former employees of Salomon Brothers who belonged to its famous arbitrage group, which was the envy of all investment banks.[3] The fund's founder and the main shareholder of the managing company was John Meriwether, who had previously been in charge of bond trading at Salomon Brothers and of the arbitrage group. Robert Merton was invited to join LTCM, along with Myron Scholes, also a famous finance professor, a Nobel laureate, and one of the authors of the Black-Scholes formula, and David Mullins, a former student of Merton's who had previously taught at Harvard and served on the Board of Governors of the Federal Reserve.[4]

Merton and Meriwether's personal connection started at Salomon. Meriwether had supported Merton's appointment as an advisor to the bank's CEO, John Gutfreund. Merton resigned from his position at Salomon in 1992, after Meriwether and Gutfreund had stepped down from their posts because of a scandal. Paul Mozer, a trader under Meriwether's supervision, had been found to have acted illegally; his actions brought the bank to the brink of collapse and Buffett's investment in the bank—under the threat of a full write-off. At that time Buffett, who had had to take charge of rescuing Salomon, made no attempt to retain Merton [Dunbar, 2000, p. 115].

The LTCM fund was opened in 1994. It attracted $1.25 billion of capital. This was the largest sum that had ever been raised, over the

---

3 According to Roger Lowenstein the group made more than $500 million over its last five years at Salomon [Lowenstein, 2002, p. 33]. Nicholas Dunbar reports larger numbers and notes that over 1990–1993 the group was responsible for 87 percent of Salomon's profits [Dunbar, 2000, p. 123].
4 He was viewed at the FED as second only to Greenspan, to whom Mullins was also thought to be a successor [Lowenstein, 2002, p. 37].

whole recorded history of financial markets, by a first-time management team. Investors in the fund included such well-known organizations as Sumitomo Bank, Dresdner Bank, Liechtenstein Global Trust, Bank Julius Baer, Garantia (the largest investment bank in Brazil at the time), the Central Bank of Italy, Hong Kong Land and Development Authority, Government of Singapore Investment Corporation, Bank of Taiwan, Bank of Bangkok, the state pension fund of Kuwait, Paine Webber (a U.S. investment firm), the endowment funds of a number of U.S. universities (including St. John's University in New York and the University of Pittsburgh), and some American celebrities—senior bankers and Hollywood stars [Lowenstein, 2002, pp. 37–38; Dunbar, 2000, p. 130].

Warren Buffett was also approached for an investment. He responded: "I am not an investor in other people's funds" [cited in Schroeder, 2008, p. 658]. "The jovial billionaire was his usual self—friendly, encouraging, and perfectly unwilling to write a check" is how Buffett's biographer describes the outcome of the meeting between the fund managers and Buffett about the potential investment [Lowenstein, 2002, p. 32]. According to Nicholas Dunbar, Buffett refused because ". . . mathematical money machines didn't impress" him [Dunbar, 2000, pp. 124–125].

Buffett probably would not have wanted other managers to capitalize on his name (Buffett did not support the Berkshire "tracker" fund ideas that we discuss in the next chapter). Although the creators of the fund were well known in the investment community and were able to raise ample capital, Buffett's participation in the venture would have added another level of respectability to it, and once he had joined, attracting any amount of capital would have been more than extremely easy. Munger admitted that these reservations were taken into consideration [Schroeder, 2008, p. 655]. Buffett's overall skepticism about becoming essentially a fund of funds, at least to the extent of the capital invested, is entirely understandable.

LTCM was planning to (and eventually did) make money on arbitrage transactions. Bets would be made (and were made) on the changes in the spreads between different securities. It was intended to locate these "mispriced" by the market opportunities through the use of advanced models that had been tested on large arrays of market data (at times the fund did get indirectly involved in the local politics of the markets in which it operated). All the other investment risks, aside from these very specific mispriced situations, were meant to be removed through hedging.

Although the fund's strategies have been widely discussed and are well understood, I will nevertheless briefly go through a simple example. For instance, if the bet is that one bond is mispriced relative to another,[5] and therefore that bond's price is going to change, as the market will seek to correct the mispricing, then that bet would consist of taking a long position in one of the bonds and a short position in the other (or in the replicating set of securities). The decision as to which bond to buy and which bond to sell, in turn, would depend on whether the spread between the two is expected to rise (widen) or fall (narrow). The exposures to market movement (whether interest rates overall would rise or fall) would cancel each other, and thus, in theory, the direction of the market movement would not be material to the bet. The return on the bet would depend only on the change in the bonds' prices relative to each other.

Since the price spreads between securities that had to be captured were small in absolute terms, in order to amplify the return on capital invested the fund intended to use leverage actively. The debt/equity ratio was to be maintained at 20 or 30 to 1. With this leverage, the highest loss that LTCM contemplated was 20 percent of its assets, and the fund estimated that the odds of this loss were no more than one in a hundred [Schroeder, 2008, p. 655]. The expected losses and their probabilities were derived from broad statistical analysis and attempts to model markets mathematically.

As another instrument of protection against losses, the fund relied on diversification, so investments would have to be made in markets, for instance, Russia and Italy, that to the managing partners appeared to be unrelated to each other [Lowenstein, 2002, pp. 94, 95].

As history knows, LTCM's venture ended in tears. An economic trouble in a single geographical market, Russia, led to a contagion throughout

---

5 The relative mispricing may occur between two bonds of slightly different durations as one may be more liquid than the other. The price of the less liquid bond may not reflect its economics accurately. See an illustration in [Lowenstein, 2002, pp. 43–44].

the financial system. Roger Lowenstein described the atmosphere of distress: "the crisis in Russia, weakness in Asia, Iraq's refusal to permit full weapons inspections, the possibility of China devaluing its currency . . . global investors . . . furiously piled into Treasuries . . . no one wanted risk" [Lowenstein, 2002, p. 141]. The spread positions widened against the fund and the synchronized movements of the securities that the fund's models expected to be uncorrelated defied the diversification of the portfolio.

It is now well understood that the correlation of prices seemingly unrelated from the economic point of view of assets may become nearly perfect during a crisis. The wide use of leverage and similar risk management systems in different institutions that compelled market participants to cut similar positions at the same time were some of the mechanisms that contributed to the sudden emergence of this strong correlation. Investors were also affected by liquidity constraints and were often able to reduce positions only in those markets where liquidity still remained. As Roger Lowenstein described it, "you don't sell what you should. You sell what you can" [Lowenstein, 2002, p. 42]. In 2003, possibly with LTCM in mind, Buffett remarked: "History teaches us that a crisis often causes problems to correlate in a manner undreamed of in more tranquil times" [Buffett 1977–2013, 2002].

The crisis forced LTCM's leverage to reach 55 to 1 [Lowenstein, 2002, p. 162]. This level of leverage may have been attained inadvertently, since on illiquid markets, the fund was unable to close out positions in order to reduce its borrowing. However, Nicholas Dunbar makes an interesting observation: when the fund was at its zenith, Scholes and Merton had a vision of zero capital and infinite leverage. This was Robert Merton's dream of a perfect world, achieved through the natural progression along the spiral of financial innovation. In this world hedging was so perfect that the need for public capital no longer existed [Dunbar, 2000, pp. 190, 210]. In practical terms, the banks lent to the fund, such was its standing in the investment community, on the basis of one to one without a haircut on the collateral bonds. This position, if taken into extreme, would result in the zero capital and infinite leverage state.

Once the fund took on unsustainable losses, if not for an intervention and a rescue package and the consequent support of the financial system by Greenspan's Fed, the fund could have affected the global financial system to the extent of over $1 trillion, as LTCM's derivatives positions amounted to a total of $1.25 trillion, or the entire annual budget of the U.S. government[6] [Dunbar, 2000, p. 191].

Despite the fund's spectacular collapse, the opinions expressed at the time were that just on the basis of that one precedent, it would have been premature to decide that the use of sophisticated financial modeling for these kinds of investment decisions would be unjustified in the future. Merton Miller, also a Nobel laureate in economics and the coauthor of the Modigliani-Miller theorem, commented on the subject: "the question . . . is whether the LTCM disaster was merely a unique and isolated event, a bad drawing from nature's urn; or whether such disasters are the inevitable consequence of the Black-Scholes formula itself and the illusion it may give that all market participants can hedge away all their risk at the same time" [cited in Lowenstein, 2002, p. 143]. Perhaps it is not only the formula that creates an illusion of everyone being hedged at the same time. The idea that it is possible for everyone to be hedged at the same time is itself an illusion. Nicholas Dunbar reports that Robert Merton avoided discussing how his theories had been "tested to destruction" [Dunbar, 2000, p. 229].

Buffett would have viewed negatively practically every element of the investment system that LTCM used. It is precisely the elements that Buffett would have disliked that eventually led the fund to its ruin.

First, Buffett would have considered a debt/equity ratio of 30 to 1 or 20 to 1 to be unacceptable. Buffett's insurance business generates leverage for Berkshire, but its levels of leverage, as calculated by analysts, are nowhere near as high. We discuss this subject in greater detail in Chapter 6.

Second, Buffett dislikes the idea of diversification. As we discussed, in his view, investing in one excellent company—for instance, a stable business that is generating real income—may be safer than holding a well-diversified portfolio of securities. LTCM relied on diversification, but the protection that this was expected to provide turned out to be a myth.

---

6 The total size of the notional value on which a derivatives contract is written is important: although physical assets are not held outright in this amount and relatively little capital is involved, it is the size of the notional value that dictates the extent of the economic power that the contract is likely to entail.

Third, Buffett relies on very simple mathematics—at most, he discounts future cash flows with risk-free rate. He minimizes risks associated with investing by managing his circle of competence, by investing in what for him are simple, understandable, and predictable businesses; by thorough study of the investment target and its history; and by selecting the "right" people to run his subsidiaries. As adherents to the new paradigm, LTCM sought to define risk in mathematical terms through the standard deviation of securities' returns, or volatility. Roger Lowenstein reports that the fund viewed the idea of volatility, as "the best proxy for risk." The fund monitored its positions through keeping track of their volatilities (volatilities of securities, reflecting arbitrage opportunities) where the expected returns on individual securities and the variability of those returns were assessed on the basis of long-term averages of historical returns and volatilities of those returns. The same principle was applied to the portfolio as a whole. The correlation between different positions was also considered. The fund increased or reduced the weighting of a particular position according to the impact it had on the volatility and return of the whole portfolio. By increasing leverage the fund could raise the return on equity that it was using. The stronger boost from leverage to the return on equity in absolute terms also implied higher absolute variability of that return, or higher volatility. Through this use of leverage the fund's managers were able to set the variability of returns to the level of their liking [Lowenstein, 2002, pp. 63–65].

The fund also used the concept of volatility to create positions directly, and not only to risk-manage them. Long dated equity index call options attached to government bonds had become popular among retail investors as the call options delivered the upside when equity markets performed well, while the bonds provided the protection of the principal investment. The retail banks and insurance companies that sold these products to retail customers were effectively short long dated equity index options where no exchange-listed comparable contracts existed. When LTCM traders examined this market, they felt that a significant arbitrage opportunity was present. They could sell these long dated options to the retail banks who would cover their exposure to the retail customers. LTCM would hold the short positions in these options and effectively act as a reinsurer to the banks. The fund was convinced that these options were overpriced and the cost of hedging them would be much lower than the price at which they would be sold.

A bet on equity volatility was born. The fund was so confident that they had a better understanding of the variability of equity returns than everyone else and they sold these long dated equity options in volumes so large, that other market participants began to describe the fund as the "Central Bank of Volatility." Sold at volatility levels that were only somewhat higher than the historical averages over the long horizon, these options contributed strongly to the fund's demise when the short-term equity volatility reached unprecedented levels, vastly superior to the long-term averages, and the long-term options were re-marked by counterparties to the comparable high levels that were almost a multiple of the original prices. Once the options were re-marked, collateral had to be posted, which the fund was unable to deliver. No other market participants were willing to sell options back to the fund to allow them to cover their positions [Dunbar, 2000, pp. 165–175, 181, 210–213]. This bet ended up being one of the trades that broke the firm.[7]

These positions, as reinsurance to the banking industry, were not dissimilar in spirit to Buffett's insurance or reinsurance business in general. Buffett also has been engaged in almost exactly the same transactions: he has been selling equity volatility. In Chapter 6 we will also discuss in detail his sale of long dated puts on equity indexes. As we will see, he may have used a different logic altogether in pricing these puts. In LTCM's case, the sale of equity volatility was a ride over a certain consumerist wave. The banks had marketed to the ordinary public and created demand in equity products with guaranteed equity upside and protected downside. Buffett might have sold his puts for somewhat, if not completely, different reasons. He also mentions that he sold the options at lower prices than otherwise achievable in exchange for agreeing with his counterparties that no collateral would need to be posted—a very different approach from that of LTCM.[8] Buffett has yet

---

7 For estimates of losses in different market areas, please see [Lowenstein, 2002, pp. 233–234].
8 At a later stage Buffett commented that since regulatory changes that forced the posting of collateral had been introduced, he would not engage in transactions where such a posting would be a requirement.

to become viewed as the Central Bank of Insurance, even though he might be that already. However, so far his judgment allowed him to sell contracts similar to LTCM's successfully. In the fund's case, personal judgment proved insufficient and volatility as the "proxy for risk" failed to protect the firm.

Buffett's understanding of risk, which we continue to discuss in the next chapter, leaves him with considerable skepticism toward investing when risk is managed through quantification. Such investing is reminiscent of driving a car on cruise control: "The driver might think he was fully alert and attentive, but would find out differently when the road turned winding, rain-slicked, and full of traffic" [cited in Schroeder, 2008, p. 654]. From the point of view of Buffett, it is possible to say that the fund failed to manage their circle of competence.

An example of the fund's departing from its circle of competence was the decision to bet on the arbitrage associated with mergers and acquisitions activity, where it lacked expertise. A large bet was made, among others, on the merger of two telecom companies, when difficulties associated with the deal were being widely discussed in the press and analysts were warning that the deal was likely to not materialize. The merger did not take place, and the fund lost $300 million [Dunbar, 2000, p. 206]. For the sake of fairness, it is important to note that Merton was against changing the investment tactics, but his voice was ignored [Lowenstein, 2002, p. 100].

Buffett's model of the market and that of Merton are also fundamentally different. Buffett believes that the market is populated by nonrational agents who act like lemmings (animals with great herd instincts) and who can all dash in one direction or another, with each of them using the behavior of the majority as her guide to action. One of the pathways for the development of this phenomenon is the manner in which the different players use information. They rely on similar models that assess reality through the prism of the paradigm of the day; as a result, they often think in the same way, and their actions may end up being similar. Such a setting, by design, leads to extreme outcomes. To avoid the lemmings, Buffett emphasizes independence of opinion. He does not belong to any group. He always maintains a high level of liquidity. He is able to buy when others are selling, and he is able to hold shares that are falling, as he is not being pressured by creditors.

Merton's model is populated by rational investors who always aim to pay a fair price for an asset, no more and no less. Arbitrage ensures the emergence of fair prices. Merton's market is also always open and always liquid. Buyers and sellers are always present in sufficient numbers that small-size lots would not create sharp fluctuations [Lowenstein, 2002, p. 68]. As Nicholas Dunbar puts it, "Merton's mantra was 'assume markets are continuous and frictionless'" [Dunbar, 2000, p. 116].

How would excess returns arise in Merton's model? Even a rational market makes mistakes. At every moment, the rational market assesses the "fair" value of securities by evaluating the discounted expected cash flows that these securities will generate. If we assume equal access to information among market participants, then the agent who creates the most advanced technical model (that is, the model that succeeds in reflecting reality most accurately) at any particular point in time will be accumulating excess returns.

In practical terms, Merton viewed the markets as still lacking efficiency. Exploiting the arbitrage opportunities on an extremely large scale was meant to force the markets to become more efficient. He disagreed with the "notion that the markets could ever be overwhelmed" [Lowenstein, 2002, p. 111]. He thought that ". . . the old institutional relationships could be overcome" [Lowenstein, 2002, p. 32]. Nevertheless, the fund relied heavily on the institutional relationships when setting up and running its business. Their trades were cleared and funded by other banks; the relationships that "could be overcome" were exploited to ensure a "no haircut" treatment or to obtain favorable credit lines. The same relationships turned against the fund when the markets ceased being "frictionless." For it is in the nature of markets to "conspire against the weak," as Roger Lowenstein describes it, in order "not to attack" them, but "to save themselves" [Lowenstein, 2002, pp. 163–164]. Instead of facilitating the efficiency of the markets

LTCM destroyed any efficiency that existed by growing so large that it became the market.[9] A single agent market probably cannot be efficient by definition.

LTCM relied on historical data to assist the traders in informing their judgment. This introduced the idea that the future would be the same as the past. The challenge hidden in this assumption was already discussed by Graham: "Nothing important on Wall Street can be counted on to occur exactly in the same way as it happened before" [Graham, 2003, p. 208]. In 1990 Buffett observed: beware of past-performance "proofs" in finance. "If history books were the key to riches, the Forbes 400 would consist of librarians" [Buffett, 1977–2013, 1990]. Examining average historical returns and volatilities is different in approach from reading old newspapers to appreciate the emotions of the market during the Great Depression or researching the whole history of annual reports of a particular company.

Models of the new paradigm often assumed that the returns were normally distributed. In reality, the returns are almost normally distributed—the distribution of returns is a Normal distribution–like bell-curve but it has "fat" tails. The extreme movements are encountered considerably more frequently. It is now well understood that when the market participants suddenly start acting in a synchronized manner, the frequencies with which particular returns occur are affected. The individual actions of market participants cannot be viewed as independent of each other. The models based on Normal distribution describe markets accurately when those are quiet, but extremely incorrectly in the times of crisis. As the models underestimate the probability of the extreme events, they exaggerate the "safe" level of the debt/equity ratio. Benoit Mandelbrot was the first to point out, already in the 1960s, that it was erroneous to use the Normal distribution of returns in the financial models.[10] He and Richard Hudson offered an in-depth illustration of the issues hidden in the

---

9 Roger Lowenstein reports that in the markets of the two bets that broke the firm (the equity volatility that we discussed and interest rate swaps) "It [the fund] got so big that it distorted the very markets on whose efficiency the firm relied" [Lowenstein, 2002, p. 234].

10 For an assessment of Mandelbrot's role in the evolution of financial theory, see *The Myth of the Rational Market* by Justin Fox [Fox, 2001].

use of the Normal distribution in their book *The (Mis)behavior of Markets: A Fractal View of Financial Turbulence*, in which they discuss Mandelbrot's theories and refute the efficient market hypothesis [Mandelbrot and Hudson, 2006].

Mandelbrot explains that models that assume a Normal distribution of returns assign very low probabilities to the large market moves that regularly take place. For instance, the probability of the DJIA falling by 6.8 percent in one day on August 31, 1998, is estimated to be 1 in 20 million, and the probability of three similar moves in a row (3.5 percent on August 4 and 4.4 percent three weeks later) is 1 in 500 billion. "Surely, August was supremely bad luck, a freak accident, an 'act of God' no one could have predicted"—Mandelbrot speaks ironically. A year earlier, the market had fallen by 7.7 percent in one day, and the probability of this event was 1 in 50 billion. In July 2003, the market moved sharply three times in several days, and the probability of that event was 1 in 4 trillion. The probability of the 29.2 percent fall on October 19, 1987, according to standard models, was less than 1 in 10 [Mandelbrot and Hudson, 2006, pp. 3–4]. Buffett has his own perspective. "Anything can happen in stock markets and you ought to conduct your affairs so that if the most extraordinary events happen, that you're still around to play the next day," he commented as early as 1988 [cited in Kilpatrick, 2005, p. 1376].[11]

It is probably unreasonable to imagine that the LTCM's partners did not appreciate the challenges associated with the models, using Normal distribution. Nicholas Dunbar observed that in practice LTCM probably attempted to test the portfolio with the help of other assumptions. "LTCM's partners were much too sophisticated to assume that the Normal distribution was an accurate description of LTCM's daily or monthly returns." At internal meetings "market monster stories" were discussed, stress testing was conducted, which showed that in the worst case scenario the fund would lose not much more than 50 percent of its value. "However, this unpleasant possibility was never taken seriously" [Dunbar, 2000, p 187].

---

11 Nassim Nicolas Taleb produced a brilliant mathematical and philosophical contemplation on the subject in a paper presented at Benoit Mandelbrot's Scientific Memorial [Taleb, 2011].

"Merton's theories were seductive not because they were mostly wrong but because they were so nearly, or so nearly often, right" [Lowenstein, 2002, p. 69]. But "underneath the mathematical elegance, underneath all those betas and sigmas, there was quicksand" described the collapse of LTCM Buffett. In his view, it is a matter of being approximately right rather then precisely wrong. Simple and possibly inaccurate mathematics but conceptually correct general approach is a better combination than exceptionally sophisticated mathematics, failing personal judgment, and broadly erroneous conceptual framework. Nassim Taleb, discussing LTCM's approach, echoed Buffett: "I want to be broadly right rather than precisely wrong. Elegance in the theories is often indicative of weakness—it invites you to seek elegance for elegance sake" [Taleb, 2007, p. 285]. On the other hand, another significant factor to consider is that Merton's ideas were implemented into the real world by his colleagues [Lowenstein, 2002, p. 55]. They used his framework to inform their decisions. The fund's partners introduced their personalities and private histories into his theoretical world. We do not know what would have happened if Merton alone (or with Scholes) was left to make all the trading decisions. After all, even though he "had a dream" of infinite leverage, he was against, as Roger Lowenstein reports, returning to the investors what the fund thought was excess capital when only several months before the onset of the crisis the fund felt it could no longer find profitable trades and it did not wish to dilute the return on equity of its existing positions [Lowenstein, 2002, p. 113].

Through his models, Merton aspired valiantly to create the ultimate perfect marketplace, one that operated with unfailing efficiency, with the price of every asset being known unmistakably and arbitrage enforcing the fair prices, liquidity, and continuity. It is impossible to know in real time whether a particular attempt to create a perfect world will succeed or fail. Even Nassim Taleb, who became the first to challenge conceptually any strategies that do not take the black swan factor into consideration, may have been unable to appreciate LTCM's true weakness at the start of the fund's activity. Nicholas Dunbar, who interviewed Taleb in April of 1998, asserts that Taleb spoke about Merton's ideas "admiringly" [Dunbar, 2011, p. 42]. Taleb seemed to have felt that the reason why the Black-Scholes model thrived was that a "transformation" was taking place in the real world. This transformation was that reality was "allowing" the model's assumptions to become true and resemble reality more closely, as if Merton had had a premonition of the changes in the real world. Merton felt that as the markets became more efficient, the continuous time model would keep becoming more accurate. In Merton's words, "Reality will eventually imitate theory" [Dunbar, 1998]. With all the wisdom from the benefits of hindsight, of course, it is possible to ask: Was it indeed that reality was changing shape? It might just be simply that all the participants in a game decided to adopt the same set of rules, and that this adoption itself created a smaller version, a subset, of reality among them, but then the natural economic forces from the wider world intervened (a faraway country defaulted on its debt and the contagion spread), and the small pocket of the newly created reality crumbled.

It has been observed that there may have been a certain contradiction in the fund's aspirations. LTCM intended to be very conservative and did not want to make any directional bets, but by betting on European interest rate convergence they ended up betting on the success of European integration, among other things, and caught the momentum when that bet was developing positively. This was a directional bet, by its nature. When, for the sake of being conservative, the fund did not want to bet on interest rates explicitly and took positions in off-setting pairs, this approach might have seemed as similar in mindset to Buffett's when he finds that there is no point in trying to forecast interest rates. In LTCM's case the self-perception of being conservative turned out to be an illusion. Perhaps, we could argue that it is the ability of seeing things for what they are that is the real difference between them and Buffett.

Buffett, with all his affection for simple and predictable business attempted to buy what could be described as the remains of the fund when its management was preparing to announce the fund's failure. The irony of fate was that LTCM had also managed to short Berkshire shares, probably because the partners thought the stock was overvalued relative to the value of the companies in the conglomerate.[12] Although different

---

12 The consequent evolution of the market suggests that LTCM might have been right (Berkshire's peak share price in 1998 was not surpassed until the autumn of 2003).

versions of events exist, it is likely that Buffett's offer to buy the management company was refused because he had asked that all its management, including Meriwether, be fired. Buffett did not wish to retain Meriwether not only because Meriwether had twice brought a business under his management to bankruptcy, but also possibly because Buffett's own reputation might have been affected had he joined forces with such a figure, the consequences of whose work he had already had to deal with at Salomon. Buffett considered this unrealized transaction as one of the great missed opportunities of his life [Schroeder, 2008, p. 663]. Perhaps he believed in the principal idea—arbitraging the spreads between bonds—but felt that the strategy needed to be more carefully executed. According to some sources, Buffett invested in a Bermuda-registered fund, West Capital, that followed the same investment idea as LTCM, and this fund lost only 10 percent in 1998 [Kilpatrick, 2005, p. 1017].

Nicholas Dunbar reports that Buffett did not manage to buy the LTCM leftovers on his terms only because the financial authorities dashed to the fund's rescue, and they were not planning to fire Meriwether. He, of course, having understood that he had a choice, preferred the option that preserved his position [Dunbar, 2000, p. 222]. Had the government not interfered, the inadvertent contest between Buffett and Merton over whose model of the markets represented reality more accurately would have ended in Buffett's victory, not with the scoreboard count, but with a knockout.

Warren Buffett and Peter Lynch

> It's far better to buy a wonderful company at a fair
> price than a fair company at a wonderful price.
>
> —WARREN BUFFETT [BUFFETT, 1977–2013, 1992]

Maybe Lynch was referring to LTCM when he mused: "The true geniuses get too enamored of theoretical cogitations and are forever betrayed by the actual behavior of stocks, which is more simple-minded than they can imagine" [Lynch and Rothchild, 2000, pp. 80–81]. (He made this comment in a book that was published in 2000, while the LTCM crash took place in 1998.) This notion of the simple-mindedness of stock behavior is something that Buffett and Lynch share. Lynch is not just a follower of the value investing approach. The nuances of his investment principles often coincide with those of Buffett.

Over the years of Lynch's management of the Fidelity Magellan Fund (1977–1990), its assets, including new fund inflows, grew from $18 million to $14 billion. Over the same period, the price of a share in the mutual fund rose by approximately 20 times, and its average annual growth amounted to approximately 29.2 percent. Over the same period, Berkshire's asset value grew by 30 times, while, the average annual growth was 30.1 percent, and the share price rose by 78 times, or 35.5 percent annually. An investment in the S&P grew by roughly 6 times, or 14.9 percent annually.

During Lynch's tenure at Magellan, it was the most successful American fund. Lynch succeeded in delivering high returns even after the fund became bigger, despite the fact that managing a large fund is much more complicated. Lynch's critics argued that Magellan, "like the Roman Empire," had become too big to succeed, since "a fund with 900 stocks in it didn't have a chance to beat the market average because it was the market average," and Lynch was reproached for managing the largest index fund on the planet [Lynch and Rothchild, 1994, p. 116].

Despite Lynch's outstanding results, comparing them to Buffett's is not really possible, as Lynch's returns were delivered over a far shorter, 13-year interval, all of which, in addition, took place during a bull market. Lynch left his position as manager of Magellan in May 1990, before the great bull market collapsed (after the correction of 1987 the market recovered very quickly) [Lynch and Rothchild, 2000, p. 9]. It is only possible to guess what his performance would have been in a stagnating or falling market. On the other hand, Lynch worked within a tougher institutional framework then the one facing Buffett. In this sense, achieving similar results on the same interval is a fantastic accomplishment.

Buffett once left the market also, in 1969, when he came to the conclusion that all assets were overpriced and that there were no investment opportunities. He liquidated almost all his investments (as it turned out later, at the peak of the market) and returned the funds to investors, so the unrealized returns became real. This was also an opportune moment to make the transition to the more beneficial organizational structure of a holding company. At the time the fund was dissolved, Buffett managed $104 million, or $640 million in today's money. Lynch regards this step in Buffett's career as the one that makes him one of the greatest investors. An investment in Berkshire Hathaway has resulted in a 700-bagger, and "that makes Buffett a wonderful investor. What makes him the greatest investor of all time is that during a certain period when he thought stocks were grossly overpriced, he sold everything and returned all the money to his partners at a sizable profit to them." In Lynch's view, "the voluntary returning of money that others would gladly pay you to continue to manage is . . . unique in the history of finance" [Lynch and Rothchild, 2000, p. 89].

Buffett and Lynch have a similar understanding of what it means to invest in stocks. Buffett regards stocks not as an instrument for speculation, something fluctuating in value that can be bet against, but as a claim against part of the company. Lynch believes the same: one of the keys to successful investing is focusing "on the companies, not on the stocks" [Lynch and Rothchild, 1994, p. 102]; "the stock price is the least useful information you can track, and it's the most widely tracked" [Lynch and Rothchild, 2000, p. 13]. "Just because a stock is cheaper than before is no reason to buy it, and just because it's more expensive is no reason to sell" [Lynch and Rothchild, 1994, p. 149]. "Rejecting a stock because the price has doubled, tripled, or even quadrupled in the recent past can be a big mistake" [Lynch and Rothchild, 2000, p. 303].

Lynch examines the quality of the business of the companies in which he invests, because eventually "superior companies will succeed and mediocre companies will fail, and investors in each will be rewarded accordingly" [Lynch and Rothchild, 1994, p. 30]. Lynch, like Buffett, seeks to find companies that have strong fundamentals, or that have a monopoly or quasi-monopoly position, which is even better. He searches for "pearls" and prefers quality to price: "When the best company in an industry is selling at a bargain price, it often pays to buy that one, as opposed to investing in a lesser competitor that may be selling at a lower price" [Lynch and Rothchild, 1994, p. 293].

While Buffett looks for great companies in great industries, Lynch is ready to acquire great companies in lousy industries. He calls these companies "blossoms in the desert." Lynch recommends waiting until the opinion that things have gone from bad to worse in a certain industry prevails, then buying shares of the strongest companies in the segment [Lynch and Rothchild, 1994, p. 161] (this is similar to how Buffett acted when he acquired Johns Manville, which we discuss in Chapter 10).

Lynch examines industries with poor prospects in order to find companies with monopoly positions: "In a lousy industry, one that's growing slowly if at all, the weak drop out and the survivors get a bigger share of the market. A company that can capture an ever-increasing share of a stagnant market is a lot better off than one that has to struggle to protect a dwindling share of an exciting market" [Lynch and Rothchild, 1994, p. 182], and "a survivor in a lousy industry can reverse its fortunes very quickly once the competitors have disappeared" [Lynch and Rothchild, 1994, p. 188]. In Lynch's view, total domination is healthier than competition [Lynch and Rothchild, 1994, p. 182].

As for cheap shares, Lynch finds that "a cheap stock can always get cheaper" [Lynch and Rothchild, 2000, p. 18], and he is again holding a view similar to Buffett's. A stock's price can fall to zero, and any particular reduction in a stock price is not a reason to buy it. However, Lynch prefers high rates of growth to low prices. He would rather invest in Body Shop, which is growing at 30 percent a year (Lynch talks about this in his 1994 book) but trades at 40 times earnings, than invest in Coca-Cola, which is growing at 15 percent a year and sells at 30 times earnings. Lynch believes that the company with the higher growth rate will outperform the one with the slower rate of growth, even if the P/E of the first is higher than the P/E of the second [Lynch and Rothchild, 1994, p. 157].

"All else being equal, a 20-percent grower selling at 20 times earnings . . . is a much better buy than a 10-percent grower selling at 10 times earnings" [Lynch and Rothchild, 2000, p. 218]. Buffett would probably agree with this in substance, but he is unlikely to have bought Body Shop's shares at a P/E of 40, and to the best of my knowledge, he has never bought anything at this level. Even Lynch believes that growth stocks that sell for 40 times the next year's earnings are dangerously high priced—and, in most cases, are "extravagant." As a rule of thumb, a stock should sell at or below the growth rate of its earnings. Even the fastest-growing companies can infrequently achieve higher than a 25 percent growth rate. A 40 percent growth rate is a rare thing; such impetuous progress cannot be sustained for a long time, and companies that are growing too fast tend to self-destruct [Lynch and Rothchild, 1994, p. 157].

During some periods, it is possible to acquire companies at far lower prices: Lynch's top 10 stocks in 1978 had P/E ratios of between 4 and 6, and in 1979, of between 3 and 5. In Lynch's view, when buying shares at these prices, "the stock-picker can hardly lose" [Lynch and Rothchild, 1994, p. 100].

Lynch also likes simple businesses. Some sources argue that the famous aphorism "I like to buy a business that any fool can run because eventually one will" was borrowed by Buffett from Lynch [Nocera, 2004, p. 246]. The former manager of Magellan also shares Buffett's reservations regarding businesses for which strong management is a necessity: "If it's a choice between owning stock in a fine company with excellent management in a highly competitive and complex industry, or a humdrum company with mediocre management in a simple-minded industry with no competition, I'd take the latter" [Lynch and Rothchild, 2000, p. 130].

Lynch also believes that it is important that investors buy only assets that they understand. One must act within one's circle of competence. "Buying what you know" is a very sophisticated strategy, Lynch finds [Lynch and Rothchild, 1994, p. 28]. Unlike many other professionals, who, in Lynch's opinion, have neglected to put this principle into practice, he never invested money in things that he did not understand [Lynch and Rothchild, 1994, p. 91].

Both Lynch and Buffett prefer to invest in companies that do not depend on capital investment [Lynch and Rothchild, 2000, p. 214]. Lynch has reservations similar to Buffett's with respect to industries that require constant capital reinforcement to remain afloat: continuous capital investment has undermined many major manufacturers—for instance, a steel company may have a $1 billion turnover, but on a cost base of $950 million [Lynch and Rothchild, 2000, p. 228].

Lynch prefers the consumer sector to cyclicals, turnarounds, and high technology. By watching the ups and downs of the various industries, he came to the conclusion that while it was possible to make up to five times your investment in cyclicals and undervalued companies (assuming that everything went well), there were bigger payoffs in the retailers and the restaurants. They grew as fast as the high-tech companies, and they were generally less risky. "A computer company can lose half its value overnight when a rival unveils a better product, but a chain of donut franchises in New England is not going to lose business when somebody opens a superior donut franchise in Ohio. It may take a decade for the competitor to arrive, and investors can see it coming" [Lynch and Rothchild, 1994, p. 108]. Lynch felt that the high-tech business was "incomprehensible and therefore untrustworthy" [Lynch and Rothchild, 1994, p. 231], and, like Buffett, he avoided investing in high-tech companies. Both investors avoided the well-known names, such as Microsoft [Nocera, 2004, pp. 241–242].

In one of his letters to Microsoft's management in 1997, responding to a suggestion that he invest in the company, Buffett said that he "prefers to structure investing as a no-called-strike game" [Buffett, 1997]. In 2011, in a CNBC interview, Buffett explained that he did not invest in Microsoft because of his friendship with Bill Gates. In the same interview, Buffett explained why he purchased a large stake in IBM in 2011 for $10.7 billion. Although Buffett does not invest in technology companies, he nevertheless had followed the company and read its annual reports over the course of 50 years. He came to the conclusion that it had become more of a service company than an IT company: it was a company that helps IT departments do their job better [Crippen, 2011]. We do not know what Lynch would have done if he had still been managing his fund.

Lynch explains his lack of affection for cyclicals by his belief that in order to succeed in investing in those companies, it is necessary to have a working knowledge of the industry and its rhythms, and that a plumber who follows the price of copper pipe has a better chance of making money on Phelps Dodge[13] than an MBA who buys Phelps Dodge because it "looks cheap" [Lynch and Rothchild, 1994, p. 234].

13 An American mining company that was one of the largest copper producers in the world. It was acquired in 2007.

It is possible that Buffett and Lynch dislike the sector because of its dependence on macroeconomic conditions, given that both Buffett and Lynch consider the macroeconomic environment to be unpredictable. Lynch has found that nobody can predict interest rates, the future movement of the economy, or the stock market [Lynch and Rothchild, 1994, p. 307], and so it is necessary to dismiss all such forecasts and concentrate on what's actually going on in the companies in which one has invested [Lynch and Rothchild, 1994, p. 307]. Buffett maintains the same thing. Once he was asked by a broker about his prognosis for interest rates. Buffett responded with a joke. He was aware of only two people who understood interest rates, however they held opposing views [Lowenstein, 1996, p. 331]. Buffett not only views macroeconomic indicators as unpredictable, but also plays a "long" game. "If [former] Fed Chairman Alan Greenspan were to whisper to me what his monetary policy was going to be over the next two years, it wouldn't change one thing I do," Buffett once admitted [cited in Grant, 1994, p. 58].

Lynch, like Buffett, refuses to invest in companies that promise a great deal but are too young to have any accomplishments. He looks for historical confirmation of past good results. Lynch urges nonprofessional investors not to trust the promises of the most positive future: "If they aren't already doing it, don't invest in it" [Lynch and Rothchild, 2000, p. 179].

As a result of his using a fundamental approach, Lynch arrives at a portfolio structure that is similar to Buffett's. For instance, in Magellan's annual report for 1978, he wrote that he had reduced his holdings in autos, aerospace, railroads, utilities, chemicals, electronics, and energy and expanded his positions in financial institutions, insurance, leasing, broadcasting, entertainment, and consumer products [Lynch and Rothchild, 1994, p. 87]. These industries can also be found in Berkshire's portfolio. Lynch, like Buffett, invested a considerable amount of capital in the financial sector during the savings and loan crisis: of the 83 new acquisitions he made in April 1983, 39 were banks or S&Ls [Lynch and Rothchild, 1994, p. 118].

Lynch often singles out the same companies as Buffett for investment. For instance, over a considerable period of time, Lynch owned a large stake in Fannie Mae. He earned more than $1 billion on this investment. He first acquired shares in the company in 1977. Subsequently, he increased his position. In 1989, he noticed that Warren Buffett had also acquired a large stake. In 1992, Lynch found Shaw Industries, one of the leading American manufacturers of carpet flooring. Commenting on the company's prospects (its management thought that by the end of the century, three or four huge companies would dominate carpet making worldwide), Lynch argued that Shaw's competitors worried that not three or four producers but a single producer would dominate carpet making, and they knew which one it would be [Lynch and Rothchild, 1994, p. 193]. In 2000, Warren Buffett purchased Shaw Industries.

Lynch holds the same view as Buffett on market timing. Lynch doesn't believe in predicting markets, but believes in buying great companies— "especially companies that are undervalued, and/or under-appreciated" [Lynch and Rothchild, 2000, p. 88]. According to Lynch, "Things inside humans make them terrible stock market timers. The unwary investor continually passes in and out of three emotional states: concern, complacency, and capitulation" [Lynch and Rothchild, 2000, p. 82].

Lynch also argues against market timing because, first, while waiting for the market to fall, it is possible to miss out on growth in companies with good prospects (several of his favorite ten-baggers made their biggest moves during bad markets), and second, following the fashionable trend may lead to serious mistakes in the choice of investment targets. In the early 1980s, the market was bullish on airlines, but investments in People Express (this airline bought a farm) or Pan Am did not pay off [Lynch and Rothchild, 2000, p. 89]. As we discussed, Buffett finds that the market is overvalued when there are no suitable investments at suitable prices. Lynch believes the same: there's no reason to worry about an overvalued market. "The way you'll know when the market is overvalued is when you can't find a single company that's reasonably priced or that meets your other criteria for investment" [Lynch and Rothchild, 2000, p. 90].

Of course, both investors prefer falling markets. While high prices are the cause of great jubilation on Wall Street, Lynch is happier with a good 300-point drop that creates some bargains that are "the holy grail of the true stock-picker." The loss of 10 to 30 percent of net worth in a market sell-off is of little importance. Lynch views a correction not as a disaster, but as an opportunity to add to a portfolio at low prices: "This is how great fortunes are made over time" [Lynch and Rothchild, 1994, p. 115].

Lynch and Buffett like investing when others in the investment community are disappointed by some temporary difficulties in a company's business—for example, a low profit in a particular quarter—if, of course, this is a passing phenomenon. The price of shares can fall when the fundamentals of the company remain the same. Lynch invested in Sunbelt Nursery, a retail chain selling gardening plants, when it had lost most of its market value after a single disappointing quarter, mainly caused by a string of natural calamities such as premature frost in Arizona and a lot of rain in Texas. "What a bonanza for the investors who had courage to buy more!" [Lynch and Rothchild, 1994, p. 167].

Lynch takes care not to pay attention to the opinion of the crowd. He refers to Buffett when he talks about the importance of this principle: professional investors relying on providers of financial information are missing the point. They find out what other professional investors are doing when they ought to be spending more time at the mall. A pile of software is worth nothing if the basic homework on the companies has not been done. "Trust me, Warren Buffett doesn't use this stuff" [Lynch and Rothchild, 1994, p. 141]. In Lynch's view, "you don't have to be trendy to succeed as an investor" [Lynch and Rothchild, 2000, p. 11]. Lynch recommends avoiding popular shares: "If I could avoid a single stock, it would be the hottest stock in the hottest industry, the one that gets the most favorable publicity, the one that every investor hears about in the car pool or on the commuter train—and succumbing to the social pressure, often buys" [Lynch and Rothchild, 2000, p. 149]. He gives the same advice to nonprofessional investors: "Dumb money is only dumb when it listens to the smart money" [Lynch and Rothchild, 2000, p. 31].

Uncertainty is a friend to both types of investors: "The greatest advantage to investing in stocks, to one who accepts the uncertainties, is the extraordinary reward for being right" [Lynch and Rothchild, 2000, p. 76]. Lynch shares with Buffett his interpretation of risk. He finds that the big winners do not come from the so-called high-risk categories: "The risks have more to do with the investors than with the categories" [Lynch and Rothchild, 2000, p. 76]. Lynch refers to the same idea as Buffett—risk is the result of the investor's not being sufficiently thorough in his research.

Lynch agrees with Buffett's position on the length of the investment horizon. Since investment is not speculation, it is important to hold investments for a long time. The typical big winner in Lynch's portfolio took three to ten years or more to play out [Lynch and Rothchild, 2000, p. 12]. Lynch realized that many stocks that he held for a few months he should have held a lot longer. "This wouldn't have meant unconditional loyalty, it would have been sticking to companies that were getting more and more attractive" [Lynch and Rothchild, 1994, p. 91].

While Lynch recommends holding shares over a long-term horizon, where "long-term" may mean more than several months, Buffett views long-term as meaning forever. He does not sell shares if a company is having only temporary difficulties. Also, Buffett assembles large stakes in public companies that may not be particularly easy to consolidate without forcing the share price considerably higher. From this standpoint, selling to buy back later may not be worth the effort. And, unlike Lynch, Buffett has the ability to acquire companies fully, although good companies rarely become available.

Lynch, like Buffett, believes that when choosing an investment, it is not advisable to place too strong an emphasis on the liquidity of the stock. This position is understandable, given his intention of holding the stock for the long term and not viewing investment as speculation. Fund managers who preoccupied themselves with liquidity "hemmed themselves in," argues Lynch, for they were limited to a pool of 1 percent of publicly traded companies and ignored very good small companies because their stocks were illiquid, although these companies could perform very well over the long term. Lynch felt that other investors would focus so excessively on finding stocks that they could get into and out of easily that they would not adequately examine whether those stocks were worthwhile investments—"in stocks as in romance, ease of divorce is not a sound basis for commitment." If a company is a loser, the fund manager is going to lose money on the stock no matter how liquid it is, and if it's a winner, she will unwind her position at a profit [Lynch and Rothchild, 1994, p. 120].

An important difference between Lynch and Buffett is in the number of stocks in the portfolio. This is not driven by conceptual disagreements. Given that both investors have a similar understanding of risk and view investment as looking for rare pearls, their attitudes toward diversification are comparable. However, Lynch's portfolio consisted of several hundred companies. In one of his books, he describes the events that took place during a holiday trip when the market was having a particularly hectic week. Far away from the office, in Yosemite National Park, he was forced to give instructions to a trader as to what to do with some of his shares while standing in a phone booth overlooking a mountain range. After two hours, he'd only gotten from the As to the Ls [Lynch and Rothchild, 2000, p. 130]. Perhaps Lynch held such a diversified portfolio not for the sake of diversification, but because he liked investing in medium-sized and small companies, which he, as a manager of a mutual fund, could not buy outright (so that he had to buy stock in a larger number of companies rather than owning fewer of them entirely) and where it could have been difficult to gather a large stake without shifting the market price. Such shares would also have been particularly hard to trade in volatile times.

Lynch also tried to overcome, where possible, the agency problems associated with the mutual fund structure. In Lynch's view, portfolio managers who care about job security tend to gravitate toward acceptable investments, such as IBM, and avoid offbeat companies like Seven Oaks,[14] because in the event of the failure of Seven Oaks, "the person who recommended putting it in the portfolio gets the blame, but if IBM fails, the blame is put on IBM itself, for 'disappointing the Street'" [Lynch and Rothchild, 1994, p. 109]. The analysts, naturally, develop a mindset that helps them avoid responsibility. To avoid risking their reputations, they do not recommend interesting but unestablished companies and advise their employers to invest in well-known companies like IBM. As a result, they do not get the blame if the fund manager ends up performing poorly. Fidelity had a different culture. Fund managers pursued their own research ideas and were responsible for their performance

---

14 A retail coupon-processing company, or clearinghouse for discount coupons redeemed by consumers at supermarkets.

[Lynch and Rothchild, 1994, p. 104]. Buffett had already spoken about this industry phenomenon in the 1960s: "To many people convention-ality is undistinguishable from conservatism." In his view, "This repre-sents erroneous thinking. Neither a conventional nor unconventional approach, per se, is conservative" [Buffett, 1957–1970, January 18, 1965].

However, Lynch's ability to invest was subject to other external limi-tations. Whereas Buffett fully controls his "investment fund." Lynch was the manager of an open-ended fund, where any owner of the fund could demand her money back at any time and compel Lynch to sell a position at an inopportune moment. Buffett insisted on not splitting Berkshire shares when they rose to high levels, even though a high share price cuts off small investors. It is possible that small-scale investors made up a more substantial proportion of Lynch's clients. A larger-scale investor is generally longer-term in his approach, and an investor with a long-term horizon (which may also mean that the investor is rela-tively well off) is likely to be more secure, and as a result will not be as affected by share price volatility. An investor with a long-term invest-ment horizon may also have a certain view of her investment choices and may be unwilling to sell if she thinks that an investment oppor-tunity has not had the chance to develop itself. A small investor may be more likely to need money unexpectedly and may be less tolerant of temporary losses.

During the large market correction in 1987, well known as Black Monday, Lynch's fund was hit by a tidal wave of selling requests to return cash to owners, and he was forced to sell part of the portfolio. He gave the traders selling instructions in alphabetical order: one trader was going to sell shares from A to D, another from E to L, and so on. At the very moment when he would have preferred to be a buyer, he had to be a seller. "In this sense," comments Lynch, "shareholders play a major role in a fund's success or failure," for "if they are steadfast and don't panic in the scary situations," there is no need to liquidate investments at unfavorable prices in order to pay them back [Lynch and Rothchild, 1994, p. 133]. These sales could have been avoided if some part of the funds had not been invested; however, the rules that govern mutual funds prohibited this. Lynch had to keep the fund fully invested even when the market was overvalued, as it was in 1987 before the dramatic fall in October of that year. In Buffett's case, the legal structure of the "fund" is more conducive to success, since a situation in which Buffett is forced to sell to satisfy investors' demands is simply not possible. Walter Schloss observed that Buffett's advantage is in that he is not afraid of the downside [Schloss, 1998].

On the other hand, the tax reform of 1986 made corporations' capital gains subject to taxation if the capital gain arose from the sale of any security in the corporation's portfolio. The capital gains of a mutual fund are not taxed. If an investment business is organized as a corporation, then two levels of capital gains taxation come into effect—when the corporation sells stock in its portfolio, and when the investor sells his stock in the corporation. Despite this, Buffett has retained Berkshire's status as a public company. Perhaps Berkshire's particular legal structure, unusual for an investment business, is connected to the long-term horizon—the investment principle that we discussed in Chapter 3.

* * *

As we saw through the comparison of Buffett and Merton, or LTCM, and Lynch, an investor's fundamental theoretical position and views on the organization of financial markets, from which follows her trading or investment strategy, are a critical factor in the investor's success. They are vital for a strategy's survival. We have already discussed some of Buffett's views. Let us now consider his position on the central questions of corporate finance in detail.

5

An Excursion Through Financial Theory and Corporate Finance with Warren Buffett

Berkshire Hathaway is a didactic enterprise
teaching the right systems of thought.
—CHARLIE MUNGER [CITED IN LOWE, 2000, P. 175]

Investment Theory (Efficiency and Rationality of Financial Markets, Risk, Uncertainty, and Portfolio Diversification)

The market is there only as a reference point to see
if anybody is offering to do anything foolish.
—WARREN BUFFETT [CITED IN LOWE, 2007, P. 129]

"My friend Warren Buffett and I"—Charlie Munger says—"entered the business world to find huge, predictable patterns of irrationality. These irrationalities were obviously important to what we planned to do, but our professors had never mentioned them" [cited in Lowe, 2000, p. 67]. Business schools teach students that markets are rational. If the markets are rational, this means that they are populated by rational investors, who value assets accurately and correctly, and that they make correct predictions, as of the time of the evaluation, with regard to the future. In Buffett's view, it is the fact that these perceptions about the rationality of the markets are held so widely that explains the success of some great investors—for instance, his friend and former colleague Walter Schloss, who managed the fund WJS Ltd Partners. When talking about Schloss after he had passed away, Buffett remarked that "tens of thousands of students were sent out into life believing that every day the price of every stock was 'right' . . . and that attempts to evaluate business—that is, stocks—were useless"; Walter's job was "made easier by misguided instructions that had been given to those young minds," and he went on outperforming the market. "After all, if you are in the shipping business, it's helpful to have all of your potential competitors be taught that the earth is flat" [Buffett, 1977–2013, 2006].

Buffett also spoke about the notion of market efficiency: "Observing correctly that the market was frequently efficient, [efficient market hypothesis proponents] went on to conclude incorrectly that it was always efficient. The difference between these propositions is night and day" [Buffett, 1977–2013, 1988].

The concepts of efficiency and rationality are interconnected. Market efficiency implies instantaneous incorporation of all available information into prices. What is meant by "all information" depends on the form of efficiency. An efficient market is not necessarily rational, because it may incorporate all available information into prices, but not correctly. A rational market is always efficient, as the concept of rational expectations, by definition, includes the instantaneous accurate incorporation of all available information into prices.

Buffett observes that irrationality finds an expression in herd behavior. "Every time it becomes fashionable to expand into something, some companies will expand into it. Then they get out of it about five years later, licking their wounds. It's very human. People do the same things with their stocks" [Buffett, 1991a]. Buffett tells a parable that he had heard from Benjamin Graham about an oilman who, upon his death, seeks to enter Heaven. When he gets to Heaven, he discovers that all places in the section set aside for oil prospectors are occupied. He shouts: "Oil discovered in Hell!" Many entrepreneurs make a dash to enter the Underworld, and an ample number of places in Heaven becomes available. Instead of sitting himself down comfortably, the oilman follows the crowd. "Where are you going?" St. Peter asks. The oilman pauses for a moment and replies: "I think I'll go along with the rest of the boys. There might be some truth to that rumor after all" [Buffett, 1977–2013, 1985].

Describing the irrationality of the market, Buffett uses the metaphor invented by his teacher, Graham, of Mr. Market, a "remarkably accommodating fellow" who has incurable emotional problems. He is the investor's partner in a private business, and he appears daily and quotes prices at which he will either buy the investor's interest or sell his interest to the investor. When Mr. Market is euphoric, he sees only the favorable factors affecting the business. He gives a very high price because he fears that his partner "will snap up his [Mr. Market's] interest and rob him of imminent gains." When he is depressed, Mr. Market sees "nothing but trouble ahead for both the business and the world" and gives a very low price because he is terrified of a potential sale of an investor's interest to him. This occurs even if the sale that is being considered is that of a business whose economic characteristics are stable.

Since Mr. Market doesn't mind being ignored and returns with a new quotation every day, the more manic-depressive his behavior is, the better it is for an investor. Buffett reminds his readers that Mr. Market should serve the investor, but not guide him. It is "his [Mr. Market's] pocketbook, not his wisdom," that is useful. If Mr. Market shows up some day in a particularly foolish mood, an investor is free to take advantage of him, but on no account should the investor fall under his influence. And if someone isn't certain that he can value his business far better than Mr. Market can, then he doesn't belong in the game. "As they say in poker, 'If you've been in the game 30 minutes and you don't know who the patsy is, you're the patsy'" [Buffett, 1977–2013, 1987].

Another interesting metaphor that Buffett uses to describe the market is that of a "voting machine." "In the short run, the market is a voting machine. In the long run, it's a weighing machine" [cited in Schroeder,

2008, p. 16]. This metaphor is also borrowed from Graham [Graham and Dodd, 2009, p. 70]. Only with a long-term perspective will the market value an asset accurately (with the true "weight" being determined). In the short term, the market will price different stocks relative to one another, as if it were an election, with the winner being the one who garners the most votes. The voting process is very "undemocratic" ("it's a very undemocratic way of voting"), and those in the electorate do not have to take literacy exams: "Unfortunately, they have no literacy tests in terms of voting qualifications" [cited in Schroeder, 2008, p. 17].

Given that markets are irrational, predicting what the market will do in the short term is extremely difficult, if not impossible. Therefore, one should not engage in forecasting. Importantly, however, since the markets are sometimes irrational and sometimes rational, sooner or later every asset will be valued fairly. Accordingly, the search for those assets that are mispriced by the market, with the expectation that in the long term they will be revalued appropriately, is a meaningful endeavor.

In addition to diverging perspectives on the market's rationality, the perceptions of risk held by traditional finance experts and Buffett are also different. According to the efficient market hypothesis, any new information that affects the value of a stock is immediately reflected in the price of that stock, and therefore the volatility of the stock price is a function of the changes in the relevant information that is available: the more frequent and dramatic the new prognoses, the stronger are the movements in the stock price.

Investors' decision to view a security as having a high or low risk is driven by this anticipation of fluctuations in the information flow connected to that security. Greater risk, or greater expected changes in the information available, requires a greater return, since investors dislike risk. The higher the risk, the greater the required discounting rate that investors would use in valuing the security. The higher discounting rate results in a lower present value for the security and greater potential income from the security in relative terms through, for instance, dividend yield. In summary, the definition of risk is designed to reflect the informational uncertainty that investors face.[1]

---

1 For practical purposes, volatility is calculated as the standard deviation of daily price returns. It is, of course, possible to calculate the standard deviation of weekly, monthly, and yearly returns. An investor would make a decision as to which returns she would prefer to analyze.

Buffett relies on a fundamentally different understanding of risk. To him, risk is not related to volatility: "We're risk averse, not volatility averse" [cited in Kilpatrick, 2005, p. 1396]. A long-term investor who intends to hold the stock "forever" and earn on the basis of economic cash flow from this security is able to take the view that for him, the falling stock price represents a risk in three circumstances: when he is compelled to sell because of margin calls, because of the time horizon of his investment, or because he did not value the stock correctly when he acquired it. This is the logic behind Buffett's common-sense definition of risk. Risk is a possibility of loss [Buffett, 1977–2013, 1993].

Buffett finds that risk "comes from not knowing what you are doing" [Rasmussen, 1994]. An investor who aims to understand what she is doing, understand the business in which she is investing, and act within the circle of her competence carries risks that are completely different from those that face an investor who operates within the conventional financial theory framework. The risk for Buffett's investor is concealed in the ability of the investor to value the cash flow that will be generated by the company accurately through exercising personal judgment and careful management of her circle of competence. We are again reminded of the importance of the perimeter of one's circle of competence that we discussed earlier. What is described as risk in traditional finance is completely unimportant, in Buffett's view.

Buffett finds that the use of a single statistic, the beta of a stock (the stock's historical relative volatility), to measure risk and construct "arcane" investment and capital-allocation theories around that statistic is an erroneous approach in principle.[2] Munger comments similarly: "People calculate too much and think too little . . ." [cited in Kilpatrick, 2005, p. 1189]. When asked to define the stock market risk at the Berkshire's annual shareholder meeting in 1997, Warren Buffett spoke about the performance of the shares of the Washington Post Company

---

2 With this approach, portfolios are created by using mathematical optimization to select stocks. These stocks are chosen to generate maximum portfolio return with minimum risk, or volatility of the combined portfolio. This is the process of diversification of risk. This approach was first proposed by Henry Markowitz in his 1952 article "Portfolio Selection" [Markowitz, 1952]. Please refer to Chapters 3 and 6 of *The Myth of the Rational Market* [Fox, 2001] for the contemporary interpretation of the portfolio theory. An emotional assessment is offered by Nassim Taleb in Chapter 17 of *The Black Swan* [Taleb, 2007]. Nassim Taleb views Markowitz's ideas as most profoundly and fundamentally erroneous.

in 1973. "When I first bought it in 1973 it had gone down almost 50 percent, from a valuation of the whole company of close to $170 million down to $80 million. Because it happened pretty fast, the beta of the stock had actually increased, and a professor would have told you that the company was more risky if you bought it for $80 million than if you bought it for $170 million. That's something I've thought about ever since they told me that 25 years ago and I still haven't figured it out." (The comment was received by enthusiastic applause from the audience) [Buffett, 1997a].

As we have discussed, since the market is not always rational, it is possible to make money by finding companies that are not valued correctly, or, in other words, by making investments that are relatively risk-free, in Buffett's sense of the word, and not by taking risks, in the traditional understanding of that term. Within Buffett's framework, not taking on risk does not mean reducing profitability, whereas in the traditional framework, taking on risk is necessary to generate return. Buffett welcomes the uncertainty that drives the volatility of stock prices. Uncertainty creates volatility that allows investors to buy stocks at a price below their fair value and sell them at a price above it. "Uncertainty actually is a friend of the buyer of long-term values" [cited in Rasmussen, 1994].

Since for Buffett risk arises from an investor's misjudging his circle of competence, the task is not to take on risk, but to elude it. Buffett finds that he has "done better by avoiding dragons rather than by slaying them" [cited in Kilpatrick, 2005, p. 13]. Discussing the qualities of character that he is looking for in his successor, Buffett said that, since one considerable mistake could wipe out a long series of successes, he is seeking someone who is "genetically" engineered to sense and avoid serious risk, even a risk which has never been encountered before [Buffett, 1977–2013, 2006]. Parallels between Buffett's conceptual approach and that of Nassim Taleb are recognizable with respect to risk first of all. To the best of my knowledge, Buffett has not discussed his views on Taleb's ideas in public. Taleb's *Black Swan* [Taleb, 2007] is not in the list of literature recommended by Charlie Munger.

In managing risk Buffett emphasizes the importance of conservatism. Not losing is more important than generating high earnings:

"I would rather be certain of a good result than hopeful of a great one" [Buffett, 1977–2013, 1996]. He aims to rely on predictability [Kilpatrick, 2005, p. 1384]. One of Buffett's acquaintances tells about their joint visit to a restaurant: Buffett "had an exceptional ham-and-cheese sandwich. A few days later, we were going out again. He said, 'Let's go back to that restaurant.' I said, 'But we were just there.' He said, 'Precisely. Why take a risk with another place? We know exactly what we're going to get.' And that is what Warren looks for in stocks too. He only invests in companies where the odds are great that they will not disappoint" [cited in Fromson, 1989].

The concept of risk that Buffett uses is not universally applicable. It is suitable specifically for his investment strategy. Market volatility is of no concern to an investor whose investment horizon is long-term and whose leverage is low. An investor who is highly leveraged is at the mercy of his creditors. Such an investor may not be free to choose when to sell specific assets. His creditors may compel him to liquidate his positions. The risk inherent in a particular investment will be different for the leveraged investor and for the nonleveraged one.

A logical consequence of such an understanding of risk is Buffett's different attitude toward diversification. A person who understands what she is doing does not need diversification, argues Buffett, referring to Keynes: "Keynes essentially said don't try and figure out what the market is doing. Figure out business you understand, and concentrate. Diversification is protection against ignorance, but if you don't feel ignorant, the need for it [diversification] goes down drastically" [cited in Lenzner, 1993]. "Diversification . . . makes very little sense for those who know what they're doing" [cited in Lowe, 2007, p. 207]. "The great personal fortunes . . . were built by someone who identified one wonderful business" [Questions Concerning Warren Buffett and Investing]. When Buffett was 20, he invested half of his net worth in GEICO [Lowe, 2007, p. 158]. In 1960, he announced that 35 percent of the assets under his management were invested in one company (he did not mention the company's name) [Buffett, 1957–1970, 1960]. During 1988 and 1989, Buffett bought 6.3 percent of the shares of Coca-Cola, and this investment represented 32 percent of Berkshire's shareholder capital and 20 percent of its market value [Boroson, 2008, p. 85].

Following Keynes, Philip Fisher, and Gerald Loeb, Buffett finds that diversification is likely to be difficult to achieve because of the relative rarity of good investments.[3] A discerning investor, who invests only in first-class companies, is not likely to find a large number of such companies in order to diversify his portfolio particularly easily: "If your only conviction is that equities over time are a good place to have your money, you probably ought to have at least 20 or thereabouts. . . . But if you really analyze businesses so that you're buying into a business and making a conscious decision about what you think the future of that business is . . . then I really think that if you can find six or eight of those, well that's plenty," declared Buffett in 1994 during a meeting of the New York Society of Security Analysts [Buffett, 1994b]. Buffett likes to say that a fund manager who invests in 40 to 80 different stocks is unlikely to be able to select such a large number of stocks with knowledge and care. "Anyone owning such numbers of securities . . . is following what I call the Noah School of Investing— two of everything. Such investors should be piloting arks" [Buffett, 1957–1970, January 20, 1966]. Investing with the Noah's Ark principle will leave the investor with a zoo [cited in Lowe, 2007, p. 165].

Buffett advises a beginning investor to imagine that she got a card with space for 20 punches on it, and that was all she would have. Every time she made an investment decision, she would receive one punch. If one had only 20 punches, she would make 20 very good investment decisions, and she could get very rich. There is absolutely no need to have 50 good ideas [Schlender, Buffett, and Gates, 1998]. Excessive diversification is meaningless in the traditional understanding also— that adding new shares to a portfolio reduces that portfolio's nonmarket risk very rapidly.[4] Owning two shares lowers the nonmarket risk by 46 percent, owning four lowers it by 72 percent, owning eight lowers it by

---

3   In Loeb's book, *The Battle for Investment Survival*, published in 1952, we find these words: "over-diversification acts as a poor protection against lack of knowledge"; "selection of too many issues is often a form of hedging against ignorance"; and "the chance of error in judgment is . . . increased by diversification" [Loeb, 2009, pp. 29, 72].
4   Nonmarket risk is exposure to a specific company. As the number of companies in the portfolio rises, the portfolio becomes the market.

81 percent, owning 16 lowers it by 93 percent, and owning 32 lowers it by 96 percent [Greenblatt, 1997, pp. 20–21].

The Stock Split

> May you live until Berkshire shares split.
>
> —WARREN BUFFETT [CITED IN LOWE, 2007, P. 176]

Buffett also disagrees with various other positions held within the financial industry. For instance, he does not accept the idea of a stock split: "Splitting the stock is like asking for a pizza to be sliced into five pieces because you can't possibly eat seven" [cited in Kilpatrick, 2005, p. 870].

Stocks with higher liquidity have higher valuations [Pratt, 2009, chaps. 5, 6, 9–15]. Stocks were traded primarily in round lots (100 shares) until Internet trading and discount brokers became common. The investment community's perception was that if the stock price rose so much that a round lot became too expensive, the company was required to do a stock split—a procedure analogous to a reduction in the denomination of banknotes in monetary circulation. Berkshire—a champion of share price growth—has never done a stock split (or almost never; we discuss the quasi split of 1996 later in this chapter). Buffett has even sent cards to wish a Happy Birthday with "May you live until Berkshire shares split" [cited in Lowe, 2007, p. 176].

Buffett's refusal to do a stock split has created a multitude of problems for the financial press, information agencies, and brokers. Berkshire's stock price is currently a six-digit figure, when stock prices are ordinarily tens or hundreds of dollars. Brokers' trading systems often are not designed to allow the insertion of six-figure numbers into the stock price field. This is, of course, of no concern to Buffett. Bill Gates feels that Buffett is doing something admirable by signaling to people that Berkshire's stock is a "different stock" and that Berkshire is a little different from a typical company [Schlender, Buffett, and Gates, 1998]. When a stock price is a six-figure number, it is indeed a signal that attracts attention to the company as nothing else possibly could.

Refusing to split the shares is not just a way to communicate a particular point or to create a certain impression. Buffett has a more important motivation. He argues that he does not believe in increasing short-term liquidity because it affects the structure of the shareholder pool. Short-term liquidity is attractive to people who are drawn to speculation, or to people who may need to sell their holdings if they need access to cash. Having such shareholders, in turn, makes the shares more volatile. Having a large number of small stockholders is probably a negative for a company rather than a positive. Berkshire's stockholders are indeed different. The average ownership period is a lot longer than that among American public companies. In 1994, Buffett commented that Berkshire has less turnover than any other stock on the NYSE [Buffett, 1994a].

Despite Buffett's dislike of the stock split idea, he was nevertheless compelled to go through a near-split of Berkshire shares in 1996. Without regular stock splits, and riding the wave of the general market rise in the 1990s, Berkshire's shares had become inaccessible to smaller investors. By March 1996, their price had reached $38,000 a share, a historical high. Berkshire shares were the most expensive publicly traded shares in the world. (By December 2014, the share price had reached $227,000.) Some fund managers saw an opportunity in the situation. They came up with the idea of setting up a new mutual fund whose profitability would track the price dynamic of the Berkshire shares; participation in this fund would be sold on the wider market at $250 to $1,000 per unit of participation. Two different fund management teams came up with this idea simultaneously. One team planned to name its fund Market Leaders Growth Trust, the other Five Sigma Investment Partners (the name of this fund is a direct reference to Buffett and his success).

At the same time, it was apparent that replicating Buffett's portfolio was impossible. First, Berkshire holds 80 percent or more of many closed companies in its portfolio, and in these cases, the rest of the shares belong to the company managers. A replicating fund would not be able to include these companies. Second, Buffett does not advertise his investments in public companies in advance. It is possible to find out about such acquisitions only post factum, if at all. Buffett does not make information about his investments public if the rules of information disclosure do not require it. Third, an important part of Buffett's profitability is tied to the use of leverage; however, his leverage is not ordinary borrowed funds but obligations from his insurance businesses. (We talk about this in detail in the next chapter.)

Nevertheless, the creators of the Buffett trackers found a solution to their problems. Their idea was simply to buy Berkshire shares and nothing else. This was nearly a genius way to create something out of almost nothing. And this something promised to provide a substantial monetary reward in the form of commissions, the magnitude of which could have been vast. Investors would have been asked to pay a load commission of 4.5 percent of invested funds on entry for Market Leaders Growth Fund and of 2.75 percent for Five Sigma Investment Partners, in addition to an annual commission for managing the funds. The managers of Market Leaders Growth Fund even announced that they had raised $60 million [Abelson, 1996].

Buffett decidedly did not like the idea of others launching funds that would piggyback on his success. First, he found the proposed commission rates nearly a robbery. Second, although Buffett does not speak about this openly, he, understandably, does not wish others to make money by using his name, if they are not Berkshire shareholders. Third, he did not want Berkshire shares to be marketed to the wider public as "hot" shares whose price "tomorrow" would only be higher. Buffett wanted to disabuse of their convictions those who believed that the phenomenal rise of Berkshire shares would continue. He thought that further growth in Berkshire's share price was impossible, given the stock price level at the time. Buffett did not want to become someone who betrayed the expectations of others. A sharp rise in demand for Berkshire shares would have resulted in share price growth, followed, most likely, by a share price fall. In his authorized biography, Buffett explained that he didn't want to have among Berkshire's shareholders people who viewed their investments as something that can double. He could have created his own market action for a while and would have been a hero for a year, as a lot of money would have poured into a fixed amount of stock [Schroeder, 2008, p. 652].

Buffett approached the organizers of the new Berkshire tracker funds and requested that they not pursue their idea. They did not heed his wishes. Buffett then decided to enter the game himself and proposed an alternative: Berkshire Hathaway announced that it would issue nonvoting Class B shares, whose economic interest would amount to 1/30 that of the Class A shares (Class A shares are those that had existed "historically" and had become too expensive). According to the terms of the issue, 30 shares of Class B stock would be convertible into one share of Class A stock, but not the other way around. Buffett set the commission rate far lower than the one established by the competing funds. Commissions paid by the investors who took part in the issue amounted to approximately $10 for $1,000 worth of shares, or 1 percent. Buffett also declared that the demand for shares would be satisfied fully. Berkshire would issue as many Class B shares as were requested through subscription: "We said we would sell as much of this stuff as the world wants, and that way there is no way it can be a hot stock" [cited in Schroeder, 2008, p. 652]. Buffett hired Salomon Brothers, a friendly investment bank at the time, to manage the offering. Brokers' commissions were set at a bare minimum in order to eliminate the motivation to market the shares aggressively to small investors.

Buffett spoke publicly about Berkshire shares being overvalued. He would not have recommended the purchase to his friends. On the first page of the information memorandum about the issue was a statement: The management does not believe that the shares are undervalued. This, of course, may have been a PR exercise directed at preventing the proxy-Berkshire funds from coming into existence. The public discussion of the excessive valuation resulted in a temporary fall in the price of Berkshire Hathaway Class A shares, but over the subsequent 20 months, the shares grew continually and quickly and, as a result, had more than doubled by January of 1998.

Altogether Berkshire issued 517,500 Class B shares at a price of $1,100. The total volume of funds raised amounted to slightly less than $600 million. Of course, neither of the proxy funds materialized, and no further attempts to create similar funds have been undertaken. Perhaps to ensure that the idea of proxy funds would not be revived, at the start of 2010, Buffett did go through a stock split for the Class B shares, which by that time had reached a price of $3,300. The split was set at 1 to 50, and after the split, the share price was reduced to $66. In December of 2014, these shares traded at $148–$152.

New Share Issues, Dividend Policy, and Share Repurchases

> If earnings have been unwisely retained, it is likely that managers, too, have been unwisely retained.
>
> —WARREN BUFFETT [BUFFETT, 1977–2013, 1984]

As we discussed, the ideal investment, in Buffett's view, is a company that is able to use the maximum amount of capital at the highest possible return. Such companies rarely exist. Usually there will be either a business that requires a lot of capital or a business that is able to deliver a high return. The second type is, of course, preferable. Businesses of the first kind are compelled to raise financing continually through stock issues and/or borrowing, where leveraging introduces its own constraints on the business. This is probably why Buffett does not like investing in companies that regularly raise new equity. The market, in his view, also values more highly, all else being equal, those companies whose managements have shown that they are not willing to issue stock at any time on terms that are not in the best interest of the owners of the business [Buffett, 1977–2013, 1982]. Buffett assures investors that he never invests in initial public offerings, as he believes that they are excessively marketed and are too much of an "it" idea of the moment, where it is not clear how the business concept may stand the test of time. Initial public offerings are the opposite of what Buffett seeks to acquire: a great company at the right price [Schroeder, 2008, p. 368].

On occasion, Berkshire has resorted to issuing stock in order to finance new acquisitions, but often this is not because of a shortage of available funds. Driven by tax considerations, the sellers of businesses often prefer to receive stock. For instance, the family businesses of Dexter Shoe and NetJets were acquired for stock. The largest secondary issue of Berkshire was a stock issue of $10.6 billion, or 6.1 percent of the share capital, in 2010 to finance the acquisition of Burlington Northern Santa Fe Railway. Buffett commented during this transaction that it was "as much fun as preparing for a colonoscopy" [cited in Stempel, 2010]. Of course, there were advantages. The acquisition of Burlington Northern allowed Buffett to use the $22 billion of dormant funds on Berkshire's balance sheet.

Great companies typically accumulate excess money that needs to be used in some way—for instance, paid out as dividends or spent on share buybacks. What determines whether a company will reinvest the profit or return it to shareholders is the rate of return on the reinvested funds. In order to make sure that shareholders are better off, earnings should be retained only to expand a high-return business; the balance should be used to pay dividends or to repurchase stock ("an action that increases the owners' interest in the exceptional business while sparing them participation in subpar businesses") [Buffett, 1977–2013, 1984].

A dividend policy in which a set percentage of profits is paid out as dividends may end up being detrimental to the business, as the company may find itself in a position where, because the company has created dividend expectations in the minds of its shareholders, it must pay out dividends at a time when it would be better for it not to pay them. If the company is able to generate more than a dollar of value for each dollar invested, then what is the point of paying out dividends? As a matter of principle, Berkshire Hathaway does not pay out dividends and reinvests all profits. The last and probably the only time when Berkshire paid out dividends, in the amount of 10 cents a share, took place in 1967. Later Buffett joked about this. He explained that he must have been in the bathroom when the dividend was declared. Walter Schloss thought that Buffett is able to avoid paying dividends because Berkshire is an insurance company. If it were an ordinary company, Buffett would have been obliged to pay some dividends [Schloss, 1993].

In its economic consequences, a stock repurchase is comparable to the payment of dividends—as a result of a repurchase, free cash is transferred from the business to the shareholders. The principal difference between a share repurchase and a dividend payment is that shareholders are free to choose to participate in the buyback (if the company is not being converted into a closed one, of course). Importantly, after the repurchase, the company's profits will be distributed proportionally to a smaller number of shares, so the net income per share should rise. Also, the tax consequences of a share buyback differ from those of a dividend payout. In other respects, a dividend payout and a share buyback are similar. In substance, the repurchase of shares is an investment of company funds in its own shares. For this reason, the criterion for whether or not this is a good decision is the same: the profitability of the investment, or, more precisely, whether the market price of the stock is higher or lower than its intrinsic value. "When companies with outstanding businesses and comfortable financial positions find their shares selling by far below intrinsic value in the marketplace, no alternative action can benefit shareholders as surely as repurchases" [Buffett, 1977–2013, 1984]. Buffett admitted that in the 1970s, he intentionally looked for companies that did share buybacks: "This often was a tipoff that the company was both undervalued and run by a shareholder-oriented management" [Buffett, 1977–2013, 1999]. "In the mid-1970s, the wisdom of making [repurchases] was virtually screaming at managements, but few responded" [Buffett, 1977–2013, 1999].

Later, Buffett's opinion on this subject was supported by the studies of economists. The 1981 paper "Common Stock Repurchases and Market Signalling," by Theo Vermaelen [Vermaelen, 1981] documented that repurchases through tender offers were followed by abnormal increases in earnings per share. In a later article [Ikkenberry, Lakonishok, and Vermaelen, 1995], it was shown that mechanical investing (without using any other measure to analyze whether a particular stock was attractive or not) in the shares of companies that bought back their shares from the market and did not raise funds through share issues delivered better returns than investing in the market as a whole. The authors analyzed the stock behavior, over the course of four years following the announcement, of 1,200 companies that had announced share buybacks over the period from 1980 to 1990. They established that the returns delivered by these shares were on average greater than the market returns over the respective periods by approximately 12 percent. This may indicate that the shares were undervalued at the time of the share buyback announcement.

However, Buffett argues, the days when companies bought back their shares because they were undervalued are over. In the 1990s, the majority of the companies that repurchased their shares did so to support their stock prices, and the buybacks were executed at inflated price levels [Buffett, 1977–2013, 1999]. Economists agree with Buffett on this. According to Robert Brenner, share repurchases became popular in the 1980s. They were often executed with the help of borrowed funds, as it was possible to account for the interest payments on these loans as costs. Share buybacks were used to create share price growth. Over the 1990–1993 period, during the recession, the popularity of share buybacks subsided somewhat, but in 1994 the practice returned with a vengeance and the stimulation of price growth became a more explicit motive. Over the 1994–1999 period, nonfinancial companies used $655 billion for share buybacks, of which about half was spent in 1998–1999. Over the 1983–1990 and 1994–1999 periods, nonfinancial corporations directed 50 percent of all their borrowing toward share repurchases. The growth in share buyback volumes at a time of sharp share price rises is driven by managers who were under pressure to produce the greatest return for shareholders over the shortest period of time and who were also motivated by the stock options in their compensation packages [Brenner, 2003, pp. 147–148, 150–151]. Nowadays the volumes of share buybacks are high also; however, let us switch from discussing the market in general to examining Buffett's views and actions.

When shares are repurchased at overly high prices, the selling shareholders win, and therefore the buyback is disadvantageous for the remaining shareholders. In order to be fair to all shareholders, Buffett does not welcome a buyback at either unreasonably high prices or artificially low prices. He deems it necessary for companies to supply all shareholders with enough information to allow them to make their own estimates of the intrinsic value of the shares. A buyback is justified only when it is an honest game—that is, when the shareholders have full information, but nevertheless have undervalued the shares.

Over a considerable period, Berkshire did not buy back its shares, although Buffett had seriously considered such an action. In 1999, he admitted that he viewed his refusal to buy back shares at certain times as a mistake. Either his own valuation of Berkshire shares was unreasonably conservative or he was too attracted to the alternative uses of the free funds. In the autumn of 2010, Berkshire attempted to buy back its stock. The repurchase price was set at no higher than 110 percent of the net book value of the assets. Berkshire ended up buying back only $67 million worth of shares, as the market price of the shares rose sharply [Buffett, 1977–2013, 2011]. In 2012, when the buyback price ceiling was raised to 120 percent of the net book asset value, Berkshire purchased a large stake from a long-term shareholder for $1.2 billion [Buhayar and Tracer, 2012]. In 2013, no shares were bought back. Since the beginning of 2013, Berkshire's share price has not fallen below 120 percent of the net asset book value. In his letter to shareholders for 2013, Buffett mentions that, in his view, Berkshire's intrinsic value far exceeds its book value [Buffett, 1977–2013, 2013].

The free funds could be channeled toward the acquisition of other businesses, but "if a company's stock is selling well below intrinsic value, repurchases usually make the most sense" [Buffett, 1977–2013, 1999]. Buffett explains that the competitive nature of the corporate acquisitions market almost guarantees the payment of a full—and frequently more than a full—price when one company buys another. At the same time, the auction nature of securities markets often creates the opportunity for well-run companies to purchase parts of their own businesses at prices below 50 percent of those required to buy equivalent earning capacity through acquisitions of other companies [Buffett, 1977–2013, 1980].

Mergers and Acquisitions and Leveraged Buyouts

> The acquirer pays for the fact that he gets to haul back
> to his cave the carcass of the conquered animal.
> **—WARREN BUFFETT [SCHLENDER, BUFFETT, AND GATES, 1998]**

Creation of value for the acquiring company—the only "lawful" motivation for a transaction, in Buffett's view—is the hardest objective to achieve. On the securities markets, shares are often traded at prices that are lower than their fair value. However, when an entire company is being sold, the sellers generally insist on receiving the full price. At the same time, to justify the high price of the transaction, the managers of the company and their advisors create optimistic financial projections that have "more entertainment value than educational value." "While deals often fail in practice, they never fail in projections" [Buffett, 1977–2013, 1982], and, "In the production of rosy scenarios, Wall Street can hold its own against Washington" [Buffett, 1977–2013, 1995].

One of the factors contributing to overvaluation is the auction nature of the mergers and acquisitions market (earlier we referred to "the competitive nature of [the] corporate acquisitions activity," but it is also a type of auction). "The smarter side to take in a bidding war is the losing side," argues Buffett [cited in Curran, 1993].

Let us consider briefly why Buffett feels that the auction nature of the securities markets allows investors to buy a stake in a company cheaply, whereas the auction nature of the mergers and acquisitions process forces an expensive purchase. As we know from game theory, more often than not the person who wins an auction overpays. The valuations of individual auction participants differ, and, as a result of the bidding process, the highest valuation wins, while the fair price is probably somewhere around the average, whether calculated as mean, mode, or median, of all the bids. (This discussion applies to auctions in general, whereas when investors bid for a company, a certain objective adjustment may be necessary, since the different companies bidding will have different kinds of synergies with the target.)

When a company buys its own shares on the open market, the company is in a position to purchase only from those who value the shares least. In an M&A transaction, a single acquisition target typically attracts multiple buyers, some of whom would value the company higher. At the same time, there will be those among the selling shareholders who also value the company more expensively, and it will be necessary to buy them out. In the case of a buyout offer on the open market, the offered price is the same for all shareholders. Those who are willing to sell cheaply will receive what they will perceive as a full or more than a full price. The buyer is a monopolist who does not have to buy out all the shareholders, and the legal framework permits him to purchase shares from different shareholders at different prices.

The problem of overvaluation is exacerbated when it is necessary to raise additional equity to be able to carry out the transaction. Buffett explains that mergers and acquisitions are often described as "the purchase of the seller by the buyer"; however, in reality, the buyer makes a partial sale of itself in order to buy the seller. The transaction makes even less sense if the marketplace is undervaluing the shares of the buying company. In Buffett's view, the decision on the issuance of new shares to finance an acquisition should be examined using the same logic as that used for the sale of the business as a whole: if you are not ready to sell your whole business at a particular price, then you should not sell a portion of your business at this price [Buffett, 1977–2013, 1982]. This principle is an extension of Graham's idea that investing itself should be viewed as buying a share in a business.

Not all transactions create value for the buyer. Buffett cites the same reasons for this as modern corporate finance theory does. Often the acquirer's managers overestimate their managerial ability, and the motivation for the acquisition is the illusion that they will be able to have the acquisition target generate more value than the original managers could. Richard Roll, discussing this phenomenon, came up with the hubris hypothesis [Roll, 1986]. In Buffett's framework, a version of hubris manifests itself in the contemplation of whether it is possible to search successfully for princes that are masquerading as toads (we discussed this in Chapter 2). Confidence that the efforts of the new management will be able to convert a toad into a prince often does not lead to this result in reality because fundamental factors, such as the nature of the industry in which the business operates, influence the profitability of the business to a far greater extent than the efforts of the managers.

Another factor that compels managers to buy companies is the desire to expand their empire, or to do a transaction for the sake of transacting. "In the excitement of the game managerial intellect wilted in competition with managerial adrenaline" [Buffett, 1977–2013, 1982]. Buffett also quotes Peter Drucker, who, in Buffett's view, "got to the heart of things": "Deal-making beats working. Deal-making is exciting and fun, and working is grubby. . . . Deal-making is romantic, sexy. That's why you have deals that make no sense" [Buffett, 1977–2013, 1995].

The problem is not limited to the emotions associated with the game. The remuneration of managers of large companies is higher than that of the managers of medium and small companies. Michael Jensen, in his 1986 paper "Agency Costs of Free Cash Flow, Corporate Finance, and Takeovers," was the first to observe that managers are unwilling to pay dividends to shareholders, as this reduces the resources that are under managerial control and, thus, the managers' power and compensation; managers prefer to use the resources to finance growth, also through mergers and acquisitions [Jensen, 1986]. It is difficult to judge whether Buffett's refusal to pay dividends is a reflection of an agency issue. Not paying dividends supports Berkshire's stock price. If dividends had been paid regularly, the extent of the stock price rise might have been more moderate. This is why the agency motive cannot be excluded. At the same time, Buffett systematically beats S&P, and in this sense the agency costs do not exist.

In some respects, Buffett's position on the driving forces behind mergers and acquisitions differs strongly from modern corporate finance theory, which considers the search for synergies a reasonable motivation for an M&A transaction. For Buffett, synergy should not be a factor. He buys businesses that have high profitability potential, but he does not integrate them into his existing businesses; instead, he leaves them with operational independence.

An example of this is the acquisition of General Re, which used to be one of Berkshire Hathaway's largest reinsurance clients. Since the acquisition, the company has been managed as an independent entity, competing with other insurance divisions of Berkshire, which also operate as free-standing units.

The four companies specializing in furniture retail that Buffett acquired at different times remain independent within Berkshire. Melvyn Wolff, the former owner and now chairman of Star Furniture, testified that Buffett had made his feeling apparent to the CEOs involved. He was not looking for synergies. Almost anyone else in his place would have chosen one CEO and let the other three go. Buffett, in fact, said the opposite: "I bought four freestanding, well-managed furniture companies; don't screw it up. Just keep running your companies like you do. I've got no objection to your meeting together and loving each other and so forth. But don't look for synergy for my sake" [cited in Miles, 2002, p. 207].

One of the reasons why Buffett refuses to merge similar companies is that the majority of the expected synergies do not materialize in practice. As Buffett puts it, synergy is a concept that is often used to justify a transaction that actually makes no business sense [Buffett, 1977–2013, 1985]. Another reason is the difficulty of transplanting or merging corporate cultures. A manager of one of Berkshire's daughter companies explains the lack of attempts to merge related businesses by the belief that corporate culture is not transferable, while at the same time there are no business cultures that are sufficiently similar [Miles, 2002, p. 207]. A further consideration is that the full merger of acquired companies would result in some of the top managers losing their positions, and this would conflict with Buffett's attitude toward the former owners who are selling him their businesses. At the point of sale, part of the sale agreement is that the old owner will continue managing his or her business as he or she did previously. (We discuss this in greater detail in Chapter 8.)

Of all the types of synergy that could arise in mergers and acquisitions, according to the standard theory of corporate finance, Buffett acknowledges as valid only one: financial synergy. Financial synergy means that leveraged financing becomes cheaper for small and medium companies once they become part of a large, diversified holding company whose cash flows are more stable and whose credit rating is higher. Accessibility and cost of financing stop being an obstacle to business development. According to Rich Santulli, the founder of NetJets, Berkshire's triple A credit rating assisted NetJets in reducing the cost of borrowing and starting operations in Europe and the Middle East; as a result, between 1998, when Buffett acquired the company, and 2000, the revenue doubled [Miles, 2002, p. 125]. We discussed earlier how this story has developed—the existence of financial synergy may have been critical to the firm's survival.

Financial synergy was one of the motives behind Berkshire's acquisition in 2003 of Clayton Homes, a company that makes mobile, modular, and manufactured homes. This company not only builds these homes, but also supplies financing for their purchase, and so the financing arm needs to raise large quantities of money. The buyers of mobile homes are often high-risk borrowers, and the number of bankruptcies among them is very high. Americans who are more financially secure buy regular homes, not mobile ones. After the events of September 11, 2001, raising funds on the wholesale market became very difficult, as the market for securitized obligations and asset-backed securities was at a standstill (and all insurers were facing large payouts). The limited funds that were available at that time came only at higher cost and on harsher terms. Had Clayton remained independent during that period, the company would have had to contend with mediocre earnings as it struggled with financing [Buffett, 1977–2013, 2004]. The company was sold to Buffett precisely because he guaranteed financing on good terms. After the acquisition, Berkshire extended loans in the amount of $7.35 billion to Clayton Homes on excellent terms—with a markup of only 0.1 percent on the cost of raising funds for Berkshire itself. For Buffett, the acquisition of Clayton meant taking ownership of a $5 billion credit portfolio that, according to estimates, was able to deliver an additional 3 percentage points over the rates at which Berkshire loaned it funds. In annualized terms, this meant a further $150 million of profit. In this way, Berkshire gained exposure to a new market, lending to individuals with low credit ratings. Buffett called this arrangement "a little synergy" and assured his shareholders that this was the first synergy in 40 years [Buffett, 1977–2013, 2004]. In the letter to shareholders of 2008 Buffett remarked that although Clayton supplied credit to subprime borrowers, the company was practically unaffected by the crisis in the mortgages market. Delinquency rate on loans it has originated was 3.6 percent, up only modestly from 2.9 percent in 2004. Clayton's foreclosures during 2008 were 3.0 percent of originated loans compared to 3.8 percent in 2006 and 5.3 percent in 2004 [Buffett, 1977–2013, 2008].

A similar logic guided the acquisition in 2001 of XTRA, a company specializing in the leasing of trucks and containers. Leasing is also a financing-intensive business, and Berkshire's credit rating was very helpful to the company.

Perhaps there is a certain synergy between Buffett's insurance business and his understanding of financial markets. For instance, in 2003, Buffett was contacted by a Wall Street firm that proposed doing a deal covering the first bankruptcy in a pool of junk bonds. In such a deal, the insurer fully covers the holder of the bonds for the cash flow that he is owed from the borrower. The insurer also acquires the rights of recovery from the borrower. Buffett carefully selected a number of borrowers and refused to look at diversified portfolios with large numbers of names. Collins & Aikman, one of the companies in the group that Buffett chose, went bankrupt in 2005. In the bankruptcy process, Buffett received 35 cents on the dollar (that is, he lost 65 cents);

however, the insurance premium that Buffett had received up front for the whole insured portfolio may have amounted on average to 75 cents on the dollar [Tavakoli, 2009, pp. 23–24]. Without including the return earned on the premium received up front and the cost of financing of the insurance payout, Buffett may have earned approximately 40 percent on the cash used. If the numbers reported by Janet Tavakoli are correct, simplifying, we may calculate that the initial "investment" amounted to $25 million (a $75 million up-front fee less $100 million for the insurance payout), and $35 million was later recovered or received as "revenue"—(35 − 25)/25 gives a 40 percent return—and if we include the return from investing the insurance premium that was received up front, the return is even higher. This is the rate of return that Buffett achieved in a bankruptcy, and it is likely that most of the companies in his portfolio did not go bankrupt. Would it be possible for an insurer to earn that much on such a deal if he were not also a professional investor?

A refusal to look for synergies, if it makes sense to put it this way, is Buffett's official strategy. Nevertheless, synergies of a different nature other than, for example, classic economies of scale, sometimes arise during acquisitions. These are the synergies with his own brand. (We discuss these in detail in Chapters 7 and 9.)

In my view, it is possible to find a number of traditional synergies in Buffett's transactions, but they did not play a critical role in his decisions. For instance, when Buffett bought a stake in Gillette, Coca-Cola replaced Pepsi in all the vending machines that belonged to Gillette [Kilpatrick, 2005, p. 841]. The largest client of FlightSafety International, a company owned by Berkshire that trains pilots for civil aviation, is NetJets, even though this would also have been the case if these companies had belonged to different owners. H&R Block, a company that specializes in the preparation of tax returns, has an agreement with Berkshire to supply the details of GEICO's insurance offers to H&R's clients, although this agreement was made before Buffett bought a large stake in H&R Block [Janjigian, 2008, p. 119].

Viewing value creation as the only justifiable motivation for a transaction, Buffett and Munger overall are negative toward leveraged buyout (LBO) transactions, as there is no value creation in such transactions. Well-known LBO specialists (Buffett referred to T. Boone Pickens and Jimmy Goldsmith) who talk about creating value for shareholders, in reality do not create value but transfer it from society to the shareholders. "It is not like Henry Ford developing the car or Ray Kroc figuring out how to deliver hamburgers better than anybody else" [cited in Lowe, 2007, p. 211]. Buffett refers to a different type of value—value not just for the shareholders of the acquiring company, but the value of a business as a whole to the broader community and the stakeholders.

For the organizer of an LBO, of course, value may indeed be created. One of the reasons is that LBO experts are free from social obligations: those to the society, the company, and its employees. LBO buyers often reduce costs mercilessly, particularly those associated with the workforce. Also, the company that is being acquired may be restructured, and during this restructuring, the attractive parts of the business may be sold to third parties. Charlie Munger criticizes the social aspects of these transactions, but he is compelled to accept that they often have an understandable rationale [Munger, 1989].[5]

This freedom from social obligations, combined with the tax advantages of raising debt financing in large volumes, explains why LBO experts are able to offer higher prices for their target companies than those that other buyers would be able to afford. The LBO organizers also invest very limited amounts of their personal funds. In Munger's view, this is another factor that drives the price inflation during the acquisition process. If the deal is a success, the fund's managing company receives a considerable part of the profit. (The partners in the investment fund receive their share of the proceeds of the sale, while the managing company receives a portion of the generated proceeds and the managing fees.) This compels the managing company to pursue projects very aggressively. In all transactions in which Buffett has participated, he took part only as a shareholder of Berkshire. This is what distinguishes him from other investors, who, particularly in the case of LBOs, receive not only a share of the profit proportional to their invested funds, but also the managing commission.

---

5 Munger's letter to Wesco shareholders 1989, where he expressed this view, used to be available on the Berkshire's website. This report is no longer in public domain.

Public versus Private Company:
The Importance of Being Private

As we have discussed, Buffett does not share the view that a public company will do the right thing when required: it will not scale down its business during difficult periods and its CEO will not promise shareholders to shrink the business in the long term, if necessary. This is an organizational weakness of a public company as opposed to a private company. In Buffett's view, public status creates the wrong incentives for the company's management. The securities market is very sensitive to short-term fluctuations, so the managers are motivated to "smooth out" the reported results; the market also likes growing companies, and this creates an incentive to acquire other companies, even if they are overvalued. Buffett does not play by the rules that the financial markets enforce. When Berkshire buys companies, it brings more to the party than just money. This is, in Munger's words, "patient" capital that allows management to pursue long-term strategies [Lowe, 2000, p. 177]. Buffett and Munger explain that by owning companies in their entirety, they minimize the impact of a whimsical stock market on Berkshire's share price [Lowe, 2000, p. 178].

Another kind of cost that is associated with public status is the cost of the time that the company's management has to invest in keeping the financial community updated about the company's performance. There are the costs associated with the reporting of results and the maintenance of listings. Ralph Schey, the CEO of Scott Fetzer, which was acquired by Buffett in the 1980s, recalled that when the company was public, he spent at least 50 of the roughly 200 working days a year outside the company. He had to talk to public relations people, investment people, and others. "We don't do that anymore, so we have more time to concentrate on growing the business" [cited in Miles, 2002, p. 275]. Buffett does not meet financial analysts and does not give many interviews. "Buffett is probably one of the few CEOs in America who spends much of the day reading" [Serwer and Boorstin, 2002].

A similar attitude toward the shortcomings of public status on the part of other CEOs makes it easier for Buffett to make acquisitions. For instance, in 1994, he decided to buy the shares of GEICO that still remained in free circulation—Berkshire already owned the majority of GEICO shares by that time. Buffett telephoned Tony Nicely, GEICO's CEO, and told him about the plan. Buffett also advised Nicely that he would pursue the idea only if Nicely agreed that it would be better for the company to become private. It turned out that Nicely had been contemplating the same idea and had also come to the conclusion that nonpublic status would suit the company better for many reasons [Miles, 2002, p. 32]. After Buffett had bought the rest of the GEICO shares, certain things changed. For example, Nicely found that he no longer had to do meetings with analysts or look for ways to smooth out earnings [Miles, 2002, p. 36].

Al Ueltschi, the founder and controlling shareholder of FlightSafety, sold his business training civil aviation pilots to Berkshire. He spoke similarly after the sale. When the company was listed on the New York Stock Exchange, he continually had to deal with questions of how much money the company would be making in the next quarter and whether it would be more than in the last quarter; after taking the company private, the management was able to refocus on the long term without having to worry continually about the next quarter. In Ueltschi's view, this was one of the best aspects of being part of Berkshire [Miles, 2002, p. 111].

Rich Santulli, the original owner of NetJets, also agrees with this view of public as opposed to private company status. Santulli was a former employee of the investment bank Goldman Sachs, and the bank became a minority shareholder in NetJets when Santulli was originally raising funds for business development. By 1998, the company had achieved a turnover of $1 billion, and Goldman began trying to persuade Santulli to consider a public offering. Santulli refused, and finally declared that he would sell the business to only one person—Warren Buffett. Santulli explained his position by saying that he did not wish to be told how to run his business by a 28-year-old analyst. Santulli viewed Buffett as a long-term player who would not be concerned with the next three or six months [Miles, 2002, p. 124].

David Sokol, the coowner of the energy company MidAmerican Energy Holdings Company, sold his company to Berkshire in 1999. As the motivation for the sale, Sokol cited his desire to convert his company from public to private. In the second half of the 1990s, when, after a deregulation, there was a bubble forming in the energy market (simultaneously with the technology bubble), financial analysts reproached Sokol for not doing one or two acquisitions a year and lacking deal velocity. He was told that his competitors were making two or three deals a month. Sokol believed that his competitors were engineering their financial reports to make it look as if their deals were financially meaningful and to assist their share price growth. Sokol argued that he did not wish to engage in the same activity [Chan, 2010, pp. 136–137].

In the early stages of developing his insurance business, Buffett preferred to invest in publicly traded companies so that his assets were sufficiently liquid in case the need for large payouts arose. As Berkshire grew, however, Buffett's focus shifted from portfolio investing to acquiring companies fully. While in the earlier years, the share of liquid assets on Berkshire's balance sheet could reach 90 percent, today it does not exceed 30 percent. Buffett converts all acquired companies in which he holds a controlling stake into privately held entities.

Berkshire is easily able to afford such a low proportion of liquid assets. Buffett mostly buys companies that could be described as cash cows, which do not need to raise new capital often, if at all, and if additional capital is required, then it can be found on Berkshire's internal capital marketplace, where the cash of the diversified company is allocated. Berkshire itself is a public company and is able to issue new shares, if necessary.

Corporate Governance and the Incentives for the Managers of the Subsidiaries of Berkshire

> Just run your business as if you own 100 percent of it.
>
> **—WARREN BUFFETT**

Buffett points out that he gives each of his managers "a simple mission." First, the manager has to run the business as if he owned 100 percent of it. Second, each manager must make decisions as if this business were the only asset that he or his family will ever have. Third, the business is not to be sold or merged "for at least a century" [Buffett, 1977–2013, 1998].

The first and second guidelines reflect a conservative approach, a corresponding attitude toward risk, and a decision-making style geared exclusively toward the interests of the owner. The restriction on merging or selling the business reflects Buffett's belief that the most beneficial strategy is long-term-focused and that any manipulations directed at increasing value in the short term will not lead to success. Also, such manipulation is not needed because Buffett intends to own any business with decent profitability for eternity. It may be meaningful to consider the third piece of advice while remembering that although it is possible to sell even a mediocre business at a good price on an overheated market, as this has an element of luck, it is better not to hope for good fortune.

It is possibly not sufficient to tell managers that they should "manage as if they are the owners." What guarantees that they will do this? Is it a question of trust? Is it possible that if one were to give the managers a set of principles, they would simply follow them? Perhaps doing what is morally right will trump monetary considerations? Buffett is a pragmatist. He does not allow matters to drift. He understands that most managers "talk the talk but don't walk the walk" and prefer compensation systems that are "long on carrots but short on sticks (and . . . [they] almost invariably treat equity capital as if it were cost-free)" [Buffett, 1977–2013, 1991].

Buffett uses very simple methods to motivate high-level managers: both carrots and sticks. His managers do not have any special arrangements in the form of options, or any special privileges in the event of their retiring or resigning (of the "golden parachute" kind).

Options do not tie together the interests of shareholders and managers. Options are a kind of "alignment" compensation plan, which is an "artful form of 'heads I win, tails you lose'" (options may lose their value, but, as they are given for free, the owner is not risking her own money), whereas true "alignment means being a partner in both directions, not just on the upside" [Buffett, 1977–2013, 1994]. Misalignment of the interests of the options owners and the shareholders also occurs when management does not pay dividends to shareholders and builds up the company's wealth through reinvesting its profits, while the strike price correction to take this into account is not included in the option terms.[6] "Indeed, the combination of a ten-year option, a low dividend

---

6 According to [Murphy, 1999, p. 2509], in 1992 such adjustments were included in less than 1 percent of the option award reward programs.

payout, and compound interest can provide lush gains to a manager who has done no more than tread water in his job" [Buffett, 1977–2013, 1994]. In Buffett's view, arrangements that pay off in capricious ways, that are unrelated to a manager's personal accomplishments are "free lottery tickets" [Buffett, 1977–2013, 1991]. When Buffett talked about his acquisition of a stake in IBM in 2011, he mentioned that IBM had reduced its option reward program from $240 million in options outstanding several years earlier ago to $30 million [Crippen, 2011].

Buffett also criticizes the widely accepted practice of option revaluation when company shares fall. In his letter to shareholders for 2001, commenting on the events related to Enron, Buffett tells a story: "A gorgeous woman slinks up to a CEO at a party and through moist lips purrs, 'I'll do anything—anything—you want. Just tell me what you would like.' With no hesitation, he replies, 'Reprice my options'" [Buffett, 1977–2013, 2001]. Given Buffett's views on matters of remuneration, no ordinary CEO would want Buffett on his compensation committee [Buffett, 1977–2013, 2004].

It is possible to name other shortcomings associated with option award schemes. When a manager shares with his company only the positive outcomes, this may lead the manager to take excessive risks and make decisions that are not optimal from the long-term standpoint and that are directed at the temporary growth of the stock price and/or its manipulation.

In Berkshire's case, an option program would not be easy to realize because the company is a conglomerate in which different managers are responsible for different divisions, no single manager is able to affect Berkshire's share price materially, and all subsidiaries are closely held companies.

Buffett does not use options but searches for other solutions. First, when Buffett buys a company from a CEO who will stay on as a manager or from her family, that seller is typically able to retain 10 to 12 percent of the company. Buffett welcomes this outcome. In exceptional cases, a proportion of the shares of the company that Berkshire is acquiring is bought by the hired managerial staff. In his letter to shareholders for 2001, Buffett discusses the terms of his acquisition of MiTek, the world leader in connector manufacturing. The management was exceptionally positive about the company's future and was keen to participate in the acquisition, and for this reason, 55 team members of

MiTek bought 10 percent of the company, with each manager paying a minimum of $100,000. All of them had to pay cash, and some of them borrowed funds in order to be able to participate. As they were not awarded options, they would take part in both the upside and the downside, and they would carry the cost of capital. Their stakes cannot be revalued, so they have to be responsible for their actions. These managers became true owners [Buffett, 1977–2013, 2001].

Second, all senior managers of Buffett's subsidiaries receive bonuses. The base salary is relatively low in comparison to the bonus part of the compensation package, as Buffett comments that "managers eager to bet heavily on their abilities usually have plenty of ability to bet on" [Buffett, 1977–2013, 1991].

The bonus part of the compensation package is a function of how diligently the managers pursue the objectives that Berkshire sets out for them. The primary task, as we discussed, is earning a high return on capital. Accordingly, "the ratio of operating earnings (before securities gains or losses) to shareholders' equity with all securities valued at cost is the most appropriate way to measure any single year's operating performance" [Buffett, 1977–2013, 1979]. For this reason, the size of a manager's compensation, as a rule, depends on the return on the invested capital. This is fairly general information on this subject, but it appears to be all that is available in the public domain regarding the contracts of Berkshire subsidiaries' CEOs.

Very recently, when answering questions about David Sokol, who was in charge of MidAmerican Energy but had to leave the company as a result of a scandal (which we discuss in Chapter 8), Buffett talked about the size and structure of Sokol's compensation plan. It turned out that his bonus was linked not to the return on capital, but to the growth of the company's profit. If the profit grew by 16 percent a year over the course of five years (after the acquisition in 1999), then Sokol would receive $37.5 million; otherwise, he would receive nothing. These were very tough conditions, given that MidAmerican Energy was a mature company that was past the initial rapid growth stage. Nevertheless, it seems, on the basis of Buffett's letters to Berkshire's shareholders, that these conditions were met.

What happens when the company earns a profit, but would be unable to deliver a high return on capital if that profit were reinvested? In this case, the capital is being deployed elsewhere by Berkshire, and therefore the managers of the subsidiary need to be motivated to return the free cash to the holding company as dividends. Ralph Schey, the CEO of Scott Fetzer, paid around $1 billion in dividends to Berkshire over the 15 years of his work as CEO after the acquisition of his company, which had been acquired for $320 million (as of the time of the interview, in which this figure was given). Some other managers have acted in this way also. As Buffett comments: "We believe in managers knowing money costs money" [Berkshire Hathaway Annual Shareholders' Meeting, 1995]. The CEOs do not need to worry about raising additional capital if it becomes required. It will be supplied by Berkshire. Therefore, it does not make sense for them to "sit" on money in case the need for it arises.

In light of this, it is clear why Buffett is also the preferred buyer for business owners who are keen to continue operating their companies but do not wish to be concerned with decisions on how to allocate capital or raise it when it becomes necessary [Lowe, 2000, p. 178]. Returning capital to the holding company, of course, reduces the amount of capital left in the subsidiary and helps to maximize the return on the capital used in the business (this affects the manager's compensation, as we discussed), while the subsidiary manager also receives the dividend payment through his ownership stake.

Buffett does not enter into lengthy contracts with his managers. The typical agreement is no more than one or two pages long, and sometimes the agreements are even shorter. The contract with John Holland, the CEO of Fruit of the Loom, a company that specializes in the manufacturing of underwear, consisted of 38 words [Kilpatrick, 2005, p. 727]. (Buffett acquired Fruit of the Loom in 2001—we analyze this acquisition in detail in Chapter 10.)

Perhaps the compensation package for Buffett himself provides an interesting insight. For a very long time, his salary amounted to $100,000 annually. He has never received bonuses. According to the latest SEC form DEF 14A, Buffett's salary remains $100,000, but he also receives "other compensation." The total amount of his compensation during the 2009–2013 period amounted to around half a million dollars a year. This is, of course, a very small compensation package for the CEO of a company of this size, particularly if we take into account that, for instance, in 2012, Buffett, who reimburses Berkshire for items such as postage and personal calls, paid back half of his salary to the firm [Condon, 2014]. Buffett's personal compensation reflects his views on the subject. There are no options. The low salary may also be a reputational issue, as it is very difficult to set an "adequate" salary level for a manager of his caliber. A high salary might also invite comments from those who are waiting for him to make a misstep. It may be sensible to set the salary at a "symbolic" level[7] for a variety of reasons, while the main source of Buffett's compensation for Buffett is his stake in Berkshire.

Buffett's views on the composition of the board of directors are also nontraditional. This is the body that controls the managers' actions. Buffett does not see the value in increasing the number of independent directors on the boards of public companies, as it is required by the Sarbanes-Oxley Act, since, in Buffett's view, an individual who is receiving 100 percent of his income from director's fees and who may wish to enhance his income by being elected to other boards is not truly independent [Buffett, 2004a]. This is Buffett's answer to the criticism of him in connection with his being a large shareholder and a board member of Coca-Cola (this role has now been transferred to his son Howard). Buffett believes that shareholders should be in charge of protecting their own interests. They are the best independent directors, not their trusted representatives, even if those representatives are nominally independent. "For where your treasure is, there will your heart be also" [Buffett, 1977–2013, 2004; Buffett is quoting the Bible].

The American press has sometimes punished Buffett for this position. The publication *Chief Executive* once reported that Berkshire's board of directors was the worst in the country. On May 6, 1994, *USA Today* published a list of boards of directors, rating them by quality. Berkshire's board came last. The list compilers criticized Berkshire's board for being small and family-oriented, and having no real outside directors [Kilpatrick, 2005, p. 288].

Modern corporate finance theory sees two potential conflicts in this area. One conflict is between shareholders and their agents, the company's managers. This is the so-called agency problem. The other conflict is the tension between the large and small shareholders. The former can afford to monitor managers and therefore are in a position to manipulate managers to their benefit. Buffett has sought to demonstrate

---

7 This is not a symbolic amount for many people, of course.

that inside Berkshire, the first of these conflicts does not exist. Buffett is both a manager and a shareholder, and as a manager, he cannot act against his own interests as a shareholder. The second conflict is mitigated. Buffett seeks to be fair toward his minority shareholders and does not discriminate against them in his position as majority shareholder.

For instance, in 1980, Buffett had to spin-off one of his companies, Rockford Bankcorp, the holding company of The Illinois National Bank and Trust Co., because of changes in the regulatory regime. Buffett calculated that the bank represented 4 percent of the value of Berkshire Hathaway and allowed each shareholder to make a choice between keeping her shares in Berkshire and her shares in the bank proportionally or taking more of one and less of the other. Buffett would receive whatever was left over after the shareholders had made their decisions. He did not leave himself any flexibility. He felt that since it was he who cut the cake, it was only appropriate that he would get the last slice. Five years later Buffett recalled the event and commented that time had shown that "the division of the cake was reasonably equitable" [Buffett, 1977–2013, 1985]. This is probably one of the finest examples of corporate management in practice ever. It is a great pity that such instances are not common.

Berkshire's corporate governance system (Buffett's simultaneous position as manager and owner; the composition of the board of directors; the system of manager motivation) makes one think of the early days of capitalism. The world has long since departed from the time when the manager and the owner of a business were one and the same and where there were no internal conflicts within this aggregate persona. The abstract microeconomic ideas that the economic agent is rational and that the figure that represents capital solely also belong to the early twentieth century. It seems that Buffett has rewound the clock and brought an old-fashioned way of running a business, and with it an old theory, back to life.

* * *

We continue the discussion of how Buffett motivates his managers to act as if they were the proprietors of their businesses in Chapter 8. Let us next consider Buffett's views and his practical actions with respect to capital structure. This may well be the most critical factor in Berkshire's success.

6

The Use of Debt by Berkshire Hathaway

Buffett's Crusade Against High Leverage

> Debt now became something to be
> refinanced rather than repaid.
>
> —WARREN BUFFETT [BUFFETT, 1977–2013, 1989]

The basics of finance teach us that debt is a cheaper financing instrument than shareholder capital. The use of debt raises the return on stockholders' equity. On the other hand, as the level of leverage rises, the likelihood of bankruptcy grows, since a smaller fall in earnings may threaten the stability of interest payments, which require an ever greater proportion of the cash flow. Borrowing becomes more expensive to compensate for the increased risk of distress. This neutralizes the positive effect of borrowing on the return on equity.

The leveraged buyout (LBO) mania of the 1980s presents an interesting case study in the use of leverage. LBO transaction volume rose from $1 billion in 1980 to more than $60 billion in 1988, the peak year.

It fell to less than $4 billion in 1990[1] [Kaplan and Stein, 1993]. Kaplan and Stein also showed that over the 1980s the buyout price to earnings before interest, taxes, depreciation, and amortization (EBITDA) ratio in leveraged management buyout (MBO) transactions[2] rose, although "not more sharply than marketwide or industrywide" P/E ratios.[3] Prices were particularly high in transactions that were financed with junk bonds. Deals were undertaken in "riskier industries,[4] and with somewhat higher leverage ratios." Buffett was sharply critical of the LBO deals at the end of the 1980s, the peak of the LBO mania. Partly, Buffett's criticism was intended to explain why it had become difficult for Berkshire to find attractive acquisition targets at justifiable prices.

The growth of leveraged buyout prices was driven largely by the proportion of debt in the financing of LBOs. This proportion often reached 90 percent. At an early stage, when leveraged buyouts first came into fashion, purchasers borrowed on a fairly reasonable basis. Conservatively projected free cash flow covered interest payments and reductions in debt. Later, "the adrenalin of deal-makers surged," as Buffett described it, and the prices paid for the acquired businesses became so high that all free cash flow had to be used for the payment of interest. Nothing was left for the reduction of principal. "A Scarlett O'Hara 'I'll think about it tomorrow'" view with regard to the repayment of debt was taken by borrowers and accepted by "a new breed of lenders," the investors in issues of junk bonds [Buffett, 1977–2013, 1989]. "Debt now became something to be refinanced rather than repaid."

1 LBO mania began to abate when Michael Milken was indicted by a federal grand jury on 98 counts of racketeering and fraud. Milken and the bank that he worked for, Drexel Burnham Lambert, controlled the market for high-yield issues and their secondary circulation. Milken was convicted. His employer filed for bankruptcy.
2 The authors focused on MBOs. Management buyouts are a subgroup of LBOs. The authors felt that they were able to obtain more reliable data for individual companies in this group of buyouts.
3 In the early 1980s, the market was still at the levels of the mid-1960s. However, over the course of the 1980s, it grew rapidly on the back of the perceived success of Reaganomics and the conquering of the double-digit inflation of the 1970s.
4 In classical understanding, some businesses are regarded as better suited for LBOs than others. Businesses with the most stable cash flows are ideal candidates. As we discussed, the more volatile the cash flow, the greater the risk that the debt payment obligations will not be met.

A company's free cash flow is assessed through EBITDA, which was viewed as a good reflection of its ability to cover interest payments. In reality, when all profit is used to pay interest, not only is it unclear how the principal amount borrowed could ever be paid off, but it is also unclear what would be the source of funds for investment in, for example, the maintenance and modernization of production facilities. As Buffett observed, in the long run, amortization is not a paper expense, but a real cash outflow. He spoke ironically of the concept of EBITDA: "Why not report earnings before wages? Why not report earnings before rent? Why not report earnings before all expenses? That is called sales" [cited in Kilpatrick, 2005, p. 1396]. "If you look at some enormously successful companies, Wal-Mart and Microsoft, I don't think those words [EBITDA] have ever appeared" [cited in Kilpatrick, 2005, p. 763].

When the proportion of borrowed funds in the financing structure is high, the use of expensive borrowing instruments with non-investment-grade ratings—junk bonds—is unavoidable. Junk bonds have a long history. Used in financing the development of certain industries, they were popular in the United States at the start of the twentieth century. During the Great Depression, high-yield bonds almost entirely disappeared. They experienced a renaissance at the end of the 1970s. In 1977, the junk bond market, whose volume amounted to $8.5 billion, consisted almost entirely of bonds that had been investment grade when they were issued, but that had had their ratings reduced during secondary trading. By the early 1990s, the junk bond market had grown to $240 billion, and downgraded bonds represented only 17 percent of its volume. The rest were bonds that had already been rated as below investment grade at issue.

Paul Asquith, David Mullins, and Eric Wolff studied the bankruptcy rate of companies with junk bonds in their capital structure [Asquith, Mullins, and Wolff, 1989]. They found that by the end of 1988, 3 to 9 percent of companies that had issued junk bonds between 1984 and 1986, 19 to 27 percent of companies whose junk bonds had been issued between 1979 and 1983, and 34 percent of companies whose junk bonds had been issued between 1977 and 1978 had gone bankrupt. Steven Kaplan and Jeremy Stein found that as of August

1991, out of 41 companies in their sample that had undergone a leveraged MBO between 1980 and 1984, only one had experienced distress [Kaplan and Stein, 1993]. Out of 83 MBOs completed between 1985 and 1989, 30 companies found themselves in a distressed situation. The deals of the end of the 1980s were considerably more risky.

Finance theory distinguishes two kinds of bankruptcy. One occurs when the business is nonviable operationally; the other occurs when the business is operationally sound, but the company has so much debt that it is unable to cope with the interest payments. If a company has a high level of leverage, then the smallest change for the worse in the operational results of the business may push it over the brink. Any bankruptcy is associated with unmanageable costs, but it is particularly disappointing if the bankruptcy is not business-driven. There is another side to the question of debt issuance. Modern financial theory recognizes the existence of agency problems. A large amount of debt attached to a company may be viewed as a helpful tool from the point of view of the disciplining effect that the debt may have on the company's managers. Oliver Hart and John Moore discussed this idea in an influential paper [Hart and Moore, 1995]. If a company has no debt, then its managers may waste resources on inefficient projects. If the debt burden is high and it is necessary to pay interest each year, then the managers will not enter into excessively risky projects.

The context of LBOs helps us look further at this idea. Ordinarily, the managers of public companies would set the level of debt themselves. It is not something that is attached to them by exogenous forces. The "discipline" is self-imposed. In the case of an LBO, the level of debt is determined by the buyer in the process of the LBO transaction. As a result of the competitive bidding process, the sale price is likely to be higher, and the higher sale price will trigger a higher post-LBO debt burden. The disciplining effect will be tainted if the debt burden ends up being excessive.[5]

Buffett seeks out businesses that are able to deliver a high return on invested capital without relying on leverage to boost those returns.

---

5 Buffett prefers to motivate subsidiary managers through compensation schemes, which we discussed in Chapter 5. He does not use debt as a disciplining mechanism.

A strong return on equity without using debt (or using little of it) is among the formal criteria that are set out for Berkshire acquisition candidates [Buffett, 1977–2013, 1987].

After the purchase of a company, Buffett recommends that the acquired company reduce and gradually end its relationship with its bank. Berkshire becomes the company's banker. This enables the company to take advantage of Berkshire's credit rating, which has remained at a maximum level over an extended period of time. Berkshire's rating was AAA from 1989 until 2009. In February 2010, it was lowered to AA+. In May 2013, it was lowered again to AA. All Berkshire's subsidiaries have retained the AA+ rating.[6] This rating allows Berkshire to raise financing on very good terms.

A business achieves its best results when both sides of the balance sheet are well managed. Berkshire Hathaway pays considerable attention not only to the searching for good investments, but also to optimizing its capital structure. This optimization requires selecting the appropriate level of debt. Although Buffett's views on borrowing may suggest otherwise, Berkshire's level of leverage cannot be regarded as very low. As estimated by Andrea Frazzini, David Kabiller, and Lasse Pedersen, the share of leverage in Berkshire's capital structure amounted on average to approximately 37.5 percent from 1976 to 2011 [Frazzini, Kabiller, and Pedersen, 2012, pp. 6, 7]. Perhaps Buffett would not have become the investor that he is if he were not using leverage with great skill. It is precisely the use of leverage that is one of the key components of his phenomenal success. The bulk of Berkshire's borrowing takes place not through issuing bonds on the debt market, but through writing insurance policies. This also happens to be the company's main business. Insurance theoretically does not require borrowing. Insurers collect premiums from their customers, and then, if and when the insured event takes place, the insurers make a payout. Premium collection may be separated from the payout by a considerable amount of time—often years. By collecting premiums, the insurance company

---

6 According to Standard & Poor's, the recent reduction in the rating is not connected to changes in Berkshire's financial position, but is the result of changes in the criteria that the rating agency uses to evaluate insurance companies.

acquires capital that it can invest. Insurers call this capital float. On the other hand, insured events are bound to happen eventually, and it will be necessary to make some payouts sooner or later. From the point of view of accounting, insurance premiums are a form of debt obligations. In Frazzini, Kabiller, and Pedersen [2012, p. 7] it is estimated that insurance premiums represent on average 36 percent of the liabilities of Berkshire Hathaway.

Insurance and Insurance-Type Businesses of Berkshire Hathaway

Float is wonderful.

—WARREN BUFFETT [BUFFETT, 1977–2013, 2004]

Since 2012, Berkshire Hathaway has been the fourth-largest insurance company in the United States in terms of the size of its nonbanking assets[7] and the largest in the world in terms of market capitalization. Buffett's first investments into insurance companies took place in 1967. Buffett acquired National Fire and Marine Insurance Company and National Indemnity Company, which specialized in auto insurance and general liability insurance. Gradually National Indemnity became the best-known player in the market for natural disaster insurance. Today, National Indemnity is a group of companies.

In the 1970s, National Indemnity bought an array of relatively small companies that supplied natural disaster and other insurance. Cornhusker Casualty Company[8] was purchased in 1970, Lakeland Fire and Casualty Company—in 1971, Texas United Insurance Company in 1972, and Kansas Fire and Casualty Company[9]—in 1977. Home and Automobile Insurance Company, Kerkling Reinsurance

---

7 This statistic is according to A.M. Best, the credit rating agency for the insurance industry. A list of top insurers is available at: http://courantblogs.com/ct-insurance/a-m-best-list-shows-top-insurers-by-assets-premium-revenue/.

8 The company changed its name to Berkshire Hathaway Homestate Insurance Company in 2012.

9 In 1993, Kansas Fire and Casualty Company merged with a newly established Oak River Insurance Company. The combined companies continued to operate under the Oak River Insurance Company name.

Corporation,[10] and Cypress Insurance Company (insurance of employee compensation) were bought in 1971, 1976, and 1977, respectively. In 1973, Cornhusker Casualty Company acquired Insurance Company of Iowa. In 1976, Buffett began to acquire the shares of GEICO. This acquisition was completed in 1995. In 1992, Buffett bought Central States Indemnity Company (medical supplement and life insurance). Berkshire also set up a couple of small companies.

In 1998, Buffett bought 100 percent of the shares of General Re. It is the largest American reinsurer for property/casualty insurance. In 2009, General Re completed an acquisition of Cologne Re, the world's oldest reinsurance company. At the time of the deal, Cologne Re was active in more than 100 countries. General Re was severely affected by the terrorist attacks of September 11, 2001. According to Buffett's estimate made in November 2001 the insurer's losses amounted to $1.7 billion [Buffett, 1977–2013, 2002]. Buffett felt that the losses had been incurred because the company had provided insurance against catastrophes resulting from human activity, but had not charged appropriate premiums for this aspect of coverage. After the attacks, these policies were reviewed. In 2002, the insurance business returned to high profitability. In 2005, however, the company was affected by a scandal connected to General Re's involvement in the sale of insurance contracts to AIG for the purposes of accounting manipulation. Following this scandal, the management of General Re was replaced.

In 2000, United States Liability Insurance Company (commercial, personal, and professional lines of property/casualty insurance), Mount Vernon Fire Insurance Company, and U.S. Underwriters Insurance Company (fire, marine, and casualty insurance) became wholly owned subsidiaries of Berkshire Hathaway. In 2005, Berkshire bought Medical Protective, the country's leading provider of healthcare malpractice insurance. In 2006, it bought Applied Underwriters Inc., the industry leader in workers' compensation solutions. Since 2007, Berkshire has owned Boat U.S., which provides boat insurance and other services. In 2012,

---

10 The company changed its name to Central Fire & Casualty Company in 1977 and to Redwood Fire and Casualty Insurance Company in 1980.

National Indemnity, a Berkshire Hathaway subsidiary, bought Guard Insurance Group, which provides workers' compensation insurance to small and midsize businesses across the country. Berkshire also owns Kansas Bankers Surety Company, which insures bank deposits in excess of the amount covered by FDIC insurance and underwrites bonds for financial institutions, directors' and officers' liability, and other risks. Kansas Bankers Surety Company is a subsidiary of Wesco Financial, itself a subsidiary of Blue Chip Stamps, which we discuss later in this section.

Berkshire divides its insurance companies into four groups: GEICO, General Re, Berkshire Hathaway Reinsurance Group, and Berkshire Hathaway Primary Group. Insurance and reinsurance against catastrophes are provided by General Re and Berkshire Hathaway Reinsurance Group, which includes National Indemnity Company.

Buffett has also owned some noninsurance companies whose cash flow model is similar to that of an insurance business. In 1970, Buffett bought Blue Chip Stamps, a large loyalty marketing company based in California. The company issued coupons that were sold to participating retail networks. The retailers gave away these coupons to their clients as gifts. Once a customer accumulated a certain number of coupons, he could exchange the coupons at a Blue Chip Stamps store for merchandise, such as a toy, a kitchen appliance, or a watch. Although this form of marketing is more than 100 years old, it became particularly popular in the 1950s and 1960s. Later it faded away as technology developments allowed other types of loyalty programs to emerge, such as loyalty cards or advertised low prices.

If customers collected coupons in only one store, then it would take them a very long time to accumulate a sufficient number of coupons to receive a gift. In order to make the program attractive, it was necessary to make it available at many different establishments. Nevertheless, it took time for people to amass enough coupons. Invariably, they would lose some of their coupons, leave them at the back of a sock drawer for several years, destroy them by laundering them in washing machines, or put them into their pockets and forget about them. For these reasons, the quantity of unexchanged coupons in circulation (company obligations) was always growing. In other words, the company raised funds up front and then later either made payouts in the form of gifts or did not make any payouts at all.

The funds that were raised could be invested. By the start of the 1970s, the annual coupon sales amounted to $120 million, and the coupons in circulation reached $100 million. By 1980, the sales had fallen to $19 million, and by 2006, they had fallen to almost zero [Buffett, 1977–2013, 1989]. The business died. Over the course of its operation, it generated large cash flows that Berkshire used to buy other companies: Wesco Financial, See's Candies, and the *Buffalo Evening News* [Buffett, 1991c].

Buffett has been deliberately targeting the acquisition of insurance and insurancelike businesses since the 1960s. Perhaps he was charmed by the idea during his first visit to the GEICO offices in 1951. As we have discussed, this is a business area in which cash is received up front for a service, or an insurance-event–related payout, that may or may not need to be delivered later. The cash raised is "stored" and managed, or invested, until the expiration of the insurance contract and after. We now look at Berkshire's insurance businesses in greater detail.

The Role of the Insurance Business in Lowering the Cost of Borrowing for Berkshire

> The business is a lemon if its cost of float is higher than market rates for money.
>
> —WARREN BUFFETT [BUFFETT, 1977–2013, 1997]

As we have mentioned, the amount of leverage in Berkshire's capital structure amounted to 37.5 percent of total capital on average. Insurance float as a portion of the total liabilities represented 36 percent. Given such a level of float in the capital structure, the cost of this float has a significant effect on the cost of leverage and therefore the cost of capital for the company.

In the insurance industry context, the cost of float is considered to be the ratio of the difference between payouts made and premiums raised in a given year to the total float as of that year. If premiums raised in a particular year exceed payouts in that year, the cost of capital is considered to be negative.

In 1997—the year he purchased General Re—Buffett disclosed data on the capital costs of the insurance companies within Berkshire

Hathaway; the cost of capital was compared with the return on long-term U.S. government bonds from 1967 on. In 17 out of 31 years, the cost of capital was negative; in 9 years, the cost of capital was lower than the return on long-term government bonds; and in only 5 years was it higher [Buffett, 1977–2013, 1997]. In substance, the negative cost of capital in the form of insurance premiums means that the policyholders were "paying" Buffett for the service of storing their money.

In Frazzini, Kabiller, and Pedersen [2012, Table 3], the cost of "borrowing" in the form of insurance premiums is calculated for the years from 1976 to 2011. The authors calculate that, on average, the cost of capital was 2.2 percent, which is 3 percentage points lower than the return on Treasury bills and 4.8 percentage points lower than the return on 10-year bonds. The proportion of years with a negative cost of capital amounted to 60 percent. This calculation may present an inflated view of the cost of "borrowing," as the authors set it to zero when Buffett reported the cost as negative.

Additional data on the cost of borrowing in years when it was reported as negative are available in the collection of Buffett's letters to Berkshire shareholders for 1965 to 2013 edited by Max Olson [Buffett, 2013]. According to the data in this collection of letters, from 1967 to 2012, the cost of "borrowing" was negative in 29 out of 47 years, and from 1998 to 2012, the cost of borrowing was negative in 12 out of 16 years. The data also show that in some years, the cost was highly negative, as payouts were far lower than the premiums collected. In 2006, the cost amounted to around negative 7.6 percent; in 1972 and in 2007, it amounted to negative 6.2 percent.

This negative or extremely low cost of float would have been impossible if Berkshire had not radically reduced its presence in the market during years in which conditions were difficult. Buffett's insurance companies attempt not to write policies if, according to management's calculations, the size of the payouts will exceed the premiums that can be raised.

However difficult it may be to time any market, and we have already discussed Buffett's views on timing the securities market, Buffett nevertheless seems to be successful at timing the catastrophe insurance business. Berkshire appears to be active after catastrophes take place, when other insurers are counting their losses. At such times, the capital pool that is available in the insurance market is insufficient to write new large policies, and, as a result, policy prices increase.

In his letter to shareholders for 2004, using National Indemnity Company as an example, Buffett paints a "Portrait of a Disciplined Underwriter." In 1986, National Indemnity raised $366 million in premiums and then began to reduce its presence in the market. Over the 1989–2000 period, the volume of premiums raised every year did not exceed $100 million. In 2001, it was $161 million; in 2002, it was $343 million; and in each of 2003 and 2004, it was around $600 million [Buffett, 1977–2013, 2004]. The decline in revenue over the 1986 to 1999 period did not occur because business was unobtainable. Berkshire could have collected many billions of dollars in premiums had it been willing to cut prices. However, the company priced its policies to make a profit, not to compete with other insurers. Berkshire never left customers. Customers left Berkshire. Buffett sharply increased his activity after the September 11 attacks.

For a while, it seemed as if Buffett's "market timing" had created a very profitable business. The profitability of supercatastrophe insurance for the 1993–2003 period amounted to 43 to 44 percent [Kilpatrick, 2005, p. 332]. In later years, the business did not fare as well: 2004, 2005, and 2010–2012 showed accounting losses; 2006, 2007, and 2009 were profitable [Berkshire Hathaway, 1995–2013].

The industry accounts for losses without including the income on invested premium, even though the amount of income may be colossal. Since 2000, the amount of investment income produced by Berkshire's total insurance business (not only supercatastrophe insurance) was larger than the underwriting loss in each year except 2001 (see Table 6.1).

Pulling away from the market in difficult years is encouraged by the company's employee compensation schemes. Senior managers are compensated on the basis of the return on capital that they deliver. The rest of the employees in Berkshire Hathaway's insurance companies are not motivated to grow the business at any cost because they are not afraid of being fired during tougher times. Buffet's strategy is to retain employees during periods of business reduction. He prefers to carry additional personnel costs rather than facing the large losses that may arise from a drive to write as many policies as possible without optimizing the return

TABLE 6.1 Net earnings of the insurance business segment of Berkshire Hathaway, 2000–2012.

	Underwriting profit/loss, in millions	Investment income, in millions
2000	−1,041	1,946
2001	−2,654	1,968
2002	−284	2,096
2003	1,114	2,276
2004	1,008	2,045
2005	27	2,412
2006	2,485	3,120
2007	2,184	3,510
2008	1,739	3,610
2009	949	4,271
2010	1,301	3,860
2011	154	3,555
2012	1,046	3,397
2013	1,995	4,735

Source: [Berkshire Hathaway, 1995–2013].

on capital. In 1991, Buffett, perhaps jokingly, promised his insurance business managers that Berkshire "will buy them golf memberships, country club memberships, if they'll promise to play golf during business hours." Buffett did not "want them in the office during business under terms that are generally available" in bad markets [Buffett, 1991c].

Comparing his approach to insurance business management with common industry practices, Buffett observes that most insurers would find it impossible to replicate Berkshire's managerial mindset. Public companies do not embrace business models that can lead to slides in revenue as considerable as those that Berkshire experienced from 1986 to 1999. "Most American businesses harbor an 'institutional imperative' that rejects an extended decrease in volume" [Buffett, 1977–2013, 2004]. In Buffett's view, no CEO will be able to find the courage to report to the shareholders that not only did business contract last year, but it will continue to drop, particularly when the consequences of underpriced policies may not become apparent for years. The agents are not motivated to shrink business, as they are afraid of layoffs. "To avoid pink slips, employees will rationalize inadequate pricing, telling themselves that poorly priced business must be tolerated in order to keep the organization intact." Otherwise, these employees will say, the company will not take part in the recovery "that they invariably feel is just around the corner" [Buffett, 1977–2013, 2004].

Buffett's insurance business is not just a function of successful "market timing," however. Insurance is a commodity business. High margins on the sale of a commodity are possible in circumstances in which demand exceeds supply, or if a producer has low costs. National Indemnity, a subsidiary of Berkshire specializing in supercatastrophe insurance, seeks to make money on timing the demand for insurance, while GEICO is an example of a company with low costs, as it does not use the services of agents.

Buffett has also succeeded in bringing an element of branding into his insurance business. Berkshire is one of the largest and, according to some opinions, the most reliable insurance company in the world.[11] This position allows the company to write policies on more profitable terms than those available to other insurers. The size of the business also plays a role. Ajit Jain, with whom Buffett jointly manages the underwriting of large transactions in catastrophe insurance or insurance against unexpected events, finds that when it comes to unique, large, or one-of-a-kind deals, Berkshire is the first to receive an inquiry [Miles, 2002, p. 79]. This may well be a contribution of Berkshire's brand.

It is not purely accidental that Buffett's insurance business is oriented toward supercatastrophe insurance. In supercatastrophe insurance, the payouts are separated in time from the moment of premium collection by a considerable period. Losses are accounted for not in the year of the catastrophe, but once the damage has been assessed. At the same time, the premiums received are invested. The longer the period that the collected funds are held, the greater the earnings on the investment of these funds. Buffett's investment capabilities allow him to

---

11 Berkshire and its five property and casualty affiliates have the highest rating among the insurers (A++, or superior), as rated by A.M. Best Company.

invest premiums with better returns than those that would be available to other insurers. The outcome reinforces itself. Premiums are invested with greater profitability, which assists the insurance business.

In this segment of the insurance market, the insurer's reputation plays the most important role. The volume of losses may be colossal, and Berkshire is able to sustain losses of $50 to $60 billion. Buffett is also skillful at marketing his company's reliability as an insurer. For instance, in 2004, he was assuring markets that Berkshire was fully prepared for a $100 billion industry loss, something that many insurers regarded as "unthinkable." Berkshire's share of such a loss would be 3 to 5 percent. The company's earnings would easily exceed that loss, and Berkshire's checks would clear "the day after" [Buffett, 1977–2013, 2004]. In recent years, Buffett has spoken of $250 billion industry losses related to supercatastrophes. This is three times as large as the total losses over the history of catastrophe insurance. Buffett assured stockholders that in such a case, while all other major insurers and reinsurers would find themselves in the red and some would face insolvency, Berkshire would show a "moderate" profit [Buffett, 1977–2013, 2011, 2012].

Berkshire's Derivatives Contracts as Quasi-Debt

> The Black-Scholes formula . . . produces strange results when the long-term variety [of options] are being valued.
>
> —WARREN BUFFETT [BUFFETT, 1977–2013, 2008]

Buffett's views on derivatives are best illustrated by his 2002 comments, made following the collapse of Long-Term Capital Management (LTCM) but preceding the recent financial crisis. He likened derivatives to "financial weapons of mass destruction" [Buffett, 1977–2013, 2002]. From an individual's point of view, trading in options entails far greater risks than trading in stocks. From the point of view of society as a whole, the en masse issuance of derivatives by the financial community generates leverage and increases the money supply, if indirectly. The mechanism of this effect on the money supply is that with the help of derivatives, it is possible to buy—or "reserve," to be more precise—the right to buy various assets without spending the money that those assets cost. It is now well understood that growth in the nominal volume of issued derivatives may result in the formation of bubbles, and all bubbles eventually collapse. The use of credit derivatives by financial institutions contributes to cycles of leveraging and deleveraging in an economy. Derivatives inherently create an effect that destabilizes the financial system. It becomes more volatile.

Nicholas Dunbar argues [Dunbar, 2011] that the issuance of collateralized debt obligations (CDOs) by large institutions, which eventually created the crisis in the financial markets, was a form of manipulation of Basel requirements for capital adequacy. This manipulation allowed the institutions to maintain the proportion of debt to equity at a high level that regulators would have considered to be too risky. However, in addition to the "mass destruction" component, derivatives also have a "peaceful" purpose. This is where Buffett gets involved.

When writing derivative contracts,[12] Buffett attempts to correct for the shortcomings of the Black-Scholes model, which is traditionally used to value derivatives. He considers the model to be not entirely accurate, but comments that its creators have held similar views. He finds that the formula works less well over long intervals because in the long term, the volatility does not influence the price of the option as much as it does in the short term. In my opinion, Buffett does not agree with the assumption that the price of an option on a stock or equity index, for instance, does not depend on its fair level.[13]

Let us consider a simple example of a share, whose price oscillates around $100, and where there are no events in the short term, and all movements are random. A call option that gives the right to buy

---

12 We have already discussed some of the contracts on the credit insurance side in Chapter 5.
13 According to the Black-Scholes model, if two shares have the same market price and volatility, then the call options on these shares will cost the same if the strike prices are the same, with all else being equal. However, if one stock is undervalued in comparison to its fair level—for instance, it is twice as cheap, and, if the second stock is trading at its fair price level, then the option on the first stock should be much more expensive than the option on the second, as it is more probable that the exercise price will exceed the strike price in the first case than it will in the second.

the share at a strike price of $110 would be more expensive if the share were moving within a $30 corridor around $100 than if the share were moving within a $15 corridor. In the first case, the maximum payout is $20 ($130 − $110), and in the second case it is only $5 ($115 − $110), less the price of buying the option. Let us imagine now that the option expires in 10 years. We are expecting that the share price will double during this time, and that the share will cost $200 at the end of the period. If the volatility remains the same, then the price will be moving between $140 and $260 in the one case and between $170 and $230[14] in the other. The value of an option with a strike price of $110 will not be influenced by the volatility when the duration is this long. Even in the worst-case scenario, the share price will be much higher than $110. The rising trend of the market will "kill" the effect of volatility on the option price.

We do not know how Buffett rationalized his option prices in the sale of the long-dated European puts on the four leading world indexes (S&P 500, FTSE 100, Euro Stoxx 50, and Nikkei 225), executed in 2006–2008,[15] but it is likely that Buffett's personal views on option valuation and true cost were reflected in the deal. Arguably, the deal would not have taken place if they were not. Buffett received $4.9 billion for the sale, and this money was invested by Berkshire. The company is not exposed to counterparty risk and is able to use the funds as it pleases. In some sense, these funds are like insurance premiums that have now been collected and may have to be distributed later. Berkshire's reputation must have played an important role in the creation of this transaction. The market, or the put buyers, placed a great deal of trust in Berkshire's ability to meet its bills.

The buyers of these instruments will be entitled to compensation from Berkshire at certain points in the future (between 2019 and 2027) should the equity indexes fall by those dates below the level of the market at the time of the sale. Should the market fall to zero or cease to exist, the maximum amount of compensation would amount to $37.1

14 The corridors of price fluctuation must widen proportionately to the price level increase for the constant volatility assumption to hold.
15 See Buffett's comments regarding the value of options and the details of the transactions in [Buffett, 1977–2013, 2008].

billion. If the market falls by, for instance, 25 percent, then Berkshire will pay $9 billion.

During 2007–2008, the world stock market fell considerably. Berkshire, which uses the Black-Scholes model for accounting purposes, had to write off $10 billion in 2008. The collected premiums reduced the loss to $5.1 billion. However, the loss existed only on paper.

The transaction attracted the attention of the Securities and Exchange Commission, and Buffett had to provide explanations to regulators. The credit agencies rushed to reduce Berkshire's credit rating[16]—this was the first time that Berkshire's rating was reduced since after the AAA rating had been awarded originally. Until this reduction of Berkshire's rating, the company was one of only six institutions that have ever held the maximum rating.

Will these losses continue to only remain on paper? Probably, yes. First, if Buffett is investing the $4.9 billion at 10 percent annually (he is able to obtain this level of return in today's conditions; besides, this is roughly the same as the historical return on the S&P[17]), then in 15 years he will have accumulated about $20.5 billion, and in 20 years he will have accumulated $33 billion.[18] Second, the stock markets will probably most likely rise by that time and not fall. In the longterm, it is not only that the current crisis will end (and many people think that it is over already) and other crises will come and go, but also that the stock market will take into account the impact of inflation and numerous rounds of quantitative easing and will incorporate the growth of companies' earnings.

Over the long term, the world stock market would have to fall very strongly in real terms in order to not grow at all in nominal terms. We

16 Analysts also link this credit rating reduction to the company's raising a large amount of debt to finance the purchase of Burlington Northern Santa Fe Railway. In my view, this transaction should not have had a significant impact on an assessment of Berkshire's credit-worthiness. This deal is not large in absolute terms in comparison to Berkshire's balance sheet asset value ($8 billion versus $372 billion as of 2010).

17 In footnote 1 in the Introduction, we cited research that substantiates this estimate.

18 In the letter to shareholders in 2011, there was a clarification: some of the contracts allow termination prior to their expiration, but then Buffett would retain part of the premium received. By the start of 2015 some of the contracts were closed out on request of the counterparties with considerable profit to Berkshire.

are able to estimate that if inflation amounts to 3 percent annually, then the fall of shares in real terms from 2008 to 2019 would have to amount to 27 percent for the index to remain stable. It is possible to imagine such a scenario. In 1982, the Dow Jones was at the same level as it was in 1966, or twice as low in real terms. The scale of quantitative easing from 2008 to 2012 has been such that in practice, a fall in the nominal prices of shares by a considerable magnitude is highly unlikely. Is it possible for the indexes to fall 25 percent in nominal terms from the historical levels at which the transactions were agreed upon? Even in this case, Berkshire will lose only $9 billion, while it is earning possibly $25 billion on reinvestment (if we assume that Buffett succeeds in investing at a 10 percent rate of return).

Not all details of the transactions have been disclosed. For instance, we do not know the precise levels of the markets at which the strike prices were set. The S&P fluctuated between approximately 1,300 and 1,500 during the period when the transactions were being agreed upon. It might be that Buffett has again found a gold mine—in December of 2014, the index rose above 2,000.

It seems that Wall Street may be underestimating Buffett's knowledge of derivatives. Here is a story told by Janet Tavakoli: "In the fall of 2006 I was talking to a friend in New York, and I mentioned that Warren Buffett and I have similar views on credit derivatives. . . . My former colleague, a Wall Street structured products 'correlation' trader, wrinkled his nose and sniffled: 'That old guy? He hates derivatives'" [Tavakoli, 2009, p. 24]. Hates? Not at all! He understands, loves, and uses derivatives with considerable success. So far, it looks as if Buffett will be the winning party in this last deal that we discussed.

* * *

In earlier chapters, we examined Buffett's investment principles: how the investment targets are selected, how an investor should conduct herself, how the principles are interconnected with one another, and what theoretical finance ideas are the foundation of Buffett's investment approach. We will now look at some examples of his investments to illustrate how Buffett uses his principles in practice and, perhaps, in hopes of locating other keys to his extraordinary performance.

7

Early Acquisitions: The Strategy Has Crystallized

Someone is sitting in the shade today because
someone planted a tree a long time ago.
—WARREN BUFFETT [CITED IN ANDERSEN, 2013]

We are moving from analyzing ideas and principles to examining their practical implementation in greater detail. We will start by looking at some of Buffett's early transactions. The first acquisition we examine was accomplished, in my view, through his astute use of his skills as a psychologist. The second case is a study of a purchase where Buffett's personal brand and assistance in marketing made a material contribution to the business's performance. Possibly, Buffett's participation improved the company's bottom line by an order of magnitude. The third acquisition is an example of the deft handling of a competitive situation by largely staying on the sidelines until all the other bidders had exhausted themselves and then acquiring the company at a very advantageous price. This last purchase is also interesting because it is a rare example of Buffett's acquisition of a public company.

Nebraska Furniture Mart

> I'd rather wrestle grizzlies than compete
> with Mrs. B and her progeny.
> —WARREN BUFFETT [BUFFETT, 1977–2013, 1992]

An interesting instance of a successful early acquisition was the purchase of Nebraska Furniture Mart (NFM) in 1983. Buffett describes the transaction in the annual report for that year [Buffett, 1977–2013, 1983]. He praises the owner, Rose Blumkin, an emigrant from Russia who had created one of the best furniture and carpet flooring stores in the United States. Mrs. Blumkin, known as Mrs. B, started her business in 1937 with an investment of $500, which she had made by selling used clothes. She once found herself practically bankrupt and had to sell her own furniture to pay her creditors. Later, on a number of occasions, she was a target of lawsuits that accused her of unfair competition and of selling goods at unreasonably low prices. She not only won those lawsuits by proving that it was possible to sell furniture profitably at her prices, but also became famous as a result of the legal proceedings. After winning one of the lawsuits, she managed to sell carpets for a total of $1,400 to the presiding judge.

In 1983, Mrs. Blumkin turned 90 years old. She still worked seven days a week, managed the business, remained the chairwoman of the board of directors, and worked as a carpet salesperson. She relied exclusively on her own capital. She had borrowed money for the last time in 1950.

Mrs. Blumkin's business model appeared to be very straightforward. She bought her stock very cheaply, ran a very low-cost operation, and sold her products with only a small markup. The strategy proved highly successful. There are no recipes for starting such a business, but once a dominant position has been obtained, then Buffett's law of the "survival of the fattest" comes into play.

We now look at how to evaluate NFM's economic efficiency and how cheaply or expensively Buffett purchased it. Berkshire bought 90 percent of the company, while the remaining 10 percent stayed with the Blumkin family. According to Robert Miles, Buffett's stake was eventually reduced to 80 percent of the company, as the family had retained an option to buy back 10 percent of the shares, and this option was exercised [Miles, 2002, p. 92]. From the letter to shareholders of 1983, we know that at the time of the sale, the company had a turnover of $100 million. The section "Sources of Reported Earnings" states that Nebraska Furniture Mart brought Berkshire Hathaway approximately $3.8 million of net profit. It is not possible to estimate the company's annual net profit, as the indicated amount refers to what the company earned after the purchase had been completed, and the date of the transaction is not given.

The profitability of a company becomes apparent to noninsiders only after a year. In the letter to shareholders for 1984, we read that the company had made around $14.5 million of profit before tax on turnover of $115 million [Buffett, 1977–2013, 1984]. Buffett also commented that this was the largest turnover in a single furniture store in the United States. The pretax profit margin of 12.6 percent is a very strong performance for a discount retail business. Gross margin amounted to 22 percent. The store achieved high profitability through low operating expenses, which were half as high as those of comparable American companies. Buffett discussed the company's business principles and commented that the management had high integrity. It is apparent that the company was growing at a phenomenal rate. In 1984, the turnover grew by 15 percent.

Finally, Buffett mentioned the purchase price. He paid $55 million for 90 percent of the shares. This implies a valuation of $61 million for the whole company. If we assume that the earnings before interest and taxes (EBIT) grew at the same rate as the turnover, then the EBIT in the year of purchase would have amounted to $12.6 million. The enterprise value/EBIT[1] multiplier at which the company was purchased would have amounted to 4.8. This is a very low price for a business that is growing rapidly and that has a dominant position in a regional

---

1 Enterprise value (EV) is the purchase price as calculated for 100 percent of the shares plus net long-term debt (long-term debt less cash). In this calculation, I set the long-term debt as equal to zero, but it may have been negative, as it is known that the company had no debt, and it may have had free cash available. If it did, the multiplier could be even lower.

market and a high profit margin.[2] How did Buffett manage to buy this business at such an advantageous price?

Buffett had been contemplating the acquisition of Nebraska Furniture Mart for some time before the purchase. He had made more than one attempt to buy the business. Buffett had found out about the store from his first wife, Susan, who was a friend of the Blumkin family. His first offer had been declined as "too cheap" [Lowenstein, 1996, p. 249]. Mrs. B's son Louie insists that he once overheard his mother saying to Buffett: "You'll try to steal it" [Schroeder, 2008, pp. 496, 896]. In his book *Supermoney*, Adam Smith tells the story of one of his interactions with Buffett:

> We were driving down a street in Omaha; and we pass a large furniture store. I have to use letters in the story because I can't remember the numbers. "See that store?" Warren says. "That's a really good business. It has A square feet of floor space, does an annual volume of B, has an inventory of only C, and turns over its capital at D."
> "Why don't you buy it?" I said.
> "It's privately held," Warren said.
> "'Oh," I said. "I might buy it anyway," Warren said. "Someday."
> [Smith, 2006, p. 190]

"That store" was Nebraska Furniture Mart. Adam Smith's book was first published in 1972, so this conversation must have taken place no later than the early 1970s.

Buffett's former daughter-in-law, Mary Buffett, mentions some interesting details about the acquisition in her recollections, published in 2002. In 1983, Buffett went to the store and sought out Mrs. Blumkin. "When he found her, he proudly announced that since it was his birthday, he wanted to buy her store. She shot back, with a thick Russian accent, that she would sell it to him for $60 million and not

---

2 Buffett does not seem to agree with the view that he bought the company inexpensively. At the shareholders' meeting of 2014, he mentions that NFM was "not a bargain purchase" because there was a second buyer. This means that Buffett was not excluding the possibility of buying the store even more cheaply ["Recap: The 2014 Berkshire Hathaway Annual Meeting"].

a penny less. Warren said, 'Deal,' walked out of the store, and came back an hour later with a check. When she inquired if he wanted his accountants to see the store's books before he handed over the check, he replied, 'No, I trust you more'" [Buffett and Clark 2002, p. 154].

Was the transaction indeed closed within an hour and entirely without an audit? According to Roger Lowenstein, Buffett had previously determined the company's position. He had examined the company's tax returns, where the profits were indicated [Lowenstein, 1996, p. 250]. It could be argued that a formal audit might not have been helpful. Even if Buffett had found inconsistencies, it is unlikely that he could have used the information to reduce the purchase price. Mrs. Blumkin might have perceived an audit as a humiliation. Any inaccuracies uncovered might have simply terminated the deal. Besides, Buffett trusted Mrs. Blumkin and had no doubts about her honesty.

Other details of this transaction come to light in Buffett's authorized biography. It turns out that Buffett had heard that Rose Blumkin was considering a sale. The family had been discussing a transaction with a German furniture retailer from Hamburg. The retailer managed the largest furniture store in the world, and the company's business model was similar to that of NFM [Schroeder, 2008, p. 496]. Buffett had conducted prior negotiations with Mrs. Blumkin's children and grandchildren. He wrote them a letter advising them that if they could delay the sale, it would be possible for them to get more money. He also discussed the drawbacks of selling the business to different types of buyers. An industry buyer, such as the Hamburg company, would be tempted to interfere with the management of the company. A financial investor ("financial maneuverer," as Buffett put it, in an interesting choice of words) would possibly be motivated to sell the company or to do an initial public offering (IPO) at a later time, since financial buyers typically used considerable amounts of borrowed funds in such transactions [Schroeder, 2008, p. 497]. In some sense, these were Buffett's routine arguments, which he used in negotiations multiple times.

In the end, Rose's family privately approved Buffett's purchase of the business. Buffett had also found out that the Germans were offering $90 million for the business, but for Rose, who was Jewish, the potential buyer's German nationality may have had emotional connotations involving German and Jewish history [Schroeder, 2008, p. 497]. It seems that it was only after Buffett had been fully armed with all this knowledge and after he had conducted extensive private discussions with her family that he showed up in Rose's store with his offer to buy her business on the pretext of its being his "birthday."

Having avoided an audit before the purchase, Buffett did not lose out. The audit was carried out after the sale, and it turned out that the value of the inventory was considerably higher than what Mrs. Blumkin had thought. She reevaluated the price of NFM as $85 million and commented: "I wouldn't go back on my word, but I was surprised. He never thought a minute. But he studies. I bet you he knew" [cited in Lowe, 2007, p. 48]. Later she came up with another value, $100 million. We can agree with this valuation also, as this is about 10 times the annual net profit. Such a price is very reasonable, particularly when the sale was taking place in a noncrisis year (1983 was such a year).

Buffett's understanding of Rose's character may also have played a role in this transaction. Buffett depicts her in his letters to shareholders as a strong-minded, stubborn, and almost authoritarian person who could not be influenced by other people. "She was a strong enough matriarchal figure" [Buffett, 1991c]; "she made her mark, and the deal was cut" [Buffett, 1991d]. After 2000, other details about the sale became public. Robert Miles, who wrote a book about the CEOs of Berkshire's daughter companies and who interviewed all his protagonists, quotes Rose Blumkin as saying: "I got tired of the kids bossing me. So I thought 'I will sell it and he'll be the boss.' He didn't bother me" [Miles, 2002, p. 91]. In the transcript of Buffett's lecture at Notre Dame University in 1991, we find that Rose owned only 20 percent of the company; the rest had been transferred to her descendants. Perhaps Buffett, genius psychologist that he is, sensed the tension between the generations and in one way or another convinced Mrs. B that he would not interfere with her management of the company. This was important to Rose, who liked being in charge. She might have been prepared to sacrifice part of the sale price for this reason.

Mrs. B already understood that she was selling cheaply at the time of the sale. In an interview for his authorized biography, *Snowball*, Buffett admitted that Rose, having sold him the company, said: "You bought an oil well on your birthday" [cited in Schroeder, 2008, p. 499].

Buffett had indeed bought an oil well that has been in operation ever since, but Mrs. B did not enjoy the peaceful running of the business for much longer. In 1989, she found herself in a serious conflict with her descendants, "who were interfering too much in her operation." As Rose told the story, at some point her relatives took away her responsibilities, and she was unable to buy anything. Her relatives informed the manufacturers that the family would not pay for her purchases and would not buy the manufacturers' products if their salespeople talked to her. This made Rose "awful mad," so one morning she walked out of the shop. "And Warren Buffett [who had] acted like he's an angel—[had] said 'there's nobody like me, I don't care how old you are, you are doing a terrific job'—he stuck up for them. He never came to say he's sorry. Never. I got fooled with him. I thought he's an angel" [Miles, 2002, p. 94].

Having walked out of the shop, Mrs. B did not retire. She set up a new store next door. She also discovered that she liked the attention of the press. She began to talk to journalists about Buffett's no longer being her friend. She declared that she had opened the new store, selling carpets, next to NFM as revenge for Buffett's mistreating her [Kilpatrick, 2005, p. 541]. By 1991, after just two years of operation, the shop not only had become profitable but also had risen to the position of Omaha's third-largest carpet outlet. On December 1, 1991, two days after Mrs. Blumkin's ninety-eighth birthday, Buffett, hoping to make peace, walked into her store. He brought 24 pink roses and a five-pound box of See's chocolates. Buffett and Mrs. B had not spoken amicably since she had opened the new place, but on this occasion, his attempt at rapprochement was received benevolently. "He's a real gentleman," said Mrs. B . . . and a few months later she sold the new place to NFM for nearly $5 million [Miles, 2002, p. 95].

After the first sale, Buffett had decided not to sign a noncompete agreement. He did not think it was necessary, given that Mrs. B was 89 at the time. After the second sale, Rose offered him a noncompete agreement, and Buffett did not refuse [Buffett, 1977–2013, 1992]. The second sale was closed in a more confidential manner than the first, so it is not possible to evaluate whether it was cheap or expensive. A "simple" lady who had never really learned to speak or write English managed to create a business that Buffett was keen to acquire not once but twice.

Borsheim's

Your Chairman, I wish to emphasize, is good for something.

—WARREN BUFFETT [BUFFETT, 1977–2013, 1992]

In 1989, Buffett bought another family business in Omaha—the jewelry store Borsheim's. The financial terms of this acquisition have never been disclosed, and it is impossible to assess whether it was cheap or expensive. The purchase of this company is an example of the type of synergy that Buffett looked for in a business. In Chapter 5, we discussed that Buffett has no interest in operational synergies but would seek out financial synergies or synergies with his personal brand. The purchase of Borsheim's could be viewed as an instance of pursuing the latter.

Borsheim's belonged to relatives of Rose Blumkin, the Friedman family. The Friedmans had purchased a small jewelry store in 1948. They captured market share by pursuing the same strategy that Rose had in her furniture business: buy merchandise as cheaply as possible, and sell it with as little markup as possible. The business attracted customers. The lower prices that they paid for merchandise allowed lower prices for the customers, the lower retail prices generated greater turnover, and the greater turnover produced greater profit in absolute terms. Borsheim's was able to keep operating costs as a percentage of revenue at approximately 45 percent of the level of other stores in the United States [Buffett, 1977–2013, 1990]. By 1990, as estimated by Buffett, the shop was second only to Tiffany's in New York in terms of turnover [Buffett, 1977–2013, 1990].

The store was owned and managed by Ike Friedman, a manager with a legendary reputation in the industry. Susan Jack, who took charge of the business after Ike Friedman's unexpected death, believes that one of the reasons behind Buffett's original interest in the store was Ike himself [Miles, 2002, p. 286].

According to Miles, the sale was negotiated in February 1989 during a meeting between Buffett and Friedman [Miles, 2002, p. 287]. The negotiations lasted about 10 minutes. Buffett asked five questions about the sales, gross profits, expenses, inventory, and whether Friedman was willing to stay on. Ike answered the first four questions from memory and confirmed that he would be willing to remain with the business in response to the fifth. Buffett stated his price. Shortly after that, Friedman and Buffett met in the latter's office and finalized the sale. Buffett bought 80 percent of the company; the remaining 20 percent stayed with the original owner's family.

In Buffett's letter to shareholders for 1989, the year when the jewelry store was purchased, we find only superlatives in the description of Borsheim's: "You have never seen a jewelry store like Borsheim's . . . an enormous selection across all price ranges" [Buffett, 1977–2013, 1989]. Further on in the letter, Buffett tells us that once every two years, he would meet informally with a group of friends who gathered to spend some enjoyable time together and to discuss different subjects. Buffett did not mention that this group consisted of people within his circle. Among its members have been Bill Gates, who joined the group after he and Buffett became acquainted in 1991, and Katharine Graham, who was part of the group until her death in 2001. After the purchase of Borsheim's, Buffett invited Ike Friedman to give a presentation before this group at its next meeting at a luxury hotel in Santa Fe, California. "To educate us on jewels" was Buffett's description of the purpose of the presentation. Ike decided "to dazzle the group" and brought more than $20 million worth of jewelry. Buffett remembers that he was concerned about the safety of the merchandise and asked Ike whether sufficient security was in place. Ike explained that he had changed the combination of the safe's lock. Even the hotel management did not know what the combination was. Two big armed fellows were guarding the safe. Besides, the jewels were not in it [Buffett, 1977–2013, 1989].

In some sense, this is a story of Buffett's assistance in the promotion of the brand. Such a presentation before some of the world's wealthiest people is the most valuable PR that a brand of this kind could possibly obtain. Borsheim's has a mail order service. Jewelry chosen from the catalog is sent to the client, who is able to return the jewels if he does not like them. Telling the story in the annual report, which is widely read, may be also a marketing exercise. After reading about Borsheim's in the letter, Buffett's shareholders are likely to order the jeweler's catalog and become customers.

Later, a new tradition was established. A day before the annual shareholders' meeting, Borsheim's would close the store for regular customers several hours earlier than the usual time, but would remain open for Berkshire shareholders. Additional discounts were applied to prices that were already low by industry standards. In Buffett's annual letters, it is possible to trace how this new tradition evolved. In 1990–1991, the hotel where the shareholders met arranged for two shuttle buses to take shareholders to Borsheim's. From 1992 on, the store would open for six hours on Sunday specifically for the weekend of the annual meeting. In 1993, both Buffett and Munger attended the jewelry sale. In his 1994 letter, Buffett mentioned that on the previous "Shareholder Sunday," the store had had its best turnover [Buffett, 1977–2013, 1994]. In his 1996 letter, Buffett tells us that on "Shareholder Sunday" of the preceding year, the store had broken every record in terms of sales tickets, dollar volume, and attendees per square inch [Buffett, 1977–2013, 1996].

In 1997, Buffett announced that Charlie Munger would be giving autographs: "Charlie will be available for autographs, however, only if the paper he signs is a Borsheim's sales ticket," said Buffett, smiling [Buffett, 1977–2013, 1997]. The following year, Buffett cited statistics showing that the 1997 "Shareholder Sunday" sales had been double those for the preceding year and that the sales volume on "Shareholder Sunday" had significantly exceeded the volume for any previous day in the store's history. "Borsheim's wrote 2,501 tickets during the eight hours it was open. For those of you who are mathematically challenged, that is one ticket every 11 seconds" [Buffett, 1977–2011, 1998]. From 2000 onward, Borsheim's has offered two events for shareholders: autographs are offered by both Munger and Buffett, but they sign *only the sales tickets* [Buffett, 1977–2013, 1999]. This is mentioned in italics in the letter to shareholders.

Buffett assures shareholders that since the store's markups in the store are low, or the lowest in the industry, then "the more you buy, the more you save." Acknowledging that this argument is a tired advertising trick, Buffett tells a joke that he, as a kid, had found fascinating. A little boy returns home and says that he missed a streetcar but saved 5 cents by doing so. His father is irate: "Why did you not miss a cab and save 85 cents?" [Buffett, 1977–2013, 2003].

In his letter of 2004, Buffett admits that sales rose by 73 percent in comparison to the previous year [Buffett, 1977–2013, 2004]. In

2004, sales grew by an additional 9 percent. The store also sold 5,000 Berkshire Monopoly games and then ran out of stock [Buffett, 1977–2013, 2005]. In the end, there were so many buyers for Borsheim's jewelry that the period of special prices for shareholders was extended from several hours in 1990–1991 to two weeks in 2005. The period of low prices lasted 13 days in 2013.

This type of promotional assistance is extended to all products manufactured by companies within Berkshire. In 1988, Berkshire shareholders who came to the annual shareholders' meeting purchased $57,000 worth of goods at Nebraska Furniture Mart [Schroeder, 2008, p. 532]. In the following years, the store has organized special events for shareholders. Berkshire arranges for buses that take the shareholders to the store after the meeting. The shareholders' weekend brings Nebraska Furniture Mart in Omaha[3] approximately 10 percent of its annual sales. For some businesses, such as Borsheim's, this marketing plays a very important role. It may well be that, as a result, the sales are higher by an order of magnitude. In shareholders letters, Buffett advises all shareholders to check how much they are paying for their automotive insurance. According to GEICO's estimates, around 40 percent of insurance holders could achieve a saving by switching to the coverage provided by the company. Buffett recommends GEICO on the Berkshire's website under the section "A Message from Warren E. Buffett."

In 2001, a short time after the acquisition of NetJets, Buffett began to advertise the company's service to shareholders in his annual letters. "I believe the Buffetts fly more fractional-ownership hours—we log in excess of 800 annually—than does any other family. In case you're wondering, we use exactly the same planes and crews that serve NetJets' other customers" [Buffett, 1977–2013, 2001]. Sometimes Buffett personally attended NetJets' road shows [Bianco, 1999].

During the annual shareholders' meeting, samples of Berkshire products are available for sale. *The World Book Encyclopedia,* See's chocolates, and shoes made by Berkshire companies are offered to shareholders. It is possible to apply for GEICO insurance. Jeff Matthews, an asset manager,

---

3 Now this brand includes three stores, one in Omaha, one in Kansas City, and one in Des Moines. Another branch is about to open in Dallas.

attended Berkshire's annual shareholders' meetings in 2007 and 2008 and wrote a book about his experiences. He observed the vast crowds jostling at the merchandise counters and wondered whether Berkshire was the only public company in the world that succeeded in earning a profit from its annual meetings [Matthews, 2009, p. 149].

The commerce facilitated by Buffett's personal presentations attracts large numbers of people. The shareholders' meeting of 2008 was attended by 27,000 people.[4] They do not come just to shop and to vote at the meeting. (Voting is unnecessary, as Buffett has control of the company and is able to push through any decisions he wants with the help of the votes of his family and Charlie Munger.) The shareholders come to spend time in the company of the world's greatest investor and socialize with one another. The annual meeting has been nicknamed Woodstock for Capitalists. It also has another sobriquet: BRKfest.[5]

The official beverage of the annual meeting is Cherry Coke. Buffett tells everyone that he is a big fan of the drink and that he keeps an ample supply of it in his office. (The billionaire's simple habits are well known. Buffett's doctor apparently finds that when it comes to questions of health, Buffett mainly relies on hereditary factors.)

Perhaps, however, to say that he does not drink anything else is an exaggeration. This is how Andrew Kilpatrick described his meal with Buffett: "He ordered a bacon, lettuce and tomato sandwich, a salad and iced tea. When I started ordering Coke, he said, 'Attaboy'" [Kilpatrick, 2005, p. 1414]. Louis Rukeyser, a well-known financial commentator, tells a similar story about his lunch with Buffett: "The one thing I have been told to view as an absolute certainty was that Buffett . . . never drunk anything but Cherry Coke. But when I ordered an iced tea, he immediately said 'That sounds good. Let me have an iced tea too'" [cited in Kilpatrick, 2005, p. 1418]. Nevertheless, Buffett is an excellent advertising executive for Coca-Cola. He had admitted to becoming a Coca-Cola fan in 1985: "After 48 years of allegiance to another soft drink, your Chairman, in an unprecedented display of behavioral

---

4 Each shareholder has a right to invite four guests to the annual meeting. The *Wall Street Journal* estimated that in 2014, the meeting was attended by 40,000 people ["Recap: The 2014 Berkshire Hathaway Annual Meeting"].
5 BRK is the Berkshire's ticker symbol.

flexibility, has converted to the new Cherry Coke" [Buffett, 1977–2013, 1985]. Buffett bought a large stake in Coca-Cola in 1989 (we discussed his investment in this company in Chapter 2).

Buffett enjoys slipping into the role of a common man. While at the opening of a new store of Jordan's Furniture, a Berkshire company, he was munching popcorn during the ceremony [Kilpatrick, 2005, p. 641]. When cutting the ribbon at the opening of a new RC Willey store in Idaho, Buffett remarked humorously and humbly: "Your Chairman, I wish to emphasize, is good for something" [Buffett, 1977–2013, 1999]. During a visit to Nebraska Furniture Mart for the annual shareholders' meeting event, Buffett lay down on a mattress and announced: "I finally landed the only job I really wanted in life—a mattress tester" [Schroeder, 2008, p. 729]. When in public, Buffett never fails to deliver an excellent marketing performance.

Scott Fetzer Company

> The smarter side to take in a bidding war is the losing side.
> —WARREN BUFFETT [CITED IN CURRAN, 1993]

At the end of 1985, Buffett made a very unusual (for him) acquisition: he bought a public company. Scott Fetzer was a conglomerate based in Ohio. The company provided financial services, published *The World Book Encyclopedia,* and produced oil and gas burners, pumps, air compressors, and household appliances (vacuum cleaners under the brand name Kirby), among other products. The conglomerate consisted of 16 companies. Its CEO, Ralph Schey, was an ambitious executive. In 1984, the conglomerate's total turnover amounted to $695 million, or $102.90 a share. This was an increase of 13 percent from $635 million or $94 a share in 1983. Net income rose 26 percent to $40.6 million, or $6 a share, from $32.2 million, or $4.80 a share ["Scott & Fetzer Co. Agrees to Be Acquired," 1984]. The company was practically debt free and had considerable cash reserves. In April 1984, the balance sheet had $97 million of liquid reserves, which amounted to $14 a share. The company's pension fund, in analysts' view, was overfunded. With the excess funds in the pension fund added, the reserves could have been valued at $20 a share. In early April of 1984, the conglomerate's shares were trading at around $45. If we subtract the conservative estimate of cash reserves of $14 from the share price, then we arrive at something that is just over five times the annual profits.

On April 16, 1984, Schey, who owned 0.9 percent of the company's shares, offered to buy out the shareholders at $50 a share as part of a leveraged buyout (LBO). This led the shares to rise to $53 a share on the open market. When the market price rises above the offer price, this means that the market "thinks" that someone else will better this offer. And, indeed, another player entered the game—Ivan Boesky, a well-known arbitrageur. He bought 5.4 percent of the shares of Scott Fetzer on the open market and offered shareholders $60 a share for the remainder. The board of directors refused the offer, as it had doubts about Boesky's ability to raise sufficient funds to complete the deal [Winter, 1984]. There may have been other reasons for the board's refusal as well. Given his reputation, Boesky may have been viewed as too aggressive and as an unfriendly buyer who would replace management. The directors may have feared that the company would be broken up and sold piece by piece.[6] Schey would have had to abandon his personal future plans with respect to the company. (Later, a senior manager of the company described the board's reaction to Buffett's offer: "When someone walks in the door with money in hand, things seem a little more certain" [Ansberry, 1985].)

On the other hand, the board's refusal of Boesky's offer could have led to legal action by shareholders, who could have accused Schey of acting out of personal interest, not in the interest of the shareholders. When the board turned down Boesky's offer, Schey had to hire an investment bank, whose mandate was to search for other offers at $60. The bank did not succeed in creating competition among serious strategic buyers. Interest in the deal was shown only by financial buyers, the little-known companies Triangle Industries and Itel [Rotbart, 1984]. Schey did not abandon his plans to obtain control of the company, but he decided to resort to an employee stock ownership plan (ESOP).

---

6 It might just have been that the board conducted a background check and ascertained that Boesky was being investigated by the SEC for insider trading.

A consortium consisting of senior company managers, representing themselves and the company employees, and a number of outside investors offered first $61 and then $62 a share. One outside investor was a subsidiary of General Electric. The consortium was subsequently joined by Kelso & Co. The founder of this company, Louis Kelso, was a pioneer of transactions involving ESOPs, in which the employees buy the employer's shares with borrowed funds. By 1984, Kelso & Co. had begun to invest in LBO[7] transactions and to compete with such well-known specialists in this market as Kohlberg Kravis Roberts (KKR).

The initial plan was that the ESOP group would obtain a loan in the amount of $182 million and buy out 41 percent of the shares at $44.39 a share. Fifty of the company managers and Kelso & Co. would receive 29 percent of the shares at a symbolic price of $1 a share. General Electric would receive the remaining shares (100% − 41% − 29% = 30%) in the form of warrants. The difference between these prices and the price promised to the shareholders would be financed by the free cash on the company's balance sheet. The members of the ESOP group would receive shares of a different class from those that would be granted to the organizers of the deal. The company management justified this asymmetry by arguing that the employees were receiving their shares for "free," since the responsibility to repay the borrowed funds rested with the company. Since "free cheese can only be found in a mousetrap," the shares designated for employees would be transferred to the employee retirement funds, though not in addition to the pension plan contributions, but *in lieu* of them.

The U.S. Department of Labor concluded that the transaction was not in the interests of the company employees and calculated that for the $182 million, the employees had to receive 66.7 percent of the shares; this allocation of shares would reduce the proportions intended for other investors. The Department of Labor also insisted that the managers should pay for their shares. Only Schey agreed to these conditions; the other top managers expressed no interest. The deal fell apart. These events unfolded during August of 1985. The official

---

7 For the history of the use of ESOPs in leveraged buyouts and Kelso's experience in these deals, see [Hoerr, Stevenson, and Norman, 1985].

announcement of the collapse of the deal was made on September 6 ["Department of Labor Ruling," 1985].

In the beginning of October, a company called Danaher Corp. expressed an interest in acquiring Scott Fetzer and offered a price that was $2 lower—$60 a share. At approximately the same time, Buffett entered the game. On October 10, he wrote Schey a letter saying that he had always liked the company and that he did not do any unfriendly deals. He also stated that he owned 250,000 shares of Scott Fetzer. Buffett also expressed an interest in a telephone conversation, in case Schey felt that it might be meaningful to consider a merger with Berkshire [Miles, 2002, p. 273]. Since Buffett had already bought some of the company's stock, it is possible that he did not initially plan to buy the entire company, but intended to act as an arbitrageur. Schey, who was not acquainted with Buffett, remembers that he telephoned Buffett, who suggested that they meet for dinner. They met the day after the conversation, and the day after that, Buffett visited the company. On the day after his visit, the deal was finalized. It was announced to the public just one day later [Miles, 2002, p. 273]. The deal to buy this company was executed in a blitzkrieg style.

Buffett bought the company at the same price as Danaher had offered—$60 a share, or $402 million for 100 percent. As part of the deal, Scott Fetzer would buy back its shares that were in free circulation and would fund this buyback program with the cash on the company's balance sheet. The company had already launched this share buyback prior to the negotiations with Buffett in order to increase the percentage of the company controlled by its management [Ansberry, 1985]. Suspending the buyback would not have made economic sense: if a company has accumulated substantial cash reserves, then a buyer who is taking over the company would be acquiring cash for cash, and so the lower the cash reserves left on the balance sheet, the cheaper the company becomes and the fewer outstanding shares need to be bought by its acquirer. The shareholders were guaranteed that if they ended up selling their shares at a price lower than the one offered by Buffett, then Buffett would compensate them for the difference between their sale price and $60. Taking into account the share buyback and the reduction of funds on the balance sheet, it is possible to estimate that Buffett paid $320 million for the whole company.

On November 18, three weeks after the announcement in the papers of Buffett's plans to acquire the company, *Forbes* published an article titled "Raiders in Short Pants" [Gubernick, 1985]. The article discredited the public image of Danaher Corp. *Forbes* discussed tax evasion and "milking" of the companies that Danaher had acquired control over without adequate expenditure. Danaher did not bid above Buffett's offer, but instead left the scene. Of course, it was also helpful that Scott Fetzer's management supported Buffett as an acquirer. The transaction is particularly interesting in view of the acquisition price, as the company had been trading on the open market and had a market value. The purchase of Scott Fetzer was purely a market transaction. There were various competing buyers, there was no controlling shareholder with whom it would have been possible to agree on a deal, and the equity was distributed among a large number of small shareholders; the transaction was voluntary for the shareholders, and it was easily approved at the general shareholders' meeting. Scott Fetzer was acquired at a price/sales (P/S) multiple of 0.58 and a P/E multiple of 10. If we subtract the reserves per share from the share price, then the P/E multiple would be between 6.6 and 7.5.

I would view this transaction as inexpensive based on any indicator. The market price of the company when the first proposal was made was low. The P/E ratio was approximately 5 without accounting for the cash reserves on the balance sheet. According to Robert Shiller, at around that time, the shares of S&P 500 companies traded on average at a P/E of 9.3, although Shiller's calculations were based on cyclically adjusted earnings ["Online Data Robert Shiller"]. Eight times annual profits (reserves subtracted) is also not a high multiple to pay to acquire 100 percent of a publicly traded company. The markup to the market price before Ralph Schey's first offer was not particularly high—around 33 percent. We also know that after the acquisition, no skeletons were found in the closet and the company was highly profitable.

How was this transaction possible in the first place? In my view, the answer lies in the company's almost excessive diversification. A company like Scott Fetzer does not attract interest from strategic buyers, as it is too diversified, and no single strategic buyer is able to make sense of it. It could have been bought by a financial investor, broken up, and sold piece by piece. This view was confirmed by Schey: no large investor was pursuing the opportunity as the company consisted of too many components. Some investors cared for certain parts of the business, but there was not anyone who had sufficient funds to take over the whole operation. Boesky and Milken regarded the sheer variety of the businesses within the company as a difficulty [Miles, 2002, p. 272].

Schey, of course, would have opposed the acquisition of the company by anyone who wanted to break it up, since he would have lost his position. All the potential buyers other than Buffett were buyers of this type. Schey admitted after the transaction that the management felt highly ambivalent about most of the acquirer candidates: "Why in the hell should I help those bastards buy it?" [cited in Miles, 2002, p. 272]. Conglomerates had been fashionable in the 1960s, but they were out of fashion in the 1980s. During the early 1990s, their shares traded at a 13 to 15 percent discount to comparable stand-alone businesses [Berger and Ofek, 1995]. The valuation at which Buffett acquired the company suggests that in Scott Fetzer's case, the discount was far higher than average.

* * *

The first two acquisitions highlight Buffett's skills as a very patient judge of human nature and his ability to drive profitability through his personal brand. The last acquisition is an instance of Buffett's acting as a fine tactician. What were Buffett's tactics in the acquisition of Scott Fetzer? He entered the game as the last player after two things had become apparent: first, the management was unable to do an LBO, and therefore would not object to being bought out by an external buyer, and second, other external buyers were not interested. The share price did not rise excessively. The external offers that were available were considered unsuitable by the directors, either because of doubts about the financial capacity of the prospective buyers or from the point of view of the reputation of those buyers. Buffett had a perfect reputation and readily available funds. The story of the acquisition of Scott Fetzer brings us to the topic of strategic positioning by Buffett in the market of mergers and acquisitions and the significance of this positioning in accessing potentially promising deals.

8

"Who Is the Fairest of Them All?": The Role of Image in Buffett's Investment Strategy

Some guys chase girls, I chase companies.
—WARREN BUFFETT [CITED IN KILPATRICK, 2005, P. 1367]

BUFFETT DOES INDEED CHASE COMPANIES. A NUMBER OF EXTREMELY successful early acquisitions made him famous among a small circle of people. His later work brought him international celebrity. He has developed such a reputation as an investor and buyer of businesses that enterprise owners, of their own volition, have been keen to sell their companies to him at below-market prices. The sellers could have achieved higher prices on the open market if they had had no specific preferences concerning the type of buyer. However, they value the fact that Buffett does not seek to replace the managers and interfere with a company's operations after the acquisition. The sellers also value the fact that he trusts them and does not care for formal due diligence prior to the purchase. However, how does this component of the Buffett phenomenon work?

205

No Hostility, No Due Diligence, No Management Change

> Nothing ever happens to our managers.
> We offer them immortality.
>
> —WARREN BUFFETT [BERKSHIRE HATHAWAY
> ANNUAL SHAREHOLDERS' MEETING, 1997]

As a young investor, Buffett purchased shares of and acquired control over companies without the consent of their owners. Roger Lowenstein tells the story of how in 1958, Buffett came across an insurance company that, in his view, was severely undervalued. National American Fire Insurance was controlled by the Ahmanson brothers, who were banking entrepreneurs. Some of the shares had been held by Nebraska farmers since the late 1920s. The brothers were quietly buying up the stock at $50 a share. This was a very low offer. The shareholders were selling the stock at this price because there was no public market in the shares. Seeking to obtain the stockholders' list, Buffett tried to attend the annual shareholders' meeting. The Ahmansons, understandably, turned him away. Buffett, accompanied by a friend, drove through all of Nebraska and offered $100 to anyone he saw in exchange for shares. He accumulated 10 percent of the outstanding equity. Eventually, Buffett sold the shares, earning $100,000 in profit [Lowenstein, 1996, p. 65].

In 1961, when Buffett was still managing the partnership that preceded Berkshire, he bought around 70 percent of Dempster Mill Manufacturing of Nebraska. He obtained operational control over the company, which produced windmills, pumps, and water well products. The company was underperforming. Having examined the situation, Buffett concluded that the working capital was being misused. He fired the CEO and put a manager he trusted in charge of the business.[1]

---

1 It was a balance sheet play. Buffett justified the acquisition on the basis that it was possible to buy the company at less than the balance sheet value of the assets. The average purchase price was $28 a share, while the balance sheet value of net assets was $75 per share. Buffett began the acquisition process in 1957 and in total spent $1 million [Buffett, 1957–1970, January 24, 1962]. The company was sold in 1963. Buffett's profit on the investment amounted to more than $3 million, of which $1 million came from selling excess inventory and more than $2 million from the sale of shares [Buffett, 1957–1970, November 6, 1963].

Buffett's acquisition of Berkshire Hathaway was also not friendly. As we discussed in Chapter 2, Berkshire Hathaway was formed as a result of a merger between two New England textile manufacturers, Hathaway Manufacturing and Berkshire. The combined company had 14 production facilities and a turnover of $112 million. The company was controlled by two large shareholders—Seabury Stanton, the principal owner and president of Hathaway Manufacturing, and Malcolm Chace, the owner of Berkshire. Stanton became the CEO of Berkshire Hathaway. Soon afterward, the position was transferred to his son, Jack.

Berkshire Hathaway was a public company. Buffett had originally analyzed its shares in the 1950s, when he was working for Graham, but Graham did not make the investment into the stock. At this time, the share price also started to fall slowly. Buffett began the buying of the shares in 1962, in those periods when they traded at the level near 50 percent of working capital per share. (He was still investing in "cigar butts," which we discussed in earlier chapters.) By 1963, Buffett had become a large shareholder. He had been acting anonymously and held the securities through Wall Street brokers. His interests were represented by a friend. Somehow Buffett's identity as the actual purchaser was leaked. One of Berkshire's managers called him and asked whether he intended to continue his acquisition process. Buffett responded open-endedly: "I may or I may not" [cited in Lowenstein, 1996, p. 127].

This story contrasts with a later instance of a purchase of shares on the open market. In 1988, Buffett started acquiring shares in Coca-Cola. Again, he acted through a broker. Coca-Cola's management suspected that Buffett might be the person who was buying up the shares. The company's president phoned Buffett and asked whether he was the buyer. Buffett did not deny that it was he, only requesting that the president not disclose anything until Buffett had to declare his stake publicly for legal reasons. Coca-Cola's president at the time, Don Keough, was also from Omaha [Kilpatrick, 2005, p. 434]. He had been acquainted with Buffett for more than 30 years. He apparently abided by Buffett's request.

In 1964, Berkshire conducted a number of share buybacks that increased the proportion of the equity held by the Stantons. Buffett seriously considered selling his stake, but he did not agree with the potential buyers on price. Subsequently, he came to feel that he preferred to remain a shareholder in the company and began attempting to influence managerial decisions through his representative on the board of directors. Jack Stanton resisted the interference. Buffett then sought to obtain a majority of the votes at the general stockholders' meeting. He offered to buy out Malcolm Chace's stake. Malcolm refused, but some members of his family agreed to sell to Buffett their shares. Buffett also persuaded Otis Stanton, Seabury's brother, to sell his shares; his condition was that the same offer be made to Seabury, who agreed to it. Purchasing these stakes allowed Buffett to reach a 49 percent share in the company. At the next meeting of the board of directors, Seabury resigned as chairman and Jack's career as CEO ended. Buffett took the post of chairman of the board and appointed as CEO a manager who was loyal to him, Ken Chace, a namesake of the Chace shareholding family [Lowenstein, 1996, pp. 121–130].[2]

Today Buffett is one of the most friendly investors toward the management of the companies that he buys. He never undertakes any hostile actions with respect to businesses that are of interest to him, and he always stands by the promises he makes before the deal. He never adjusts the price that he offered for the company downward, and he is critical of the common practice in which the original price is corrected or the offer is recalled if unexpected risks are uncovered during the due diligence process. There is "no chance" that Berkshire would back away or insist on changing the terms after the deal was announced— "with apologies, of course, and with an explanation that banks, lawyers, boards of directors, etc. were to be blamed" [Buffett, 1977–2013, 1990].

Buffett guarantees his price, but he does so within his framework of paying low prices, below those that would be achievable on the open market. (We discuss the issue of the low acquisition price in greater detail in the next chapter.) He finds it significant when the owner of a business agrees to sell his company at a price that is lower than that

---

2 The Chace family probably does not regret not selling all of the shares to Buffett. In 1998, *Forbes* reported that value of those unsold shares, controlled by the family heir Malcolm Chace III, amounted to $850 million [Setton, 1998].

available on the market because it means that the owner prefers to sell to the "right" buyer. "We like to do business with someone who loves his company, not just the money that a sale will bring him (though we certainly understand why he likes that as well)" [Buffett, 1977–2013, 2000]. This emotional tie between the selling owner and the company is an indirect confirmation that everything inside the company is likely to be in order. Honest accounting, pride in one's product, respect for customers, loyal employees, and a strong sense of direction will be present. The reverse applies also. When an owner exhibits a lack of interest in the business's future, it is possible that the company has been dressed up for sale, especially if the seller is a financial investor. The owner's attitude will often permeate the company [Buffett, 1977–2013, 2000].

Not only does Buffett not adjust the price downward as a result of due diligence, but also he often avoids due diligence altogether. "If you have to go through too much investigation, something is wrong" [cited in Lowe, 2007, p. 163], and there is simply no point in investing. We have already discussed some of the numerous accounts of Buffett's buying companies without any due diligence whatsoever. He did not do due diligence on RC Willey or Star Furniture, which were recommended to him by Irv Blumkin. Buffett described the process of purchasing Star Furniture from Melvyn Wolff as perfect. The transaction was agreed to "in a single, two-hour session." There was "no need to check leases, work out employment contracts, etc." Buffett knew that he "was dealing with a man of integrity and that's what counted" [Buffett, 1977–2013, 1997]. Wolff was left with similar impressions. Buffett had not done any due diligence, had not requested a noncompete agreement, and had not even sent anyone to look at the company [Kilpatrick, 2005, p. 614]. According to another source, Wolff felt that "it was love at first sight" [Elder, 1997].

Helzberg Diamonds were also purchased in a similar manner. When the owner of Helzberg Diamonds asked about due diligence, Buffett replied: "I can smell these things. This one smells good" [cited in Helzberg, 2003, p. xviii]. The transaction to buy Executive Jet (now NetJets) took 15 minutes to agree on at a meeting at Teterboro Airport in New Jersey. Rich Santulli later remembered that it took less time to sell Buffett the business than it did to sell him a share in a plane

[Kilpatrick, 2005, p. 628]. Clayton was bought over the phone. Buffett had not seen the company. He did not request an audit when buying Jordan's Furniture from the Tatelman brothers. The brothers informed their lawyers, "who were big attorneys in Boston," about this. They replied that they had never encountered anything of this kind. One of the brothers later observed in an interview: "It's a new concept in business. It's called trust" [cited in Miles, 2002, p. 221]. This comment echoes an earlier remark by Charlie Munger: "The economics are irrelevant if you don't have trust" [cited in Lowe, 2000, p. 121]. Buffett spoke about his due diligence–free acquisition style. He commented in *Aviation International News* that he would never do what people call due diligence. He would simply seek to find people who genuinely love their businesses [Kilpatrick, 2005, p. 631]. As his business expanded, often finding a humorous response to invitations, Buffett stopped the practice of personally visiting the companies that he was buying. On account of the purchase of the Israeli company ISCAR, Buffett remarked that its owners "tried to get me to Israel to see the operation there before I bought it. I knew it would be wonderful, I just thought I would pay more money if I saw just how wonderful it was, so I did not go" [Buffett, 2008].

Ordinarily, Buffett does not change the management of the companies that he buys. The selling owners remain in their positions. "Nothing ever happens to our managers. We offer them immortality." He finds that this is important to the former owners. Although they are able to afford not to work, they love what they do. In one of his letters to shareholders, Buffett advises them that Berkshire has and will have no one—family members or recently recruited MBAs—to whom it has promised a chance to run a business that it has bought from owner-managers [Buffett, 1977–2013, 1990].

Those with whom Buffett wishes to work feel very comfortable with being part of the group. In 2001, Buffett remarked that in 37 years, not a single CEO of an operating business had elected to leave Berkshire to work for a competitor. Managers left only to retire, and they retired at a very advanced age [Buffett, 1977–2013, 2001]. Buffett does not compel his managers to retire at 65, although this is a common practice in many corporations. Most of his managers are over 70. The record was set by Rose Blumkin, who retired at 104. Once Buffett explained his policy through a metaphor: "It's difficult to teach a new dog old tricks" [Buffett, 1977–2013, 1988]. These comments may also have a marketing purpose. Buffett needs to reach out to potential sellers of businesses, who are frequently in advanced years. One of the main motivations for the sale is often transferring the family fortune to the next generation. At the same time, Buffett also aims to buy a business that is not subject to change and will remain the same tomorrow as it was yesterday. Old dogs may be unable to learn new tricks, but there may well be no point in their learning them.

Retaining the services of the old owners and managers is one of the key elements of Buffett's investment strategy. After all, as an owner, he is in need of excellent management. There is a certain synergy between Buffett's needs and those of the family business owners, who may wish to sell the business that they have built to a "worthy" buyer through arrangements that are as painless as possible from a tax liability standpoint, but who still want to remain at the helm. Buffett, understanding this dilemma, offers the original owners the opportunity to continue to manage the business. This concept of a good home for the right people and the right business is extremely attractive to those who are perhaps more interested in the business itself than in money. The concept draws the kind of people who are able to create an excellent business in the first place and then are ready to sell it at a price that is less than the maximum achievable because they value a broader range of parameters, such as the character of the incoming buyer and the future of their business. Once connected to each other, these different ideas form a highly effective tool that helps generate successful investments. Buffett does not buy businesses where he would need to replace the managers after having become a controlling shareholder. Since he invests in companies that have excellent management, Buffett does not need to replace it, with rare exceptions, after the purchase. The need to replace the managers may also indicate that the business may have difficulties and Buffett avoids such businesses. Owners of good companies prefer Buffett as a buyer because he does not replace the management. Buffett ends up with a choice of good companies from which to select an investment. A virtuous circle is created.

No tool or framework is entirely failure-proof. When problems with management arise, Buffett may decide to resolve the issue in an unusual manner. He was not satisfied with the quality of leadership of George Aderton, the president of a tiny Buffett holding, Citizen State Bank of Mount Morris, Illinois, in the 1970s. Buffett felt that Aderton's reporting lacked accuracy. In the end, instead of firing the CEO, Buffett disposed of the bank [Lowenstein, 1996, p. 290]. In 1981, Buffett hired Michael Goldberg, a McKinsey consultant, to organize the various insurance assets that belonged to Berkshire. Over the following 11 years, Goldberg remained the de facto CEO of Berkshire's insurance business. However, his management style was creating an atmosphere of tension among his subordinates, so in 1993, Buffett moved Goldberg to work on special projects and eliminated his position [Bianco, 1999].

In a rare instance of publicly interfering with the running of a subsidiary, Buffett dismissed the managers of Dexter Shoe after its losses snowballed out of control. He transferred the company to the management of H.H. Brown [Buffett, 1977–2013, 2001]. Later, Dexter Shoe was shut down altogether. We discussed both companies in Chapter 3 in the section on the circle of competence.

The story of General Re also offers an insight. Ron Ferguson, the CEO of General Re, was dismissed "gradually" after Buffett's acquisition of the company in 1998. The company's condition turned out to be much worse than expected. However, Buffett did not fire Ferguson immediately. Perhaps Buffett wanted to give the manager a second chance. Losses of $1.5 billion followed. Then came further losses. Of $2.3 billion of losses generated by the September 11 attacks, $1.7 billion fell on General Re. Buffett transferred part of General Re's insurance business to Berkshire and terminated a number of contracts. The losses were not only monetary; Berkshire's reputation suffered. Nevertheless, having been semifired—dismissed from his position as CEO but appointed as a consultant—in 2000, Ferguson initiated the very contracts with AIG that were later found to be fictitious and fraudulent. Ferguson and other managers of AIG were prosecuted and found guilty (but had their convictions suspended as part of a deferred prosecution agreement). Joseph Brandon, who replaced Ferguson, also resigned under pressure from federal prosecutors and the SEC [Calandro, 2009, p. 102]. Buffett had to appear in court as a witness. General Re eventually paid more than one settlement to resolve the matter. On this occasion, Buffett's remaining faithful to his principles led to considerable costs.

In 1999, Buffett dismissed Douglas Ivester, chairman and CEO of Coca-Cola, under whose tenure the company had not been performing well, as we discussed in Chapter 2. Buffett and Herbert Allen, who was also a large shareholder of the company, met Ivester on December 1, 1999, after having requested a meeting over the phone several days earlier. "Moments into the meeting, it was clear that they were not there to pay him compliments. They never sat down, never even removed their overcoats. In tones frostier than the air outside, they told him that they had lost confidence in him. . . . They made it clear that they wanted him to leave the Coca-Cola Company" [Hays, 2005, pp. 309–310]. The recommendation had not been agreed to by the other members of the board of directors, but Ivester did not put up any resistance. He called a directors' meeting and announced his resignation.

In 2009, Richard Santulli resigned from his position as CEO of NetJets, using the standard rationale that he wanted "to spend more time with my young family and pursue other interests" as an explanation of his resignation [Crippen, 2009]. By that time, the company had found itself in a cul-de-sac. Buffett had dispatched David Sokol, the CEO of MidAmerican Energy, to improve NetJets' performance. Santulli's resignation took place within a week of Sokol's arrival. A number of sources confirmed that Santulli was unhappy that Berkshire had brought in another executive to provide oversight [Fabrikant, 2009]. In 2011, officially on his own initiative, David Sokol, in turn, resigned from Berkshire. He was seen as one of Buffett's possible successors as CEO of Berkshire, and, in addition to his position as CEO of MidAmerican Energy, he was also the chairman of the board and CEO of NetJets and chairman of the board of Johns Manville, which we discuss in Chapter 11.

Sokol tendered his resignation after a series of possibly unremarkable events that somehow metamorphosed into a scandal. Sokol had spent $10 million of his personal funds to buy shares of Lubrizol and recommended the investment to Buffett. Berkshire acquired the company, and, according to some estimates, Sokol made about $3 million from selling his stake to Berkshire. The circumstances became public. Both

Buffett and Sokol explained in their press releases and interviews that Sokol had informed Buffett that he owned the stock, that until that episode, Buffett had rarely paid attention to Sokol's recommendations, that Sokol could not have influenced Buffett's decision to buy the company, and that, even more, Sokol could not have affected Lubrizol's decision to sell itself to Buffett. Buffett's press release also stated that this was not Sokol's first attempt to resign. The first time, Buffett had managed to persuade Sokol to stay with Berkshire. On this second occasion, Buffett accepted Sokol's resignation. Sokol explained that he had never been interested in being the CEO of Berkshire. He did not have that much time left in his life to invest his personal funds—a substantial sum that he, as a cofounder of MidAmerican Energy, had received after that company's sale to Buffett.

Upon Sokol's resignation, there seems to have been a change for the worse in Berkshire's stance toward him. Berkshire's internal investigation concluded that Sokol had not apprised Buffett of the size of his position in Lubrizol with sufficient clarity. Analysts suggested that Berkshire's conclusions may have been structured to protect Buffett. In early 2013, after an extensive investigation, the SEC confirmed that Sokol would not be charged with insider trading. After the SEC announced its decision, Sokol spoke about having been treated unfairly by Berkshire.

Buffett reflected on the changes in his management style. Over the years, the stance "I do not fire" has changed to "Occasionally, I have to fire somebody" [Buffett, 2003] and "I am slow to make personnel changes" ["Recap: The 2014 Berkshire Hathaway Annual Meeting," 2014]. These cases are an exception to his rule.

Hands-Off Approach

> He creates the image of ownership without having it.
>
> —RALPH SCHEY [CITED IN MILES, 2002, P. 278]

Buffett follows a policy of noninterference even when he disagrees with the decisions of his subordinates. And he disagrees often: "With almost every one of the companies Berkshire owns, I think I would do something different if I was running them—in some cases, substantially different" [cited in Bianco, 1999].

This policy of not interfering with the day-to-day running of operations requires a closer examination. Conglomerates often have a de facto top-down management structure. Jack Welch has been known for this kind of management style. Managers of Berkshire's subsidiaries are fully autonomous. If managers of subsidiaries need Buffett's help in managing the enterprise, "probably both" are "in trouble" [cited in Kilpatrick, 2005, p. 1380].

Buffett appreciates that managers who are natural entrepreneurs and members of the founding family are more likely to respect somebody who intimately understands the laissez-faire management style [Miles, 2002, p. 360]. He does not impose Berkshire's corporate culture on the subsidiaries. The only requirements are that the subsidiaries report their performance results and coordinate two types of decision at the conglomerate level: substantial capital expenditures and changes to their postresignation compensation packages. Buffett describes: "We centralize money. Everything else is decentralized" [Berkshire Hathaway Annual Shareholders' Meeting, 1998]. Buffett believes that in running businesses, "the best results come from letting high-grade people work unencumbered" [cited in Loomis, 1989]. Trying to implement a lot of changes does not work "any better in investments than it does in marriages" [cited in Loomis, 1988]. This policy creates a level of comfort for the original owners, who have a habit of making independent decisions. With a lifetime of such experience, it would be very difficult for them to switch to being salaried employees within a framework of defined reporting channels and without the right to make final decisions.

Rich Santulli explained his motives for selling NetJets to Buffett. He sold his company to somebody who was "one of the greatest guys I've ever met" and not to "a guy with a lot of money." Santulli observed that people who buy businesses often have large egos and believe that they can run those businesses better than the original owners. Buffett's position could have been described as, "I am buying it, but you are running it." Santulli valued the fact that being part of Berkshire meant that if he wanted to buy a billion dollars' worth of airplanes, Buffett would say, "Why are you asking me? Go do it" [cited in Miles, 2002, pp. 130–131]. Another aspect of Buffett's personality also resonated with Santulli. Buffett admitted: "I love every day. I mean, I tap dance in here and work with nothing but people I like. I don't have to work with people I don't like" [cited in Lenzner, 1993]. Santulli also felt that he did not want to do business with people with whom he did not want to do business [Miles, 2002, p. 131].

The former owner of H.H. Brown, Frank Rooney, who also sold his business to Buffett, speaks similarly to Santulli. When asked whether Buffett's company was an acquirer of choice, Rooney remarked that being part of Buffett's organization is "the next best thing to being in business for yourself" [cited in Miles, 2002, p. 172]. Rooney and Buffett agreed on a price of $200 million, or approximately 83 percent of sales and eight times the annual profit, on revenue of $240 million and pre-tax profit of $24 million [Miles, 2002, p. 171]. This could be viewed as inexpensive for a noncyclical business with a positive growth rate.

It was important for Bill Child, who sold his company RC Willey, a furniture retailer in Utah, to Buffett, not to work on Sundays because of Child's Mormon faith. He was confident that having sold his stores to Buffett, he would still be able to keep the stores closed on Sundays and manage them the same way he had previously.

To an even greater extent, if Buffett disagrees with the decision that is being taken, he does not interfere with the running of operations of companies where he is only a shareholder and a member of the board of directors. For instance, as a large shareholder in Capital Cities, while once visiting New York, he attended negotiations that ABC, a channel belonging to Capital Cities, was conducting to acquire the broadcast rights to a National Football League (NFL) championship. In the opinion of Capital Cities' director, Dan Burke, the channel could lose up to $40 million on the purchase of the rights. Nevertheless, ABC did not want to miss the opportunity to broadcast the prestigious sporting event. Roger Lowenstein relates Burke's recollections of the negotiations: Buffett arrived and it was apparent that he did not approve of the idea, however he refrained from expressing his views directly and only said, as the Cap Cities executives were waiting for the call from the NFL to close the deal, something to the extent that he hoped that the NFL would change their mind and not call back. The NFL did call back. The eventual losses on the contract ended up being worse than had been anticipated [Lowenstein, 1996, p. 271]. In 1996, Roger Lowenstein commented that there had been only a single instance of Buffett's opposing his managers [Lowenstein, 1996, p. 374]. Buffett objected to the bonus plan at Salomon after he had bought a large stake in the bank (see details of the story in [Schroeder, 2008, chapter 47]).

Randy Watson, the head of Justin Brands, which Berkshire purchased in 2000, made an accurate observation as to the essence of Buffett's approach: "He sells the incredible features and benefits of Berkshire ownership, and that attracts the willingness of like-minded owners and other good companies to be part of the Berkshire family" [Chan, 2010, p. 32]. Ralph Schey, the CEO of Scott Fetzer, also formulated a poignant description of Buffett's style of doing things: "He creates the image of ownership without having it, and that's hard to do." Schey found that he viewed his job as if he were the owner of the business with the exception of two days a year when he had to transfer profits to Berkshire [Lowenstein, 1996, p. 289]. This made him feel that he would not take risks that were greater than those that he would have wanted to carry personally. "I think the issue of ownership is the most critical thing that you can give to someone. I just see a huge difference between people who own a business, even if it is a small business, and professional managers in big companies" [Miles, 2002, p. 279].[3]

In addition to making his managers feel as if they own their businesses, Buffett also appears to inspire deep personal loyalty. Bill Child remarked that he was motivated not only by the professional challenge, but also by the desire to not let Berkshire down [Miles, 2002, p. 192]. Similar themes appear in descriptions of Buffett's relationship with Schey: ". . . Schey was also motivated by Buffett personally . . . he hated to bring Buffett bad news" [Lowenstein, 1996, p. 289]. Walter Schloss opined that, when buying companies, Buffett, being a good judge of people, is aware that "the guy's killing himself working for Warren" [Schloss, 1998].

---

3 Note the comment of Tony Nicely on the role of image: "We don't only want to be the fairest organization that we could possibly be; we also want to be *perceived* as the fairest organization possible" [cited in Miles, 2002, p. 39; italics mine]. I believe that this creation of the sense of ownership and, in parallel, of the perception of being a fair organization—and this perception, of course, is a reflection of reality—are the most important aspects of Buffett's strategy.

Buffett has created an outstanding company, and all the subsidiary managers are keen to sustain and develop its success. Nobody wants to let down the side. This is a very powerful nonmonetary motivation.

In the early days of his career, Buffett did not always give his managers a lot of independence. After he acquired control of Berkshire Hathaway, as chairman of the board of directors, he demanded reductions in administrative expenses and inventory. He closed down the investment programs in research and development on the basis that the return on that investment in R&D would remain low. He personally controlled all expenses, including those on pencil sharpeners. In the published minutes of the meetings of the board of directors, we find approval of the purchase of various equipment and the repairs to buildings with costs of individual items of as little as a few thousand dollars [Lowenstein, 1996, p. 137]. Buffett personally supervised the use of working capital. He demanded that the shipment of goods to those who had not yet settled their previous bills be suspended. The CEO of the company remembers that one thing that Buffett wanted to come up with was cash [Lowenstein, 1996, p. 132]. All the cash earned was used for purchases of companies in other industries.

Buffett actively participated in managing See's Candies after its acquisition. The company was a large buyer of sugar. Buffett took a crash course on trading sugar futures and subsequently felt in a position to advise See's CEO on how to time the sugar market [Lowenstein, 1996, p. 165].

The story of Buffett's participation in *Washington Monthly* also sheds some light on the evolution of his managerial style. Buffett invested $82,000 in the idea proposed to him by Charles Peters. A consultant had been hired to evaluate whether the publication was viable. Had the magazine become successful (it did, but not in a financial sense), it would have provided Buffett with exposure and connections. Despite the fact that the magazine was unprofitable and desperately short-staffed, and despite the fact that Peters worked for a very small salary, Buffett demanded annual financial reports that Peters could not prepare. Buffett was annoyed, although this was a small investment for him. "Even in a venture that couldn't possibly make a buck, he needed that yardstick" of financial statements being sent out [Lowenstein, 1996, p. 145].

Eventually, Buffett reduced his involvement in the running of the companies that he was acquiring. He introduced compensation packages for his CEOs that motivated them to reduce expenses and maximize their return on capital. This policy lessened the need for Buffett to monitor the subsidiaries closely. As a result, he not only achieved his objective of maximizing return on capital, but also created an image of a person who does not control his subordinates and does not interfere in their affairs. Why was this scheme not introduced at Berkshire Hathaway right after its acquisition? There may have been many reasons. When Buffett owned just a few companies, he had the time to evaluate the capital expenditures at all his subsidiaries personally. He may not have wished to pay bonuses to his CEOs when his investment portfolio was relatively young because he wanted to accumulate cash for further investment. As Buffett's investment portfolio grew, he gave the directors of Berkshire's subsidiaries more and more freedom and created a management model of almost complete noninterference.

Compensation packages based on return on invested capital may have their drawbacks. This compensation structure may have promoted under-investment. Roger Lowenstein observed that individual subsidiaries earned great returns but they expanded only at a slow pace. Perhaps still haunted by the memories of his failures in textiles, Buffett was not keen on reinvestment. World Book took too long to digitize its content. Borsheim's failed to take advantage of its fame and open branches. Buffett did not rule out expansion; he simply demanded to be convinced that the capital investment projects that his CEOs proposed would deliver greater returns than the investments that Buffett could make himself [Lowenstein, 1996, pp. 290–291]. In some sense, this is a prohibition on investment. Would anyone try to convince Buffett that she could invest better than he could?

Another analyst who has studied Buffett's investment approach raises an important question: "How long, I wonder, can a good business carry an owner who does not reinvest in that business?" [Matthews, 2009, p. 153]. See's Candies has "no stores East of Chicago, while Starbucks . . . is an authentic worldwide brand"; the venues of Dairy Queen stores "look so down"; a Nebraska Furniture Mart has opened in precisely two new locations—it "never took its big-box model across the country, the way Best Buy did," "the business is a shadow of what it might have been in different hands" [Matthews, 2009, pp. 142, 261]. This assertion is probably correct. At the same time, if, for instance, NFM had developed more stores and paid less dividends to Berkshire, there would have been fewer other acquisitions. NetJets did not spare funds for business development, but in the end it was Berkshire's deep pockets that saved the company from bankruptcy.

The hands-off approach is useful in yet another way. As we discussed in some detail in Chapter 3, Buffett invites the CEOs of Berkshire's subsidiaries to look for suitable companies to buy. "Several of our businesses have successfully completed such tuck-ins and they almost invariably added to our intrinsic value," commented Buffett in a letter to Berkshire managers [Buffett, 2001]. This capacity to act as sources of intelligence on suitable acquisitions in their industries is closely intertwined with the CEOs' ambassadorial role as marketing agents of Buffett's positive investor image. It is, of course, an accomplishment that Buffett's relationship with his managers is such that they are willing to perform these diplomatic duties as advertisers and business procurers.

The purchase of Jordan's Furniture in Boston was arranged by Irv Blumkin. He met the owners—the Tatelman brothers—at a dinner party and recommended that they speak with Buffett. Later, the brothers admitted that they had not intended to sell their business. They simply wanted to meet Buffett. They had turned down several prior offers to take the company public, as they did not want to lose managerial control. They were aware of Berkshire's noninterference policy. One month after the meeting, they advised Buffett that they would be willing to discuss the sale of their company. They were concerned about the transfer of the business and assets to the next generation. Buffett asked for the financial data. The brothers sent over the reports, but they were still not sure that they would be willing to sell. Two days later, the brothers received a letter that started with positive comments about their business and ended with a price offer. A short while later, a finalized deal was officially announced [Miles, 2002, p. 220].

Irv Blumkin also helped Buffett buy RC Willey in 1995. This company was the largest furniture retailer in the state of Utah, with a market share of more than 50 percent and turnover of $257 million. Bill Child controlled the company. Buffett wrote about the acquisition of RC Willey in his letter to shareholders in 1995. It was Irv Blumkin who "did the walking" around RC Willey. Irv told Buffett about the strengths of the company. He also told Bill Child about how pleased the Blumkin family had been with its relationship with Berkshire. In early 1995, Bill mentioned to Irv that for estate tax reasons, he might be interested in selling. "From that point forward, things could not have been simpler." Bill sent Buffett some figures, and Buffett wrote him a letter, indicating his valuation. The parties quickly agreed on a number. They found their personal chemistry to be perfect. By midyear, the merger was completed [Buffett, 1977–2013, 1995].

Generosity with Compliments

> You have a jewel of a company.
>
> —WARREN BUFFETT [CITED IN MILES, 2002, P. 187]

The transaction with Bill Child is interesting from yet another point of view. Although he did not want to sell the company, Child was nevertheless interested in researching the possibility of a sale. By the time of his first conversation with Buffett, he had already had several offers. In January 1995, Child met Irv Blumkin at a furniture industry conference and asked Blumkin whether he thought Buffett might be interested in buying the company. Blumkin said that he needed to speak to Buffett about it. Three days later, Child received a phone call from Blumkin, who advised him that Buffett was going to call Child. Buffett called five minutes after the phone call from Blumkin. Child said that he wanted to talk about the sale of his company and asked whether Buffett had a few minutes. Buffett responded that he had "all the time in the world."[4] Child and Buffett then chatted for 25 or 30 minutes. Some of Child's reasons for selling were the estate tax and growth. Buffett asked how much Child wanted to receive for his company. Child responded

---

4 Buffett quoted a line from a Louis Armstrong song that was used in a 1969 James Bond film, *On Her Majesty's Secret Service.*

that he wanted a fair price. Buffett requested financial statements for the last three years and promised to get back with an answer. A few days later Child received a FedEx that said: "Bill, you have a jewel of a company. It fits our mold perfectly. I'll have you a price in three days." As promised, in three days, another FedEx arrived. It included Buffett's price. Child thought that the offer was appropriate. He called Buffett and advised him that he was satisfied and that he would talk to the family. He invited Buffett to visit the company. Buffett assured Child that he did not need to see it. Child felt that he could not sell the company without the buyer having seen it. They debated the subject for a few minutes, and finally Buffett said that he was going to stop by while he was on his way to play golf with Bill Gates in Palm Springs [Miles, 2002, pp. 186–187].

A personal telephone call from Buffett is a genuine sign of respect for the business owner. The James Bond–style "I've got all the time in the world" for a conversation communicates to the seller that Buffett appreciates the value of the company that the seller has created, even though Buffett may not take the time to visit the production facilities. Cathy Baron Tamraz, the chief executive of Business Wire, which Buffett purchased in 2006, "was shocked" when she received a phone call from Buffett: "The moment is unforgettable! Warren was so down to earth and unpretentious that the phone call wasn't even dialed in by his assistant" [cited in Chan, 2010, pp. 13–14].

When acquiring (also with the help of Irv Blumkin) Star Furniture, a furniture retailer in Texas, Buffett sent a telegram to Melvyn Wolff, the company's owner: "MELVYN . . . MY ENTHUSIASM FOR OUR MARRIAGE DWARFS THE SIZE OF THIS TELEGRAM. YOUR PARTNER FOR LIFE. WARREN" [cited in Miles, 2002, p. 199]. Buffett is certainly appropriately positioned to create a sense of camaraderie in his relationships with other successful businesspeople.

Expressing admiration for an entrepreneur's work may have helped Buffett to sell an unsuccessful investment. Longing for a compliment from Buffett may have led to unreasonable transactions. When Buffett owned Salomon, the Travelers Group (then a large insurance company and the parent of Smith Barney) showed interest in acquiring the investment bank. The head of Travelers, Sanford Weill, insisted on becoming the head of the combined organization after the merger.[5] Buffett was indifferent as to who would take charge; he simply wanted an exit from the investment. Weill offered Buffett $9 billion. Buffett found this offer satisfactory. "Ever diplomatic, Buffett praised Weill as a 'genius' at building shareholder value. 'Weill's underlings were aghast that he had paid so much for a second-rate firm, particularly one in which the primary' source of profits was arbitrage which the chairman detested. One house jester snickered, 'Sandy spent nine billion dollars to get a piece of paper from Warren Buffett saying what a great investor he was. He was running around showing it to people like a kid in a candy store,'" wrote Lowenstein [Lowenstein, 2002, p. 115].

It turns out that it was Weill himself who asked for this piece of paper:

> Just before the Salomon directors were to vote on the deal, Sandy asked Bob Denham to get a quote from Buffett to put in the news release that was being prepared. Buffett took a piece of paper and began writing by hand: "Over several decades, Sandy has demonstrated genius in creating huge value for his shareholders and skillfully implementing . . ." He stopped to scratch out "implementing" and wrote "blending" over it, then continued, "and managing acquisitions in the financial-services industry. In my view, Salomon will be no exception." Denham took the paper back to the telephone to read the quote to Sandy. "Will you save it for me, the actual piece of paper?" Sandy implored. As soon as he got his hands on it, Sandy had the paper framed for his office. [Langley, 2003, p. 269]

Another commentator offered an explanation as to why Weill overpaid for Salomon. Under Buffett's supervision, Salomon's financial results were lackluster, as they had been influenced by the preceding scandals, which we discuss in Chapter 11. Weill may have seen this as a chance to beat Buffett at his own game [Schroeder, 2008, p. 655].

Not sparing compliments, Buffett also publicly admired John Gutfreund, the chairman of Salomon's board of directors, under whose

---

5 In recent years, the company has proceeded to acquire and merge with other businesses in the financial sector.

supervision the bank had been nearly bankrupted. Buffett remarked a number of times that he had invested in Salomon not least because the bank had been headed by "an outstanding, honorable man of integrity" [cited in Schroeder, 2008, p. 543]. The *Los Angeles Times* observed that Buffett "hit the roof" when Gutfreund came to Salomon's board of directors' compensation committee with a plan to boost bonuses by $120 million at a time when Salomon was struggling [Grant, 1992]. Of course, Buffett must have been aware of the Gutfreund couple's extravagant lifestyle. Gutfreund's wife, Susan, "led 'nouvelle society.' Whether redecorating her Fifth Avenue apartment at a reputed cost of $20 million, booking two seats on the Concorde to fly a cake to Paris for her husband's sixtieth birthday, or sending out invitations styled 'At home' to a party at Blenheim Palace, the extravagances of 'Social Susie' became the talk of the town. The former air-hostess amused the world with the gaucheries. 'It's like living in a fairy tale,' she told the *New York Times*" [Chancellor, 2000, p. 261]. For this lifestyle, the press christened Gutfreund's wife "Marie Antoinette" [Schroeder, 2008, p. 615]. Buffett, who leads an almost ascetic lifestyle, is unlikely to have admired this.

The story of Buffett's acquisition of a large stake in American Express in 1991 is poignant in light of the aspects of his strategy that we have been discussing in this chapter. Roger Lowenstein provides a detailed account. After the start of the Iraq War of 1991, the stock market collapsed. The CEO of American Express, Jim Robinson, called Buffett and proposed that Buffett buy a large stake in the company. American Express was in difficulties because its CEO had misspent the profits on ill-judged acquisitions in insurance, brokerage, and an art gallery. Robinson also had succumbed to the fashion for financial supermarkets and, spending $4 billion, bought Shearson. The managerial oversight of Shearson was weak; for example, it had managed to buy a conference center at a ski resort. Shearson continually needed cash infusions. American Express also had a penchant for pretending that nothing was amiss. Robinson kept up appearances with the help of a vigorous PR department and overly friendly board of directors. Buffett could hardly have been uninformed of Robinson's exploits. At an earlier time, when GEICO had bought a stake in American Express, Buffett had expressed his reservations to GEICO's management: "Robinson's record was a compendium of the managerial sins" that Buffett despised. However, when Robinson reached out to Buffett, it was as if no transgressions had ever occurred. Buffett came to New York immediately after hearing that the company's credit rating had been lowered. "Robinson asked for a $300 million investment, Buffett quickly agreed" [Lowenstein, 1996, pp. 365–366]. Buffett proposed $500 million, but Robinson refused. In Lowenstein's view, "It is hard to account for his [Buffett's] saying 'We're buying to be in with Jim' [Robinson].[6] Buffett's friends were stunned" [Lowenstein, 1996, p. 366]. Buffett did not join the board of directors of American Express, as he would ordinarily do when he made such a substantial investment. Robinson was politically correct when he expressed his opinion on Buffett's decision in *USA Today*. Robinson felt that there was no need for Buffett to join the board. His advice would have been listened to in any case. The board would have welcomed Buffett, but he was already serving on a number of boards, including Salomon's, which was a competitor of Shearson. Buffett's calendar would already have been full [Kilpatrick, 2005, p. 854].

Buffett bought preferred shares with a guaranteed dividend of 8.85 percent and obligatory conversion in three years. The conversion coefficient would be reduced so that the market price of the stake at conversion would not exceed $414 million if the share price should rise. In the event of the share price falling below a certain level, the conversion could be postponed for a year, but no floor was provided for the value of the stake [Buffett, 1977–2013, 1991]. Buffett explained his investment in American Express by saying that "it's what's available at the time" ["For Buffett, Amex Is a Great Place to Stash Cash," 1991].

Soon after Buffett became a shareholder in American Express, the company started restructuring. In 1992, a new CEO, Harvey Golub, took charge of the company. Jim Robinson moved to head Lehman Brothers, which was leaving the group. In 1993, Shearson was sold to Primerica. The spin-off of Lehman Brothers, which had originally been acquired in 1984, was announced the next year. In 1994, Buffett's stake in AmEx was converted into common shares. American Express

6 Interview with *BusinessWeek* magazine [cited in "For Buffett, Amex Is a Great Place to Stash Cash," 1991].

refocused on its main business—travelers' cheques, credit cards, and tourist services. As a result, the company's share price rose by five times over the period from 1994 to 2000. As part of the spin-off of Lehman Brothers, the shareholders also received its shares.

Joel Greenblatt offers an excellent study of the American Express story. He argues that the magnitude of the stock price growth resulting from the restructuring could have been quantified with the help of a calculator [Greenblatt, 1997, pp. 94–99]. In his assessment of Lehman Brothers, Greenblatt does not cover the bank's financials; however, taking them into account would make his argument even stronger. Lehman's profits were very volatile and often negative. Spinning off Lehman undoubtedly made American Express's shares more attractive. Buffett not only still owns his original AmEx stake, but also has increased it to 14.2 percent [Buffett, 1977–2013, 2013]. He describes his investment in the company as permanent. Since 1994, the shares have risen by approximately 10 times if we take stock splits into account. The company has regularly paid dividends. It is understandable why Buffett has viewed this investment as economically reasonable, although at the outset he seemingly acted against his own principles. The ending of Lehman's story requires no retelling.

Indirect Influence

> This guy made a lot of money by backing up the truck.
> —JOHN BYRNE [CITED IN LOWENSTEIN, 1996, P. 199]

A nonfriendly acquisition is not negative in and of itself. Nonfriendly acquisitions are a threat to a company whose management is ineffective, so that a change of management could lead to an increase in company value. Nonfriendly acquisitions are nonfriendly with respect to the management, but may be very friendly toward the shareholders, who gain from the increase in the stock price. Nonfriendly acquisitions can be a healthy market mechanism for transferring organizations from ineffective to effective managers. The buyer acts as the agent of positive change. In my view, it is unlikely that Buffett's personal, ethical, or other convictions do not allow him to engage in nonfriendly acquisitions. Perhaps he does not pursue these opportunities because it is a different kind of strategy altogether. It is not a matter of leaving everything as it is with the same manager, who remains a minority shareholder, but one of possibly intensive restructuring and implementing a new management structure that lacks historical ties to the business. Buffett has created a very specific niche that has practically become a self-perpetuating moneymaking machine. Engaging in other kinds of investing might disturb his preferred niche. Also, perhaps there is a white-knight-in-shining-armor element to Buffett's strategy, and it may be valuable to him to ensure that this image remains untarnished, although a reputation for being a skillful hostile acquirer does not necessarily clash with that of a parent company owner who entrusts the managers of his subsidiaries with a job for life.

In fact, Buffett does make money on hostile takeovers, but mostly as a neutral participant. He made a profit on acquisitions by others of Beatrice, Federated Department Stores, Kraft, Interco, Southland, and other companies. He also profited from KKR's purchase of RJR Nabisco [Kilpatrick, 2005, p. 353].

In Chapter 2, we discussed an insightful example of a situation in which Buffett started buying the shares of a public company that was, in his view, undervalued, but stopped the acquisition process at the request of the controlling manager-owner. Buffett began buying the shares of the Washington Post Company in 1973 during a period when the share price was slumping. He quickly built up a stake of approximately 12 percent of the outstanding equity at a cost of $10.6 million. This implied a total capitalization of the company of $88 million. Buffett valued the company at upwards of $400 million. He became the largest shareholder of the Washington Post Company after the Graham family, the main owners of the holding.

Katharine Graham started managing the holding company in 1963. Her father, Eugene Meyer, had bought the paper in 1933. Mrs. Graham hardly knew Buffett. Although he had acquired Class B shares, which had far more limited voting rights than the Class A shares that the Graham family owned, she was concerned. Buffett, aware of her reservations about his purchase, wrote her a letter in which he reminisced that as a boy, he used to deliver her paper, the *Washington Post*, and assured her that he did not intend to seek control of the company. The letter did not allay Katharine's concerns. Her advisors recommended that she keep her distance from Buffett. Nevertheless, she asked him for a meeting, which soon took place.

Buffett had been seeking to meet Graham for a long time. In 1971, he asked Charles Peters of the *Washington Monthly* to introduce him to her. At the time, Buffett owned a small stake in the *New Yorker* magazine. He thought that the magazine might become available for sale and that Graham might turn out to be the natural buyer [Kilpatrick, 2005, pp. 409–410, 413].

After the meeting, Buffett offered to suspend his buying of the shares. Buffett's biographers comment that he felt that the personal meeting and various assurances on his part would not be sufficient to calm the situation. However, his offer to abandon his buying program broke the ice, and Buffett and Graham developed a close friendship. Buffett did not try to increase his stake in the Washington Post Company, but he did recommend the shares to his friends.

Graham had become the head of the company by accident after her husband's untimely death following a mental illness. She turned out to be a successful business manager, but she felt that there was no one in her entourage whom she could rely on entirely [Lowenstein, 1996, p. 185]. Those who knew her mention that she "desperately needed a friend" [Lowenstein, 1996, p. 187]. This is understandable, especially given the tense political and economic situation that we discussed in earlier chapters. Buffett acted simultaneously in all three capacities— friend, confidant, and expert advisor. Soon Graham invited Buffett to join the company's board of directors. His shares did not give him the right to vote, but his membership on the board did. In essence, Buffett was invited to walk in through the wide-open gate after he had declared that he was not going to climb over the fence.

Buffett assisted both Katharine and her son, Don, with managerial decisions. They turned out to be keen students of his teachings and became converts to his philosophy. Don Graham mentions that first his mother and then he discussed all significant decisions with Buffett before taking any action. The family found that "fortunately" Buffett did not disagree with them when they felt particularly strongly about doing something, but that Buffett materially "influenced" their opinions on valuations. He openly expressed his views when he thought something was overpriced. This prevented the family from overpaying. Invariably, Buffett proved to be right. Those who overpaid eventually ended up regretting the acquisitions [cited in Miles, 2002, pp. 145–146]. Katharine refused the offer to purchase a regional paper, the *Louisville Courier-Journal*, when another large publisher, showed interest. In Buffett's view, the price was catastrophically high [Lowenstein, 1996, p. 187]. When the Washington Post Company avoided unintelligent purchases with Buffett's help, this positively influenced the share price performance of his holdings. We have already discussed another aspect of Buffett's assistance to the company: with Buffett's advice, the *Post* took market share from its competitor in Washington.

The extent of Buffett's influence on the Graham family becomes apparent through examination of the structure of the company's board of directors. At some point, the board was made up of Don and Katharine Graham; Buffett; Dan Burke, a former CEO of Capital Cities/ABC, a major Berkshire investment; Don Keough, a former president of Coca-Cola, another major Buffett investment; and Bill Ruane, manager of Sequoia Fund, a large Berkshire shareholder, and Buffett's Columbia classmate. "It's as if Buffett picked the board of directors"[7] [Miles, 2002, p. 140].

It is in Buffett's style to offer a view on price, but not to comment directly on whether an acquisition is worthwhile. This is how he assisted the management of other companies in which he was a shareholder. John Byrne, the CEO of GEICO in the 1970s, remembers that Buffett showed him "sensible ways to finance. He was generous with his time. But he never—ever—made suggestions" [Lowenstein, 1996, p. 199]. In Byrne's opinion, this was a conscious choice on Buffett's part: it was apparent that Buffett felt that it was possible to make a lot of money by being a benign presence [Lowenstein, 1996, p. 199].

Buffett's friendship with Katharine Graham must have been fair compensation for all the uncollected dividends and profits. Given

---

7 In more recent times, the composition of the board has changed. Buffett left in 2011. See, for instance, http://www.diversityinc.com/diversity-recruitment/melinda-gates-leaves-post-board-after-report-criticizes-kaplan/.

family connections, Katharine was able to introduce Buffett to a wide circle of people. She would have recommended him as a helpful and loyal investor. Those who knew Katharine thought that she "widened his circle enormously"; "the Washington Post really changed his life" [Lowenstein, 1996, p. 188]. A very successful but nevertheless provincial businessman from Omaha was introduced to Henry Kissinger and others in the political elite. Roger Lowenstein comments that Buffett "did not like splashy affairs, but he liked meeting bigwigs in the controlled setting of Graham's home" [Lowenstein, 1996, p. 188]. No doubt Katharine would have made inquiries about Buffett prior to their first personal meeting. It is likely that she would have received only positive references. This must have helped her decision to allow him into her personal circle.

*   *   *

Perhaps Buffett has achieved his extraordinary investment success precisely because his strategy is very complex. It involves deep understanding and use of psychology. Walter Schloss was right when he said that Buffett is a very good judge of people. The strategy also includes a powerful self-promoting PR operation. Never failing to express admiration for a furniture store, Buffett does not discount the slightest aspect of his strategy, however apparently insignificant. At the same time, he does not seem to bet on any one factor in particular, whether it is his ability to analyze a business or the psychology of his counterparts in his transactions, even though he is able to do both of these with formidable accuracy.

9

Buffett as a Strategic and Portfolio Investor

For the right business—and the right
people—we can provide a good home.

—WARREN BUFFETT [BUFFETT, 1977–2013, 1983–1987]

Strategic or Financial Investor?

We don't sell. We have an entrance strategy,
but we have no exit strategy.

—WARREN BUFFETT [CITED IN KILPATRICK, 2005, P. 770]

Financial theory argues that the best price for a business will be paid by the investor for whom the business has the highest value; such an investor is typically a strategic buyer, one who, unlike a financial investor, may have a synergy with the business that is being acquired. For this synergy to be realized, however, the investor must integrate the acquired business into the structure of the investor's existing business. For the great majority of companies, this strategic buyer is another company from the same industry—a direct competitor. A financial investor aspires to add value to the business fairly quickly either by making investments that stimulate growth or by improving the business in the areas where the financial investor may have particular expertise, for instance in financial management. The financial investor will sooner or later sell the business to a strategic investor. For the financial investor, this resale is the objective of the original acquisition.

An entrepreneur who has given all her life to growing her business and has become very wealthy in the process, even without including the funds that she could obtain if she sold her creation, would prefer that her business continue to operate as an independent entity and retain its name. If the business under consideration is truly excellent, then its sale to a competitor may be too generous a gift. The situation is aggravated if the competitor buying the business intends to restructure it in order to reduce competition with its own products. In addition, business proprietors may also feel responsible for their employees. As for a sale to a financial investor, if all is well with the business, then what is the point of giving someone else the opportunity to earn a substantial amount on a resale in three to five years after some restructuring? Buffett's strategy of acquiring family businesses relies on the pool of business owners for whom the sale of the business to a competitor may be psychologically too difficult. Here Buffett's neutrality plays a role. He is the most acceptable buyer because he is not a strategic investor in the strict sense of the word, as he is not a competitor. Buffett is not a financial investor, either. He promises to own the business for eternity. Buffett interacts with the emotional affection of the business founder for her creation.

As we have discussed, Buffett is not a financial investor because he will not sell the acquired asset. At the same time, however, he is a financial investor because he is not a competitor of the company he is buying. He is not a strategic investor because he does not choose to pursue the synergies among his subsidiaries, but he is a strategic investor because he intends to own his companies forever. This position is critically important to his strategy of inexpensive purchases. The motley collection of companies that he owns form a conglomerate—the type of organization that financial theory views as the most deserving of criticism. In Buffett's case, the structure is beneficial. He created a market niche: a "home" for mature companies whose owners wish to convert their business assets into a liquid form. Perhaps this is where Buffett's true genius resides. He emphasizes this specificity of Berkshire's in a letter to a business owner who was interested in selling his company. Indeed, Buffett points out, if "the sole motive" of the owners is "to cash their chips and put the business behind" them, then "either type of buyer . . . is satisfactory." But often price, while very important, is not the most critical aspect of the sale. The type of buyer is most important "if the sellers' business represents the creative work of a lifetime and forms an integral part of their personality and sense of being" [Buffett, 1977–2013, 1990].

The purchase in 1986 of 84 percent of the shares of Fechheimer, a manufacturer of work clothes and uniforms, is a good example of Buffett's unique positioning as a buyer. The company belonged to a family of entrepreneurs who had been managing it for several genera-tions. The owners wanted to withdraw capital from the enterprise, but they also wanted to retain a small stake and continue exercising opera-tional control. The owners insisted that the buyer not sell the business after the purchase, even if she would receive an attractive price. Buffett commented that from the point of view of the seller's motivation, this acquisition was the same as the sale of Nebraska Furniture Mart. In my view, the valuation was also similar. Fechheimer had pretax earnings of $8.4 million. Buffett bought it at a valuation of $55 million [Buffett, 1977–2013, 1986], or at a price to pretax earnings multiple of 6.1.

Ed Bridge, the owner of Ben Bridge Jeweler, a chain of 65 jewelry stores in the western part of the United States, sold his business to Berkshire in 2000. He noted that he sold his company at a low price. Negotiations with Buffett had already begun when a strategic buyer who was able to offer 20 percent more than Berkshire was offering showed an interest. Although Bridge was confident that the other buyer would pay substantially more, Bridge also felt that he probably would have "destroyed the business" if he "had gone that way" [cited in Loomis, 2001].

The Tatelman brothers, who sold Jordan's Furniture to Buffett, admit that they could have sold the business for a higher price. One of the brothers explained: "Barry and I realize we can have pretty much any-thing we want. But it reaches a point where you ask yourself, 'How much more do I need, and for what?' We like doing this—we are still negoti-ating deals, we're doing; we like the challenge and the excitement of it, but it's not so much the money anymore" [cited in Miles, 2002, p. 221].

The owner of Helzberg Diamonds, Barnett Helzberg, who wanted to sell his business specifically to Buffett, spoke similarly. He was con-fident that he could trust Buffett to keep the headquarters in Kansas City, not alter the company's character, and continue to provide jobs to all its employees. Helzberg felt strongly that he "did not want my associates spitting on my grave." It might have been easier to sell the company to the highest bidder, "but this notion seemed as sensible as choosing a brain surgeon based on the lowest price rather than on talent and reputation" [Helzberg, 2003, p. xvii].

Let us look at some of the reasons behind the sales and why it may be so important to sell to a certain kind of buyer. Forward-looking entrepreneurs sell their businesses when they still have the energy and interest to remain in charge, rather than near the natural end of their professional life. An earlier sale is also more beneficial from a tax point of view. If a company is sold after the owner's death, it is very hard for that business to survive. The heirs are likely to have to pay two taxes: the capital gains tax and, from the remaining sum, the inheritance tax. In most cases, high taxes make it impossible for family companies to be inherited, as the heirs do not have sufficient resources to keep the company going and pay the taxes. The business has to be sold at a time when the new owners are in constrained circumstances. The sellers do not have a strong negotiating position. When the business is sold before the death of the owner, the capital gains tax and the inheritance tax are separated in time, and it is easier to pay the taxes, as the capital is liquid. In addition, some of the cash can be transferred to heirs without paying taxes. From a tax point of view, a sale through a merger is better still, as the business is "sold" in exchange for shares of another company and the sale is not subject to capital gains tax. Only the inheritance tax remains upon the owner's death. Buffett has sometimes agreed to buy businesses in exchange for Berkshire shares. For instance, Dexter Shoe (1993), Dairy Queen (1997), Star Furniture (1997), and Executive Jet (1998) were purchased fully or in part in exchange for Berkshire shares.

The owners of Star Furniture, Melvyn Wolff and his sister Shirley Tomin, describe their motives in selling the company to Berkshire in exchange for Class B shares. "This was an opportunity to get liquidity without losing control and management," says Wolff. "I think the federal estate tax [the inheritance tax would have amounted to 55 percent] is a concern of all family-owned businesses" [Elder, 1997]. If the inheritance had been in the form of shares of the company itself, then the heirs would have had to sell the company to pay the inheritance tax. It would have been a forced sale, and it would have had to be done quickly. The buyers, most likely, would have been leveraged buyout (LBO) specialists who would have burdened the company with substantial amounts of debt, and the business would have ceased to function in its original form. After the sale to Berkshire, should the need to pay inheritance tax arise, the heirs could sell some of their Berkshire shares, and this sale would not affect Star Furniture's business [Miles, 2002, p. 205].

Berkshire shares are well suited for such transactions. First, they are highly liquid. Second, given Berkshire's broad business diversification, holding shares in the conglomerate exposes the holders to the more reliable parts of the stock market. Third, through the transaction with Berkshire, the business seller receives a large stake in Berkshire at a fixed price. Accumulating such a stake on the open market would possibly result in a higher weighted-average purchase price. Fourth, until recently, Berkshire shares have always beaten the market. A transaction with Berkshire also solves the problem of investing the free cash that is received during the sale of the business. There are so many advantages that it may make sense to sell one's business to Berkshire at a discount.

Buffett has been aware of the potential tax advantages involved in selling a business to Berkshire. In November 1985, he advertised that he was ready to buy businesses valued at more than $100 million and close the transaction by the end of the year. The deadline was very important. In 1986, the taxes on the sale of a business would rise to 52.2 percent. A significant savings on taxes would have been possible if a business could be sold by the end of 1985. Buffett advertised himself as a buyer who had cash ready and could act with extraordinary speed [Kilpatrick, 2005, p. 1223]. This particular advertising campaign was not successful. Subsequently, Buffett closed many transactions in which the seller's main motive was the transfer of family assets between generations. In addition to the Star Furniture and Fechheimer acquisitions, these transactions included, according to the business sellers or CEOs, Justin Industries, Jordan's Furniture, and Pampered Chef [Chan, 2010, pp. 63, 70, 107]. Borsheim's was probably also a sale of this kind. Its owner died shortly after the transaction.

Of course, the acquisition of other companies in exchange for Berkshire shares dilutes Buffett's ownership in the conglomerate. In order to encourage those who are more neutral with regard to the tax question to receive cash, he sometimes suggests asymmetrical pricing. For example, for one share of FlightSafety International, Buffett offered one Berkshire share, which at the time traded at $48, or $50 in cash [Kilpatrick, 2005, p. 610]. For one share of Dairy Queen, he offered $27 in cash or $26 in Berkshire stock [Kilpatrick, 2005, p. 619]. Now he uses Class B shares, which are nonvoting.

Buffett has other competitive advantages as a buyer. He has deep pockets. He would never finance a transaction through borrowing and use the acquired shares as collateral, nor would he borrow against the acquired assets after a transaction. Borrowing against assets can lead to the destruction of those assets. It is this mindset that distinguishes Buffett from other buyers of companies and from funds in particular. This was the decisive factor for Bill Child when he was contemplating the decision to sell RC Willey. Child remembers that he had had more than one other offer to buy his company, but he did not like them because none of them was bringing a lot of cash. One buyer was offering a split, with approximately 50 percent of the purchase being financed by cash and the rest being borrowed against the company. In this case, the company would end up burdened by a substantial financial obligation. Others were willing to talk to Child about stock, but he did not feel "comfortable" about their businesses [cited in Miles, 2002, p. 186]. In the end, the company was sold to Berkshire Hathaway in exchange for Berkshire shares. This arrangement avoided taxes on the transaction. For the sake of preserving some residual ownership and as a motivation for the managers, one of the stores remained with the Child family and was leased to Berkshire.

Buffett offers his own summary. Berkshire "can do things other companies can't do" and "no American company can do," specifically, "arrange the transfer of some of the ownership of the business to another generation." Buffett "can promise it [the business] won't get resold" [Buffett, 1991b]. He controls Berkshire's board of directors, so no one will be able to tell him to dispose of any particular business.

Buffett's acquisition of 50 percent of Heinz in 2013 is an interesting diversion from this type of acquisition. The other 50 percent of the company was acquired by the fund 3G Capital, which was known for its aggressive management style. During the sale, it was announced that the future management of the company had not been determined and that the fund would manage the company [Jargon and Ng, 2013]. After the sale, a *Wall Street Journal* article reported: "Just a few days after the deal closed in June, Heinz executives gathered for their annual leadership meeting at a swanky San Francisco hotel. The newly named chief executive, Bernardo Hees, announced the replacement of nearly all the top executives with subordinates or 3G's own people" [Gasparino, 2014]. The article continued with a dramatic account of drastic personnel reductions and plant closures. Analysts attributed the necessity for deep cost cuts partially to the changing consumer preferences toward fresh foods, consumer expenditure reductions during the financial crisis, and other economic factors. This was probably the first M&A transaction in which Buffett was not selling the idea of a good home for the right companies. Buffett's strategy may be changing with his age. Naturally, the older one becomes, the more complicated it is to issue personal guarantees. By extension, is it arguable that the core of Buffett's business is personal guarantees?

White Knight Defense

> You better have a nine-hundred-pound gorilla.
> —**WARREN BUFFETT [CITED IN LOWENSTEIN, 1996, P. 261]**

Buffett buys minority stakes in large public companies when they are attractive from an investment point of view but may be too large for him to buy them in their entirety—they would be too expensive, or it would be too difficult to gain control. Sometimes he buys shares on the open market. Sometimes he reaches an agreement with the issuer directly about buying a stake through a private investment in public equity (PIPE). Analysts debate whether Buffett succeeds in buying these stocks on better terms than other investors and whether he is able to achieve these terms because of his reputation.

Linda Sandler, a journalist, thought that the answer to these questions was yes. In 1989, she published an article in the *Wall Street Journal* titled "Buffett's Savior Role Lands Him Deals Other Holders Can't Get" [Sandler, 1989]. She referred to three well-known PIPE transactions with convertible preferred stock: the investments of $700 million in Salomon Brothers in 1987 and of $358 million and $600 million in USAir and Gillette, respectively, in 1989. All the transactions were "white knight" defenses against hostile takeovers. Sandler explains that Buffett acted as a protector against the "so-called quick-buck artists." He did not show "any inclination to pursue a Trojan Horse strategy." Had he tried to gain control, this would have tarnished his image as a friendly investor.

Until Buffett acquired a stake in the company, USAir was viewed as a target for a hostile takeover by a hedge fund managed by Michael Steinhardt. Salomon Brothers was also concerned about the risk of an approach from Ronald Perelman. Gillette had been targeted a number of times. Convertible bonds or convertible preferred stock became widespread in the 1980s as a defense mechanism against nonfriendly LBO takeovers financed through junk bonds [Dunbar, 2000].

In Sandler's view, all three transactions were completed at prices lower than what would have been achievable on the open market. The dividends on the preferred shares (9.25 percent for USAir, 9 percent for Salomon, and 8.75 percent for Gillette), according to analysts' estimates, were high. Conversion premiums (15 percent for USAir, 12 to 13 percent for Salomon, and 20 percent for Gillette) were low. Sandler thought that in a market placement, the convertible preferred stock could have been sold with a premium of 20 to 25 percent. Indeed, in the case of Salomon Brothers, Perelman was proposing to buy the convertibles on better terms than those at which the bonds were sold to Buffett: he offered the same price for a smaller stake—10.9 percent vs. 12 percent

[Coles, 1987]. Carol Loomis, a friend of Buffett's, observed that within Salomon, the opinion was widespread that "Buffett had exploited Gutfreund's fear of Perelman and had secured a dream security, with a too-high dividend or a too-low conversion price or some combination thereof. Over the next few years, this opinion did not die at Salomon, and more than once executives of the firm (though never Gutfreund) came to Buffett with propositions for deep-sixing the preferred" [Loomis and Atanasov, 1997]. Indeed, in this transaction, it was certainly taken into account that he was friendly toward the management of the bank, since he bought the securities on terms that were less beneficial for the company than those offered by Perelman.

Another analyst who shares the view that Buffett entered into these transactions on highly beneficial terms is Allan Sloan, a former *Newsday* columnist and currently a senior editor at large at *Fortune* magazine. According to the terms of Buffett's investment in Gillette, one preferred share, costing $1,000, could be converted into 20 ordinary shares at $50 a share, with mandatory conversion in 10 years. The guaranteed dividends on the preferred shares were 8.75 percent (on $50), or $4.375 annually [Buffett, 1977–2013, 1989]. Sloan argued that since the stock was trading at $41⅝ at the time of the deal, the difference between the stock market price and the implied stock price was $8⅜, or 20 percent. Regular dividends that the company paid on common stock amounted to $0.96 a share. Dividends on the preferred stock were approximately $3.40 higher than the dividends on the common stock. Buffett would have been compensated for the difference between the common stock price and the implied stock price in less than 2½ years. In Sloan's view, on average, the payback period for comparable instruments would have been 3½ years. For the payback period for Buffett to equal 3½ years, the preferred-to-common stock conversion price should have been set at $53¼. Buffett benefited by 7 percent in comparison to market conditions. Both Buffett and the management of Gillette commented on Sloan's calculations and agreed with his numbers, but not with his conclusions. In Gillette's view, some specific conditions of the deal (in particular, the issuer's ability to call for an early redemption and the right of first refusal to buy Buffett's stock should he decide to sell) balanced out the relatively high interest and the low conversion price.

Thus the terms of the transaction were not dissimilar to market valuations [Kilpatrick, 2005, p. 840]. In fact, Gillette asked for the redemption in 1991, and Buffett converted his preferred stock into common shares. Robert Hagstrom reports that the $600 million of the original investment was valued at $875 million as a result of the conversion [Hagstrom, 2005, p. 53].

In order to get a better sense of the conditions of the deal, let us examine Gillette's circumstances at the time. James Altucher, an author, investor, entrepreneur, and connoisseur of Buffett's investment strategy, found that Gillette was operating under difficult conditions. The revenue was growing at a rate of 1 percent a year, the share price was stagnating, and the company had been forced to increase its debt burden to fend off hostile takeover attempts. Altucher believed that this company did not fit Buffett's investment criteria [Altucher, 2005, p. 133].

Many analysts felt that Gillette was not realizing its potential. Starting in 1986, Ronald Perelman made three hostile attempts to gain control of the company. He had previously taken over Revlon. Gillette won the battles against him at a huge cost, buying out Perelman's stakes at a premium. In 1988, Perelman was followed by Coniston Group, which wanted to gain control of the company through the board of directors. Gillette won the proxy battle by only a small margin [Ricardo-Campbell, 1997, p. 7].

An insider—a Gillette director, Rita Ricardo-Campbell—later disclosed that the investment bankers advising the company thought that $600 million would be a hard amount to find. There had been no placements in this volume, and an investor would be likely to demand 25 percent annually. In addition, Gillette did not have alternative offers, and Buffett was attractive as an investor because he did not engage in unfriendly takeovers. In a standstill agreement, he promised Gillette that for at least 10 years, he would not join with any other group holding 5 percent or more of the stock [Ricardo-Campbell, 1997, pp. 208, 212, 214]. Coniston Group's ability to influence the board's decisions would be sharply curtailed by Buffett, who would hold 11 percent of the stock and be a member of the board. "By one major investment he could remove Gillette as a target of the takeover wars" [Ricardo-Campbell, 1997, p. 209]. "I do not recall long discussions during the

June and July board meetings that Gillette would gain because of Buffett's investment. Probably it was so obvious to all concerned that it did not warrant discussion. Gillette needed a quiet period to conduct its business. Gillette had continued to be a target of takeover speculation up to the Buffett investment. . . . To me it was amazing how many of the board members knew of the reputation of Warren Buffett" [Ricardo-Campbell, 1997, p. 214]. Perhaps it is not surprising that the members of the board were aware of Buffett's reputation: he had already defended Salomon from the same attacker through the same means.

According to *Warren Buffett Speaks: Wit and Wisdom from the World's Greatest Investor,* by Janet Lowe, Buffett's investments in USAir and Salomon Brothers ended up being, by his standards, relatively unsuccessful [Lowe, 2007]. USAir found itself in near bankruptcy and stopped paying dividends on the preferred stock. Buffett wrote off $268.5 million of the $358 million original investment [Buffett, 1977–2013, 1995]. Subsequently, the company's operations improved, the previously unpaid dividends were paid, and the paper loss became an accounting transaction. Buffett admitted that he had "bought into a high-cost airline thinking it was protected . . . but that was before [the low-cost airline] Southwest Airlines showed up." USAir's costs amounted to 12 cents per passenger-mile, where Southwest's were 8 cents [Matthews, 2009, p. 84].

The Salomon Brothers investment was affected by the 1991 scandal, which we touched on briefly in Chapter 4. The scandal was widely publicized. The SEC accused one of the bank's traders, Paul Mozer, of trading government bonds in a way that breached regulations. The violations were so serious that they could have led to the bank's liquidation. The managers of Salomon reached out to Buffett, with his superb reputation as "Mr. Clean," and asked him to become chairman of the board of directors. Buffett was compelled to agree. As a result of his running the organization for a number of months—his description of the experience to Berkshire investors as "far from fun" became well known—the bank was saved from liquidation. Buffett held part of his Salomon investment for 10 years, until the company was acquired by Travelers Group. According to some estimates, he increased his investment by 2½ times [Janjigian, 2008, p. 127], or achieved a 10 percent annualized return—the minimum required return for an investment, from Buffett's point of view at that time.[1]

In both of these cases, USAir and Salomon, Buffett did not convert all of his investment into common stock after the company's performance improved. Perhaps, this is an indirect indication that Buffett did not view the common stock as being able to deliver his required returns.

In 2005, Buffett had to convert his Gillette shares into those of Procter & Gamble after it acquired Gillette. Buffett's stake amounted to $5.6 billion [Buffett, 1977–2013, 2005]. Pretax return on the investment amounted to 14 percent annualized. This return resulted from the share price growth and the 20 percent premium that was paid for Gillette shares in the acquisition. Buffett had also been collecting dividends. This was, indeed, a very good investment.

In Lowenstein's view, Buffett's terms may have been viewed as more beneficial than those that could have been attained by a more ordinary investor, but nevertheless his terms were not as advantageous as various critics wanted to imagine. He had to commit for 10 years in each deal. Such duration would have been regarded by the investor community as extremely long and many investors would have likely passed by such opportunities [Lowenstein, 1996, p. 356].

A lesser-known investment in Champion International, a pulp and paper company, was also a defense against a takeover. In 1989, Buffett bought $300 million of preferred stock with a 9.25 percent dividend, a conversion price of $38 (the market price of the stock was $30, so the conversion price implied a 27 percent premium), and a term of 10 years. Substantial timber reserves with a market value of approximately $2.5 billion guaranteed that the company would be able to pay off its debt. The reserves also served as a hedge against inflation. In 1995, the

---

1 I found it difficult to locate the data to calculate the return accurately. The preferred shares carried a 9 percent dividend, which was paid. A portion of the preferred shares was converted into common stock. Some stock was sold. Buffett also bought additional stock once Salomon's circumstances began to improve. It is this total stake that was eventually converted into the Travelers stock. The *New York Times* assessed the investment. It thought that Buffett kept $420 million out of the original $700 million investment, and on this residual stake he earned 16 percent as of the time of the company's sale to Travelers. The Travelers stake was not reflected in Buffett's annual reports after 1997.

preferred shares were converted into common stock and then sold back to the company. Berkshire achieved a return on investment of around 19 percent after tax, or 4.4 percent annualized through the sale, in addition to the main part of the income that was received through the dividends [Buffett, 1977–2013, 1995]. The return on this transaction could be viewed as acceptable. Eventually the company was acquired by International Paper.

In 1997, Austin Murphy, Robert Kleiman, and Kevin Nathan published an article in which they attempted to analyze the accuracy of the pricing of preferred stock issues based on the reaction of the securities markets [Murphy, Kleiman, and Nathan, 1997]. They evaluated the common stock price fluctuations around the date of the public announcement of new issues. Buffett made five deals involving preferred shares between the end of the 1980s and the early 1990s: American Express, Gillette, Salomon, USAir, and Champion. The shares of Gillette and Salomon reacted positively to the news. In the opinion of the researchers, this may have happened not only because the conditions of the share placement were more beneficial for the seller of the paper than for the buyer, but also for other reasons. The buyer's investment may have increased the value of the company or brought it positive publicity, since a professional investor had signaled to the market that the company was an attractive investment. In other cases, the market did not react to the news in any way. Overall, the research showed that if Buffett did receive any beneficial treatment in terms of pricing, then, in the market's view, he deserved it; however, why this is the case is a different question. Reputation, after all, costs money.

Buffett began acting in the capacity of a "white knight" at the end of the 1980s, when LBO-style acquisitions became fashionable. LBO specialists focused on buying large companies using little equity capital. These purchases were financed mainly through issuing junk bonds. Buffett was ideally positioned for the role of the defender. He had an excellent reputation. He did not need to raise capital from external sources, and he was able to act quickly. Roger Lowenstein commented: "For a desperate CEO, selling to Buffett could be a third route between succumbing to a raider and resorting to self-immolation via greenmail" [Lowenstein, 1996, p. 264].

Defense against unfriendly investors was also the reason why some family companies were acquired by Berkshire. In the case of FlightSafety International, the controlling shareholder's stake amounted to 37 percent. A biographer of Buffett reports that the purchase of this company in 1996 was a defensive step against a nonfriendly investor [Schroeder, 2008, p. 650]. The owner of one of the largest stakes in the company expressed his views more obliquely: "In recent years, I became concerned that once I exited the stage—say, maybe a hundred years from now—the company that we've built so carefully and so well could be taken over and parceled out by outsiders. I didn't want that to happen but wasn't sure what to do about it. Fortunately, my good luck held once again. Warren Buffett called" [Ueltschi, 1999]. The principal shareholder, Albert Ueltschi, was 78 years old at the time of the transaction, which could also have been a preparation for the transfer of inheritance. Ueltschi passed away in 2012.

We have already discussed Buffett's acquisition of Capital Cities in 1985 in some detail. Roger Lowenstein describes the conversation that took place between Buffett and the directors of Capital Cities, Thomas Murphy and Daniel Burke. By buying ABC, Cap Cities would have, oddly, made itself a target. Thomas Murphy wondered what to do about it. Buffett suggested that having a "gorilla" among the shareholders might help. By "gorilla" he meant somebody who would hold a large amount of stock, which he or she would be willing to sell under no circumstances. The executives asked whether Buffett would care to perform the "gorilla" service and he agreed. Later, Buffett commented that he had not been imagining himself in that position until the idea appeared, however the executives felt that indeed the opposite was the case [Lowenstein, 1996, p. 261]. Buffett might have deliberately prepared himself for this position. He made a price offer for the Capital Cities stake on the same day. This may possibly indicate that he had thought through the subject previously, and not only as part of his continuously ongoing marketwide due diligence, which we have discussed. After the transaction with Capital Cities, Buffett issued a power of attorney allowing Burke and Murphy to vote his shares. He legally agreed not to sell the shares without their permission.

In this light, the story of how the idea of investing in Gillette emerged is also insightful. Buffett was the party who initiated the deal.

One evening, when he was reading Gillette's annual reports—reading company annual reports is his favorite activity—he noticed that the company's net worth was negative and came to the conclusion that some additional shareholder capital might be of use to the company. He then proposed himself to Gillette as an investor [Buffett, 1991c].

Buffett's private investments in public equity at the start of this century had a different economic rationale: supplying companies and banks with financing when they were affected by crisis conditions in the economy. This was the motivation for his investments in Level 3 Communications, a telecom company that provided broadband (the company had been founded by one of the Berkshire directors); in Williams Companies, specializing in natural gas exploration; and in Goldman Sachs, a well-known investment bank.

Buffett's investment in Level 3 Communications took place in July 2002, after the collapse of the telecommunications bubble. The company's stock price had fallen from $100 to $2.89. The total investment by the investor consortium amounted to $500 million. Buffett's stake was $100 million. The interest was set at 9 percent, while the conversion price was $3.42 (an 18 percent premium to the market price at the time of the transaction). When the deal was announced, the market price rose to $4.26. In 2003, or 16 months after the deal, Buffett converted his shares and sold them. He explained his sale by saying that he did not feel comfortable holding telecom shares, as he did not know how to value them. In the opinion of analysts, Buffett made a 100 percent return on this deal ["Telecommunications: Buffett Company Cuts Level 3 Stake," 2003].

Buffett's investment in Williams in 2002 in the amount of $275 million was assistance to an energy company whose shares were under pressure after the collapse of Enron. The interest rate was set at 9.875 percent, and the conversion price at $18. The shares were trading at $16. Eventually Buffett exited this investment successfully, despite the fact that for part of this time, the company had been sustaining losses, and at one point the shares had fallen to $1. During this period of distress, an investor consortium again provided the company with an emergency loan. Buffett took part in this consortium, but his share was not disclosed.

In March 2007, Buffett was approached by Lehman Brothers, which asked for $4 billion. Buffett indicated the conditions on which he would be prepared to do the deal: preferred shares with a dividend of 9 percent and warrants to buy common shares at a price of $40. At the time, Lehman's shares were trading at a little less than $39. Having studied Lehman's financials, however, Buffett changed his mind. Andrew Sorkin, in his book *Too Big to Fail*, explains that after reading the reports, Buffett had too many questions. It is one of Buffett's principles that if there are a lot of questions, then it is better not to invest, even if these questions have answers [Sorkin, 2009, p. 74]. By autumn, the crisis had escalated. Lehman filed for bankruptcy on September 15, 2007. The crisis intensified further.

The next notable bank to ask Buffett for money was Goldman. This time Buffett did not refuse. The deal was signed for $5 billion in preferred shares, with dividends set at 10 percent. Buffett was also granted the right to buy, but no earlier than in 2013, common shares for another $5 billion at $115 a share. At the moment of the deal, Goldman shares were trading at approximately $110. The premium to market price amounted to 4.5 percent. In April 2011, Goldman requested the redemption of the preferred stock prior to term—this option had been agreed upon in the conditions of the deal—at a premium of 10 percent to the par value of the preferred shares. Buffett earned around $1.75 billion on dividends and premium for the early redemption. This amounted to 35 percent over 2½ years, or around 12.5 percent annually, which is a very good return on an investment in preferred shares. At the same time, the investment was made at the bottom of the market, when many investment banks were on the verge of bankruptcy and a number of them subsequently ceased to exist.[2] In 2013, Buffett exercised his right to buy Goldman shares at the pre-agreed-upon price. Having previously peaked at $170, the stock price at the beginning of the year had fallen to $130. The terms were adjusted. Goldman sold Buffett far fewer shares than had originally been agreed on, but at a lower price, so that the difference between the sale price and the market price created the same amount of profit as he would have received had

2 And it is, of course, doubtful that Goldman would have been able to survive without Buffett's investment and the government bailout of AIG, to which Goldman was exposed contractually to a considerable extent, as has been widely discussed.

he been able to exercise his right under the original agreement. As of the end of 2013, Berkshire holds on its balance sheet Goldman Sachs shares with a cost value of $750 million and a market value of $2.3 billion.

We can probably agree with Michael Lewis in that in such transactions the funds, coming from Buffett, were "not just money," they were "also an ethical imprimatur" [Lewis, 1992]; at the same time our explorations into performance of his investments do not allow us to conclude unequivocally that, borrowing from Lewis, "Buffett's reputation as the soul of integrity enabled him to charge the embattled CEO extra for his capital" [Lewis, 1992].

A Nonnegotiable Deal

Now, I am a "one-price" guy.

—**WARREN BUFFETT [CITED IN MATTHEWS, 2009, P. 150]**

When Buffett acquired popularity and it became prestigious to sell to him, he established an acquisition procedure to be followed by anyone who was considering bringing him in as an investor. The seller must name the price first. In game theory, the optimal solution, maximizing proceeds for the seller, is the Dutch auction. In this type of auction, it makes sense for the seller to start with a price that is as high as is reasonably possible. In negotiations with Buffett, after the seller states her price, Buffett makes his final decision and does not review it, even if the seller reduces the price in response. If Buffett had not declared his "transaction" rules and stuck to them without fail, then sellers would try to extract from him a sense of the maximum price he would pay. "Over a lifetime, you'll get a reputation for either bluffing or not bluffing" [cited in Schroeder, 2008, p. 468]. One seller of his business to Buffett commented: "To negotiate with Buffett means not to negotiate at all; he gives you the terms of the deal and these are the terms of the deal." Game theory describes this formally. If the seller is able to name the price only once, then she will state a lower price than the one that she would have stated had she been able to negotiate down if necessary.

The head of the insurance company Central States Indemnity, which Buffett acquired in 1996, describes his experience of negotiating with Buffett: "The price he quoted us was that he buys companies for 10 times [annual] earnings. I suggested, 'Well, last year we made $10 million, so if my multiplication is right, that's $100 million,' and he said, 'OK,' And I said, '$125 million?' He said, 'You are too late'" [cited in Kilpatrick, 2005, pp. 337–338].

Buffett speaks ironically of his principle "I do not bargain" when he tells the story of the $35.05 a share that he paid for the acquisition of MidAmerican Energy in 2000: "Why the odd figure of $35.05? I originally decided that the business was worth $35.00 to Berkshire. Now, I'm a 'one-price' guy . . . and for several days the investment bankers representing MidAmerican had no luck in getting me to increase Berkshire's offer. But, finally, they caught me in a moment of weakness, and I caved, telling them I would go to $35.05. With that, I explained, they could tell their client they had wrung the last nickel out of me" [cited in Matthews, 2009, p. 150].

Of course, it has not always been, "Now, I'm a 'one-price' guy." In 1977, when Buffett was acquiring the *Buffalo Evening News*, he first offered $30 million for the paper, but his price was refused. He then raised the bid to $32 million. When the offer was again rejected, he offered $32.5 million [Lowe, 2000, p. 142]. Buffett was also persuaded to raise his price somewhat by the bankers who represented Capital Cities in the 1985 deal that we discussed in Chapter 3. The negotiations on the final acquisition of GEICO lasted for more than a year. Buffett periodically suspended the discussion to convey the impression of lack of interest. In the end, the two sides met at a price that was very different from what Buffett had originally envisaged. Buffett accepted the sellers' conditions [Schroeder, 2008, p. 648]. This took place in 1995.

In the earlier days of Buffett's career, when he was still building the backbone of his "money printing press" by buying companies, delivering return on capital, and accumulating insurance businesses, a tough negotiating stance was not always appropriate. Alice Schroeder relates an account of his acquisition of National Indemnity in 1967. Buffett heard from a common acquaintance that although the company's owner, Jack Ringwalt, did not want to sell his firm, every now and then something would upset him to such an extent ("some claim" would "irritate him") that he "would convince himself he was better off without" his business. Having once heard through his intelligence source that Ringwalt was in a bad mood, Buffett swiftly arranged a meeting. Ringwalt, who had not sold the company before because all the offers he had had came from "crooks," asked for $50 a share and set out his conditions: that the company had to remain in Omaha and that all employees had to be retained. Buffett, sensing that Ringwalt's spleen was about to pass, consented to all the terms immediately, even though the price was more than 40 percent higher than he had wanted to pay. The instant Buffett agreed, Ringwalt regretted the sale, but, being "an honest guy," "wouldn't back out of a deal." After shaking hands, Ringwalt asked whether Buffett cared to see the financial statements. Buffett felt that had he said yes, Ringwalt would use it as a pretext to pull out. Buffett declared that audited statements were "the worst kind" and that he had no need of them. Ringwalt then asked whether Buffett wanted to buy the insurance agencies also. Buffett suspected the same trap and refused the idea of buying the agencies, although they would have been very useful, as they handled some of the key client relationships. Buffett finalized the terms the same day, as Ringwalt was leaving for a trip the next morning, and "freight-trained" him to close the deal a week later, upon Ringwalt's return. Having liquidated Berkshire's original business, Buffett was in the process of putting a new structure together. The insurance businesses that were being placed at its core would bring in capital and earn returns. Buffett would use these to fund acquisitions of other moneymaking businesses that could supply capital back to the insurance core, if necessary [Schroeder, 2008, p. 301]. While he eventually became a tough "one-price" man, in this case Buffett went to great lengths to practically fish a business out of an unwilling emotional seller.

Although Buffett did not use his one-price approach in this particular early purchase of an insurance business, the method was nevertheless useful in the subsequent campaign of building up the insurance core that we discussed in Chapter 6. In 1985, Buffett published an advertisement inviting large commercial clients to insure risks with a premium of over $1 million. The insurance buyer had to give her price, and her proposal would be considered only once [Lowenstein, 1996, p. 296]. Buffett counted on the difference in the evaluation of risk by him and by the potential client. Which one of them would be more experienced and would end up evaluating the risks more accurately? A one-time consideration of each deal prevented the insurance buyer from asking for too low a premium, and Buffett received information on the maximum price that the insurance buyer was prepared to pay. If his evaluation of the same risk was different from that of the insurance buyer, then he would take a positive decision on the deal when the difference was in his favor. Buffett relied on his judgment being better than that of the insurance buyer. The method punished the insurance buyers for any miscalculations, but those who applied for the insurance did so on their own initiative. As a result of this advertising campaign, Buffett collected insurance premiums of $100 million.

Sometimes there are situations in which Buffett is obliged to name the price first: for instance, when he acquires a public company or a company that is going through bankruptcy. In these cases, he follows the same strategy: he names his price and states that this is the final price and it will not be amended. When buying Clayton Homes, Buffett published a press release one day before the vote on his offer (July 15, 2003) at the shareholders' meeting. He used both a stick ("Berkshire will not raise its price now or in the future"; "Berkshire hopes that Clayton shareholders accept our offer. But it is not one that we will renew") and a carrot ("Berkshire will not become a lender to the mobile home industry except through Clayton") [Berkshire Hathaway, 2003]. Such negotiating tactics are very effective when another, less friendly buyer is catching up and there is a risk of losing Buffett as a buyer altogether.

When he was trying to buy Burlington Industries,[3] which had gone bankrupt in 2003, Buffett rescinded his offer when the bankruptcy judge did not approve one of his conditions—a penalty in the amount of $14 million in the event that the seller chose a different buyer. "We are sorry to have to terminate our offer. We trust and admire the Burlington team and hope the company can emerge

---

3 In Munger's words, Buffett was interested in Burlington because of the possibility of cooperation between Burlington and Shaw Industries, which belonged to Berkshire. Given how easily he pulled out of the contest, perhaps he doubted the wisdom of this acquisition.

from bankruptcy debt free," was Buffett's response to the judge's decision [Berkshire Hathaway, Form 8-K, 2003]. Game theory tells us that he who buys at an auction overpays (we discussed this in Chapter 5). Buffett exercises great care in transactions where the procedure requires an auction, as is the law in bankruptcy cases. He always tries to convert the auction into an exclusive transaction, for instance, with the help of high breakup fees. From the point of view of maximizing the price for the company, in the case of Burlington, the judge turned out to be right. Buffett was offering $579 million, and the company was sold for a cash payment of $615 million.

Buffett's "I do not bargain" policy is supported not only by his reputation, but also by his financial position. He told a story at the shareholders' meeting in 2008: "We got a call [from Mars, to finance the purchase of Wrigley] and we said 'yes.' I can tell people 'yes,' and that won't change. The $6.5 billion will be available whether a nuclear bomb goes off in New York City, or whether Ben Bernanke runs off with Paris Hilton" [Matthews, 2009, p. 267].

* * *

The image of a friend and a desirable buyer, or, at worst, a neutral one, combined with an acquisition procedure that steers the final price in Buffett's favor, allows Buffett to enter into transactions on terms that are very profitable for him. Next, we examine some other acquisitions in which Buffett fully uses his methodology in its mature form.

10

Reputation at Work

If you want to shoot rare, fast-moving elephants,
you should always carry a loaded gun.

—WARREN BUFFETT [BUFFETT, 1977–2013, 1987]

IN THE 1970S, BUFFETT USED TO SAY THAT HE WAS NOT INTERESTED IN companies that were going through turnarounds because "'turnarounds' seldom turn." He argued that the same energies and talent would be much better employed in a good business purchased at a fair price than in a poor business purchased at a bargain price [Buffett, 1977–2013, 1979]. Later, Buffett changed his opinion. "Great investment opportunities come around when excellent companies are surrounded by unusual circumstances that cause the stock to be mis-appraised" [cited in Fromson, 1988]. Later still, Buffett arrived at the conclusion that it might be best of all to buy companies that are "on the operating table" [cited in "Homespun Wisdom from the 'Oracle of Omaha,'" 1999]. Buffett is acquiring these companies more and more often. Some notable acquisitions of this kind are the purchases of Johns Manville, a producer of building insulation, commercial roofing, and roof insulation, and Fruit of the Loom, a manufacturer of underwear and activewear for adults and children. In this chapter, we discuss Johns Manville, Fruit of the Loom, and Benjamin Moore. These purchases provide insight into the full spectrum of Buffett's acquisition techniques. Benjamin Moore is an example of an "old economy" purchase during beneficial market conditions, when the broader investment community was infatuated with the "new economy" technology companies. Benjamin Moore and Johns Manville were formally public companies; however, their circumstances were somewhat different from those of Scott Fetzer.

Fruit of the Loom

> He who laughs last laughs longest.
>
> **—PROVERB**

Fruit of the Loom, a well-known brand of underwear, was part of the conglomerate Northwest Industries. The conglomerate was acquired by William Farley in 1985 for $1.3 billion through a leveraged buyout. Farley provided $70 million of equity capital, which he had borrowed. The rest of the financing was arranged by the investment bank Drexel Burnham Lambert through various securities and bank loans ["Making a Merger," 1985]. The transaction was based on a price/sales (P/S) valuation of somewhat lower than 1 and a P/E valuation of around 20. In 1984, the revenues reached $1.3 billion. Net profit amounted to $77.5 million ["Northwest Industries OKs $1.4-Billion Merger Offer," 1985].

When the transaction was being closed, analysts commented that the company might face difficulties in servicing its debt. *BusinessWeek* was critical of Farley's projections, which envisaged operating earnings of $117.3 million and cash flow of $159 million for the second half of the year. "That would be twice what Northwest would need to meet the period's estimated interest expenses. But hefty charges associated with the acquisition—$21 million in severance benefits and $50 million in fees to advisers, banks, and others—will quickly gobble up the extra cash. And if the projections turn out to be too rosy, as the company's first half suggests, Farley could find himself cash-starved" [Spragins, 1985].

William Farley, the son of a postman, was very ambitious. Having started his career as a seller of encyclopedias, he built his financial empire by buying first small, then larger companies with borrowed funds. He made his first acquisition at the age of 33, using all his personal savings of $25,000. Nine years later, at the time of his purchase of Northwest, Farley was managing a $2 billion business. Northwest was his largest acquisition and one of the largest LBOs of the time. He also brought some of his family members into the company. His wife became director of wellness for Fruit of the Loom, and under his 68-year-old father's supervision, the company employees sang hymns: "No scrap, no scrap: We're for quality" [Spragins, 1985]. Some analysts felt that Farley would not succeed with this purchase. He had previously managed only relatively small companies and had had little experience in running large businesses. He was also somewhat extravagant. He took part in underwear advertising for Fruit of the Loom and at some point toyed with the idea of running for president of the United States [Snyder, 1986].

After the deal, Farley sold some of the company's assets in order to reduce the debt burden. This is a standard practice after an LBO where the proportion of borrowed funds is high and financing is expensive. The asset sale brought the company around $200 million.

In 1986, the company's revenue amounted to $690 million, and pretax profit was $147 million. Farley planned an initial public offering (IPO) for the autumn of that year; $15.25 to $18.25 a share was the price corridor indicated in the preliminary prospectus. Eventually the price was set closer to the lower end of the corridor, at $15.50. This was equivalent to a P/E of 30. Farley wanted to raise more than $400 million [James, 1986]. Wall Street did not seem to be interested in the deal, and setting the price near the lower end of the range failed to generate excitement among market participants. The placement was postponed. Farley resumed his IPO efforts the following spring. This time the price was set at $11 to $12 a share. On March 3, 1987, the company was listed on the American Stock Exchange, a smaller exchange that was later purchased by the NYSE, but at only $9 a share ["Fruit of the Loom Initial 27 Million Class A Priced at $9," 1987]. The offering raised around $246 million. The company issued 27 million shares of Class A, each of which had one vote. Farley owned 15 million shares of Class B, each of which had five votes. Another 3.7 million shares of Class B belonged to shareholders who had invested in the company during the LBO—Drexel Burnham Lambert and some of its employees. By structuring the IPO in this manner, Farley retained a controlling stake of 67 percent of the votes. Fruit of the Loom also issued about

$310 million in bonds to replace a more expensive loan ["Fruit of the Loom Back as Farley Makes Changes," 1987]. Over the next 10 years, the company was quite successful. In the middle of the 1990s, its shares rose to a peak of $50 a share.

The first signs of negative developments in the company surfaced in 1996. The CEO of the company, John Holland, retired. He had been with the company for 34 years, of which 21 were as CEO. It was owing to his efforts that Fruit of the Loom had become a well-known underwear brand and the key asset of Northwest Industries. Buffett reported that after Holland's departure, the management raised the debt levels in order to finance new acquisitions, all of which ended up being unsuccessful. "Bankruptcy followed" [Buffett, 1977–2013, 2001].

Over the next three years, the company continued to relocate production facilities from the United States to the Caribbean in hopes of reducing expenses and increasing competitiveness. Fruit of the Loom Ltd. was reincorporated in the Cayman Islands, a jurisdiction with lower corporate taxes. The measures did not help the company. The restructuring did not seem to work. The company had difficulties with the sourcing of raw materials and the organization of its product range. There were quality concerns. The company was unable to meet its own deadlines for supplying the retail market. An analyst commented: "They did a lousy job at buying cotton, a lousy job at manufacturing, a lousy job at logistics. They just didn't execute" [Ryan, 1999]. The business went from profitable to barely breaking even and then to operating at a loss.

In the opinion of some analysts, reincorporating in the Cayman Islands was an attempt to increase the company's attractiveness to a strategic buyer. Indeed, shortly after its reincorporation, the business was put up for sale. The company was examined by all its major direct competitors, but not one of them expressed an interest in acquiring it, despite the fact that in 1998, with revenue of $1.94 billion, the company controlled 32 percent of the underwear market for men and 15 percent for women. It seemed logical that taking over such a market share would be worthwhile. Furthermore, Fruit of the Loom was still profitable at that time. In 1998, it earned a profit of $136 million. An anonymous source at one of the potential buyers explained their refusal to buy Fruit of the Loom. The buyer's company did not wish to find itself entangled with a vertically integrated structure that included its own production facilities. Such structures often operated at a loss [Cunningham and Monget, 1999]. The company was unlikely to be competitive with companies that outsourced their merchandise production to China and other countries with cheap labor forces.

In 1999, the market realized that Fruit of the Loom was having serious difficulties in servicing its debt. By July, the total debt burden had grown to $1.3 billion. At the end of September, the revenue for the first nine months of the year had reached around $1.5 billion, but the company had a loss of $253 million. In the fourth quarter, the situation took an even more horrific turn. Full-year sales amounted to $1.78 billion, but the loss was a colossal $669 million. Under pressure from creditors, Farley was compelled to resign as chairman of the board. In the middle of December, the company invited John Holland to return to the position of CEO. It was hoped that under his leadership, the company might be able to avoid bankruptcy ["Ailing Fruit of the Loom Files for Bankruptcy Protection," 1999].

On December 21, the credit rating agencies reduced their ratings on the company's bonds to just above the bankruptcy level (S&P reduced its rating to CCC). The share price fell to $1. This brought the market capitalization to $54 million. On December 30, the company filed for bankruptcy under Chapter 11. In 2000, Fruit of the Loom continued its attempts to reduce costs. The company closed its design printing and embroidery workshops; suspended loss-making lines of clothing, such as denim and some other types of products; and sold parts of its warehousing and production facilities in the United States. These measures led to a reduction of sales to $1.55 billion, or 13 percent lower than 1999 sales. However, Fruit of the Loom did not manage to return to profitability. In 2000, the losses, though lower than the year before, still amounted to $226 million [Fruit of the Loom, Forms 10-K and 10-Q, 1999–2000].

The restructuring plan was presented before the bankruptcy judge only in March 2001. On August 9, 2001, the court received offers to buy the company from two investor groups. Blackstone was leading one, and Texas Pacific Group (TPG) was leading the other. Blackstone was in alliance with a small company called Russell Corp., which had a market capitalization of $400 to $450 million. Russell specialized in manufacturing T-shirts and activewear clothing. The company had previously bought some of Fruit of the Loom's assets. TPG also had a partner—a Canadian company, Gildan Activewear [Anderson and Kosman, 2001].

The initial offers were in the range of $650 to $800 million. Both investor groups wanted to finance the deal with borrowed funds. This would have been another LBO transaction. Since the banks were not prepared to lend on the basis of the company's cash flow, the loans had to be backed by its working capital. According to some unnamed sources [cited in Anderson and Kosman, 2001], such a financing structure would have allowed the company to raise $550 to $600 million. The company had around $1 billion in working capital assets whose collateral value would have been marked to 50 to 65 percent of their market value. During the negotiations with the company's creditors, both consortia raised their prices. At the moment when Buffett came on the scene, both offers were in the $800 to $900 million range. The Blackstone Group's price was closer to $800 million. The precise value of the second offer was not disclosed [Anderson and Kosman, 2001].

Buffett made his offer on November 2. In the press release, he indicated that he wanted to buy the company for two reasons: the strength of its brand and the managerial talent of John Holland [Berkshire Hathaway, 2001]. Buffett offered $835 million for the company's assets. Furthermore, 100 percent of the offer was to be paid in cash, whereas the other buyers would be paying with a combination of cash, shares, and borrowed funds. The investment bank Lazard Frères, the organizer of the tender, evaluated the restructured company at $920 to $1,150 million [Braine, 2001]. Buffett insisted on a special condition. He wanted $30 million in compensation in the event that he was outbid by other buyers or Berkshire's recovery plan was rejected. The final decision rested with the judge, as the bankruptcy procedure was conducted through the court. The judge was alarmed by the size of the penalty; in response, Buffett reduced it insignificantly, to $22.5 to $27.5 million, with the final amount depending on the timing of the decision. Having remarked that "if you want to keep a purchaser on the hook, you're going to have to pay the price," the judge approved the amended condition ["Fruit of the Loom Is Ripe for Picking," 2001].

The final phase of the tender took place on November 30, 2001. No new offers appeared, and the old participants did not increase their bids. Blackstone Group left the tender once Buffett had joined the process, and Russell Corp. had to abandon the project because it could not raise the required financing without a financial partner. Since Buffett was offering 100 percent of the amount in cash, it would have been difficult for another bidder to top his offer. When a transaction is financed through a combination of cash, shares, and debt and the proportion of cash is not substantial, it is necessary to offer considerably more than a cash offer, since pure cash is always preferable to the seller. The cash compensation to Buffett would have amounted to approximately $25 million, and this money would have had to be subtracted from the funds paid by the buyer. Therefore, the competing offer would have to top not the $835 million that Buffett was offering, but $860 million. The precise terms offered by TPG are not known. However, the offered sum would have had to be greater than Buffett's offer in order to be "equivalent" in overall value.

The creditors had been exhausted by the process and wanted it to be completed as soon as possible. Buffett received the business at his desired price. In terms of multipliers, this price implied the ratio of enterprise value (EV) to earnings before interest, taxes, depreciation, and amortization (EBITDA) of approximately 7 (when the business is purchased at an auction, the buyer receives it free of previous debts, and the EV coincides with the price of purchase, making the calculation in this case $835/120 = 6.94$). This is not a very high valuation for a company with a strong franchise and a great manager as CEO. The valuation, however, takes into account the bankruptcy situation and the need for restructuring. Besides, by the time Buffett made the investment in Fruit of the Loom, his required return for acquisitions had been reduced from 15 percent to 10 percent.

In the letter to shareholders for 2001, Buffett wrote that Fruit of the Loom's bankruptcy was an "unusual" one. Interest payments on senior debt had somehow continued "without interruption," and Berkshire had earned about 15 percent "current return" on the bonds, as "early in the bankruptcy," Buffett had bought up "public and bank" debt of the company at about 50 percent of its face value. Berkshire's debt holdings of Fruit of the Loom rose to 10 percent of all senior debt outstanding. Buffett felt that the senior debt that Berkshire held would "probably" return around "70 percent of its face value." The cost of purchase of Fruit of the Loom was reduced because of this debt holding [Buffett, 1977–2013, 2001]. If this factor is incorporated into the valuation, then Buffett may have acquired the company for $730 million [Kilpatrick, 2005, p. 727]. In part this explains why he was able to offer a more attractive price than his competitors. The risk profile of buying up the company debt was interesting. Knowing the volume of debt outstanding and the prices that other buyers and he were prepared to pay for the company, Buffett knew approximately how much he would receive for his investment in the company debt. It is possible to estimate this only roughly, since the seniority of debt holders during bankruptcy is not necessarily observed strictly.

The purchase of Fruit of the Loom had many features of Buffett's acquisition style. First, the target company satisfied a number of Buffett's criteria for attractive companies. It was a strong brand, and it had a strong manager. Second, Buffett was aware that all strategic buyers had walked away from the company. Buffett entered the tender process at a very late stage, when the maximum prices that the other buyers were prepared to pay had been disclosed. He also knew that he was able to offer better terms, as he would be paying 100 percent in cash. Other buyers were not able to match this condition. Buffett's ability to pay cash and transact quickly also helped in 2002, when MidAmerican, a Berkshire subsidiary, invested in Northern Gas Natural, which had been part of the bankrupt Enron and desperately needed cash.

Were Buffett's expectations in this acquisition realized? We do not have much detail. Berkshire's reports do not contain data on the profitability of individual companies. The indications that are available are probably positive. According to the 2004 annual report, the company was profitable that year. Sales reached $1.3 billion, while sales in 2001 had been $1 billion. This rise in sales implied an average annual revenue growth rate of 8.4 percent between 2002 and 2004. In 2005, Fruit of the Loom's market share for men's underwear rose to 47.8 percent and its market share for women's underwear rose to 24.7 percent. When the company was going through bankruptcy in 1999, these shares were 32 percent and 13 percent, respectively [Buffett, 1977–2013, 2002, 2004, 2005]. In 2006, Fruit of the Loom bought Russell Corp.—the very company that had earlier tried to buy Fruit of the Loom. No further data are reported, as this is a relatively small business in Buffett's conglomerate.

Benjamin Moore: The Purchase of Shares That Have Fallen into Oblivion

> ... when the market plummets ... neither panic nor mourn. It's good news for Berkshire.
>
> —WARREN BUFFETT [BUFFETT, 1999]

Buffett, who is an "old economy" aficionado, made a number of acquisitions of this kind in 2000–2001, when the stock market corrected after the collapse of the new economy bubble. During the preceding boom, the high market levels had been driven by technology company valuations. Most traditional industries were out of fashion with investors. The collapse of the bubble pushed the old economy companies even lower. Buffett took advantage of this situation. He made acquisitions of public companies or almost public companies. These purchases are a rarity in Buffett's portfolio because private companies are often less expensive to buy than public ones. Also, it is difficult to buy a public company through Buffett's preferred method of declaring his price and asking the company to take it or leave it. The board of directors of a public company is obliged to act in the best interests of the stockholders, and, when considering whether to accept or decline an offer, the board has to do its utmost to draw the buyer into a negotiation in order to compel him to increase the price. If the board does not do this, it may face litigation from stockholders.

Nevertheless, Buffett succeeded in his acquisition of Benjamin Moore, a company with a more than 100-year history. Benjamin Moore was a paint manufacturer with a strong eponymous brand and a turnover of $780 million. In 1999, the net profit was $78 million, or $2.93 a share [Caulifield, 2000]. In 1999, the revenue had grown by 10 percent and net profit by 30 percent, the net profit margin had reached around 10 percent, and the return on stockholders' equity had reached 18 percent. These were very strong numbers. In the first half of 2000, the financial results weakened. The profit fell by 52 percent to $19.2 million [Caulifield, 2000]. Although this was a purchase of a public company, the attributes of Buffett's distinct style, refined during his acquisitions of private companies, were clearly visible: a carrot-and-stick-style offer, blitzkrieg speed, and a relatively low price.

Buffett's bid was announced on November 8, 2000, after the close of the market. At their peak several years earlier, the shares had cost $90. One year prior to the deal, they had cost $35, in May 2000 they had cost $28, and on October 23 they had cost $19, which implied a P/E multiplier of 6.5 based on 1999 earnings. In comparison, during the Internet boom, Berkshire shares fell "only" by 44 percent, while over the 12 months prior to the purchase of Benjamin Moore, S&P chemical stocks fell by 17 percent [Cheddar, 2000]. Benjamin Moore's shares had been sliding downward without any material reasons. One explanation for the low price, aside from the shift in investor interest toward the new economy companies, could have been Benjamin Moore's low liquidity. The shares were traded over the counter and not on an exchange. The controlling stake in the company was consolidated; analysts regarded the company as de facto closed. Some observers even rated it as one of the most closed public companies. Benjamin Moore also had an employee stock ownership plan (ESOP) that helped the company management to remain in control [Caulifield, 2000]. The company's shares were not covered by market analysts [Dorfman, 2000].

On November 8, 2000, the shares closed at $25. Buffett valued the company at $37.82 a share, or at a P/E of 13, a P/S of 1.28, and a 51 percent premium to market price—this was a high premium in comparison with average premiums, which fluctuate from year to year and from industry to industry, but on average are in the range of 30 to 40 percent. The multipliers were not particularly high if it was assumed that the fall in profit was temporary.

A formal tender offer was announced. Understandably, a majority of the small shareholders agreed to sell their shares. In the prior years, the share price had been falling, and the premium offered in relative terms was high. Buffett had reached an agreement with the large stockholders prior to the announcement of the tender offer. In the press release of November 8, it was mentioned that 18 percent of the shareholders had already agreed to sell their shares. This must have been a persuasive argument for the undecided [Berkshire Hathaway, 2000]. There were rumors that Buffett had advised the main stockholders of his price late Friday evening and obtained their consent by Monday morning. If the rumors were true, Buffett might have aimed to make it difficult for the stockholders to seek investment banking advice. It might have been more complicated to obtain the opinion of relevant experts over the weekend. Buffett also demanded a breakup fee of $25 million should the transaction fall through. The acquisition ended up being successful.

Johns Manville, the Play on a Cyclical Decline

> Don't worry. Our check will clear.
> —WARREN BUFFETT [CITED IN MCGHEE, 2000]

In December 2000, only a few weeks after the deal with Benjamin Moore, Buffett acquired Johns Manville, a company specializing in the manufacture of insulation materials and roofing and in the development of engineering solutions. Buffett's buying technique was again at the forefront. When he acquired Benjamin Moore, although it was formally a public company, Buffett was in practice buying a company whose structure was closer to that of a private one. Johns Manville could be viewed in the same light. It was a public company, but 76 percent of its shares belonged to a single legal entity—Manville Personal Injury Settlement Trust.

The trust had been created in 1988 by a federal bankruptcy court as a route for the company to exit Chapter 11 bankruptcy. Johns Manville had filed for bankruptcy in 1982 after it had become apparent that the company would not survive the lawsuits from customers who were accusing it of having harmed them. Johns Manville had used asbestos in its insulation materials. In the 1980s, it was discovered that asbestos was so harmful that it was not simply a matter of its having negative effects on human well-being. Exposure to the material could lead to cancer and death. In 1985, the sum being sought through the lawsuits exceeded $100 billion, and the company's net assets amounted to $1 billion. The company emerged from bankruptcy freed from its obligations in the lawsuits. All claims had to be addressed to the trust, which was funded by Manville with cash, insurance payments, stock contributions, profit sharing, investment income, and two bond issues with a face value of $1.8 billion. From 1992 onward, Manville would pay 20 percent of its earnings to the trust for as long as any compensation to the victims remained due. The trust would pay the claimants out of its income. Over 12 years, it paid out $2.16 billion. By 1999, the trust had accumulated 76 percent of the company's shares [Berg, 2000], while the remainder were quoted on the exchange. In the same year, the management of the trust decided to sell its stake in the company to expedite payment of the claims.

In 2000, an investor consortium consisting of Bear Stearns & Co., now defunct but at the time one of the largest brokerage houses, and Hicks, Muse, Tate & Furst Inc., an LBO specialist (now called HM Capital Partners), offered $2.85 billion, or $15.63 a share. This offer implied a premium of 27 percent to the market price of $12.30. The consortium planned to finance the majority of the deal through borrowed funds. The equity capital was going to amount to $500 million, of which $150 million were to be provided by Bear Stearns and the rest by Hicks. The $2.35 billion of debt financing was to be raised through senior debt of $1.75 billion and junk debt of $600 million. The trust accepted the offer [Alm, 2000].

In October, the consortium withdrew its initial offer, as it had been unable to raise funds for the project. The reason for the difficulties was that in the second and third quarters, the company's financial results were worse than expected as a result of the slowdown in the U.S. economy and poor market conditions in the construction industry [Green, 2000]. The company shares fell considerably—to $8. The banks' refusal to supply credit to finance the deal was also driven by the bankruptcy of two direct competitors of Johns Manville, Owens Corning and Armstrong World. Owens Corning declared bankruptcy in the beginning of October; Armstrong World did so a little later, but by October this company was already near bankruptcy, and this was known to the market. All these difficulties were driven by asbestos-related litigation. Johns Manville was in a better position in this respect, as the company did not have to deal with the claims because of the outcome of the bankruptcy procedure. All the obligations rested with the trust.

The consortium had to lower its original offer and brought the price down to $1.92 billion. The shareholders who were selling their shares were supposed to be paid in a combination of cash and preferred shares with a guaranteed dividend. This offer did not satisfy Johns Manville. On December 8, the suspension of negotiations was announced [Tsai, 2000].

When the potential sale fell apart, the trust asked the company to pay the annual dividends in the amount of $150 million. This payment essentially would have rendered the future of Johns Manville uncertain. The CEO spoke of the trust in unfriendly terms. In his opinion, the only material contribution the trust was capable of making to the future of the company was to fire its CEO [Kilpatrick, 2005, p. 714].

Buffett then joined the proceedings. He offered literally only a few cents more—$1.96 billion, or $13 a share—but 100 percent of it would be cash. During negotiations with the management of Johns Manville, Buffett remarked: "Don't worry. Our check will clear" [cited in McGhee, 2000]. He might have been referring to the difficulties of the consortium that had bid for the company earlier. On December 20, the formal announcement was made. Buffett's offer had been accepted.

In the end, Buffett bought the company with a premium to its share price of only 21 percent. This is a relatively modest premium over the market price when a public company is being acquired. The company was bought at a P/S of 0.87, an EV/S of 0.75 (the company carried debt of $300 million), and a P/E of 9.75. This was inexpensive. Even the analysts, who were often skeptical about Buffett's acquisitions, declared that this purchase was very modestly priced.

At the moment of the transaction, Johns Manville had a net loss carryforward of $1.5 billion. The buyer of the company could offset these losses against future profits for tax purposes. A company the size of Berkshire could use up this loss in one year because Berkshire's net profit amounted to $3.3 billion in 2000. The accounting loss of $1.5 billion would have affected the purchase price by $600 million (the tax on profits in that year was 40 percent), or $3 a share. Tax savings allowed Buffett to buy the company at a price that was effectively 30 percent cheaper [Bary, 2000]. This is an instance of financial synergy. As we discussed, Buffett argues that he does not look for operational synergies, but he does not object to financial ones.

Should Johns Manville have accepted a higher offer, the company would have had to pay Berkshire a breakup fee of $44 million. As in the cases of Scott Fetzer, Benjamin Moore, and Fruit of the Loom, Buffett entered the game at the last moment, when other suitors had either abandoned the idea of buying the company or declared their maximum offers. As usual, Buffett was paying cash.

Why were these companies sold so inexpensively? Scott Fetzer was a kind of conglomerate that did not have a suitable strategic buyer. Fruit of the Loom had fundamental problems. It was incurring losses, and it needed assistance in its transition from a crisis state. Benjamin Moore was not as diversified as Scott Fetzer, was problem free, and was acquired at higher multiples. What was different about Johns Manville? Buffett succeeded in taking advantage of the depression in the industry. Johns Manville, having gone through bankruptcy in 1988, was one of the pioneers of asbestos-related bankruptcies. In 2000, 24 companies filed for bankruptcy on the same basis. All these companies ended up being controlled by trusts that could not buy other companies because their purpose was different. Poor market conditions and asbestos-related lawsuits destroyed the stock prices of even those companies that were not bankrupt. Conditions in the industry were so poor that no company was able to think about an acquisition. No strategic buyer who would have been willing to pay a high price was available. All the companies involved had to focus on their own survival. A financial investor would not have been able to raise funds because of the industrywide poor financial results. These circumstances made it relatively easy for Buffett to act. This is one of the examples of his being prepared for the moment when the right deal comes along. "If you want to shoot rare, fast-moving elephants, you should always carry a loaded gun" [Buffett, 1977–2013, 1987]. The gun was fired.

Later, the company management admitted that it had been informed of Buffett's intentions of making an offer to buy the company.

John Cumming, Johns Manville's director for public relations, had noticed that somebody had been buying up the shares in large quantities. Having researched the issue, Cumming figured out who this buyer might have been and shared his suspicions with Jerry Henry, the company CEO. Henry decided to call Buffett, although he was not sure that Buffett would engage in a conversation. Buffett answered the phone call and admitted that he was indeed the buyer of Johns Manville shares. When Henry asked Buffett about the purpose of his acquiring a position in the company stock, Buffett laughed and, as Henry described it, said that if the offer from the consortium fell through, he would consider making an offer for the company [Kilpatrick, 2005, p. 713].

Later, when the deal with the LBO group did fall apart and the trust asked for $150 million in dividends, Henry again called Buffett, who had kept up his share purchasing in the meantime. Buffett laughed again and said: "Yeah, I'd like to buy your company." Henry relayed to Buffett the trust's plans with respect to the dividends. Buffett remarked in response: "Hey, you can't let that happen" [cited in Kilpatrick, 2005, p. 714]. Henry had prepared the ground for accepting Buffett's offer before the offer was made. He convinced the board of directors to rescind the dividend demand and consider Buffett's proposal. Was it really just a lucky coincidence that Cumming was so easily able to establish who had been buying the shares? Did Buffett leak the information? Why did he admit that he wanted to buy the company? Could this have influenced the disintegration of the consortium's offer?

* * *

Buffett enters the game once it becomes clear that all the other buyers will not be able to deliver. Their offers are either unsatisfactory or unsupported financially. Buffett acts fast; offers 100 percent cash, available immediately; and demands a breakup fee. This is all there is to Buffett's tactics. A walk in the park.

11

Beyond the Frontiers of Investment Theory

My father . . . had powerful friends and
access to almost everyone.

—PETER BUFFETT [BUFFETT, PETER, 2011, P. 67]

Outstanding Abilities

The smartest investor in the country.

—JOHN LOOMIS [CITED IN LOOMIS, 2012]

Buffett's natural talent came to the fore when he first showed interest
in investing at the age of six or seven. At about that age, he read his
first book on financial markets, *Bond Salesmanship*. He had been beg-
ging Santa to bring him this particular book for Christmas [Schroeder,
2008, p. 130]. In 2000, he reflected that he had always regretted that he
had not turned his attention to investing earlier. This is a very Buffett-
like remark. By the age of eight, he had read all the books about the
stock market that his father kept in his home library [Kilpatrick, 2005,
p. 78]. By the age of 10, he had read every book with the word *finance*

in the title in the Omaha public library. In fact, he had read some of those books twice [Matthews, 2009, p. 76]. At 11, he bought his first book on investment. In 1940, when Buffett was 10, his father took him to New York. Warren told his father that he wanted to see three things in the big city: Scott Stamp and Coin Company, Lionel Train Company, and the New York Stock Exchange [Schroeder, 2008, p. 62]. Scott Stamp and Coin published catalogs of stamps and coins.[1] Lionel Train Company made toy trains. Buffett wanted a toy railroad, which his father refused to buy him. Later Buffett acquired one himself— Burlington Northern Santa Fe Railroad [Merced and Sorkin, 2009]. "This is all happening because my father didn't buy me a train set as a kid," Buffett joked in an interview. In the letter to shareholders for 2009, when this acquisition took place, Buffett wrote: "Come by rail!" [Buffett, 1977–2013, 2009].

Buffett made his first investment while he was still at school. At the age of 11, he bought three preferred shares of Cities Service at $38 a share. The price fell to $27, but Buffett waited out the low price period and sold his shares at $40. He made $6 (or probably nothing, or even a loss, if the transaction costs are taken into account). The share price rose further and eventually reached $200 [Boroson, 2008, p. 18]. In 1945, when Buffett was 15 years old, he was able to save enough money to buy an undeveloped 40-acre farm in Nebraska for $1,200. He rented the land to a tenant farmer [Kilpatrick, 2005, p. 83] and later sold the property for a good profit. Buffett's interest in investing did not abate as he grew older. At Columbia University, when he started the entry-level course on finance with David Dodd (Graham's coauthor on *Security Analysis*), Buffett realized that he knew the book better than Dodd did. He could quote from any part of the 800-page book, and he was closely familiar with all the case studies [Schroeder, 2008, p. 130].

Buffett's intelligence is practically legendary. He is often described as the smartest man in the room. Rich Santulli, who, in his own words, had been around investment bankers his whole life, concluded that there was no other person who was more intelligent than Buffett. Had Buffett

---

1 At some later point, Buffett invested in stamps and tried to corner the market in a particular stamp. See the story, for example, in Chapter 22 of [Schroeder, 2008].

been 40 or 50 years old, Santulli would have borrowed all the money he could and bought more Berkshire stock [Miles, 2002, pp. 134–135]. Charlie Munger, who was acquainted with all the best students in his Harvard Law School class of 1,000 people, felt that "there was no one as able as Warren" [cited in Kilpatrick, 2005, p. 52]. John Loomis, the husband of Carol Loomis,[2] after meeting Buffett for the first time in the 1960s, declared to his wife: "I think I just met the smartest guy in the country" [cited in Loomis, 2012]. Buffett is also referred to as a "genius when it comes to numbers" [Kilpatrick, 2005, p. 183].

Those who are acquainted with Buffett note his ability to analyze information deeply and quickly and his unique conversance with the business world. There are many testimonies to Buffett's impressive erudition. David Strassler, one of the early investors in Buffett Partnership, tells the story of his first meeting with Buffett. Strassler had felt that his encounter with Buffett would be a meeting between a knowledgeable and experienced New Yorker and somebody provincial. However, Buffett began asking questions about a company that belonged to Strassler's family and to Strassler's immense surprise he realized that Buffett knew more about the business than he did. In fact, Buffett was closely familiar with the balance sheet, while only 2 percent of company stock was in free circulation [Lowenstein, 1996, p. 73]. This meeting must have taken place in the middle of the 1960s.

John Forlines, chairman of a small bank, Bank of Granite, speaks in similar terms about his interaction with Buffett in 1996. Forlines and Buffett had exchanged a few letters before the meeting. When they met, Buffett said: "I just read your report." Then Buffett began citing figures from the report for the first quarter of 1996. "He was right. I was surprised. I was overwhelmed, to say the least," Forlines described [cited in Kilpatrick, 2005, p. 1039].

A Wall Street broker who knew Buffett and tried to find interesting investment ideas for him relays a story of how he once told Buffett that a certain cement stock was cheap relative to its book value. Buffett only shot back that, in his view, the book value was not correct and advised

---

2 A journalist and a friend of Buffett. Carol Loomis edits Buffett's letters to shareholders and is the author of a number of articles about the investor.

that broker to examine how cement plants sold in the last several years [Lowenstein, 1996, p. 91]. John Byrne, a friend of Buffett's and an insurance industry executive, whom Buffett called "the Babe Ruth of insurance," found that Buffett would always manage to bring up details from some annual report that would prove important and that Byrne had forgotten or missed entirely [Kilpatrick, 2005, p. 862].

A Bear Stearns banker remembers how he brought to Omaha one of his clients who was selling a natural gas company. The meeting lasted three hours. During the first half hour, Buffett listened and asked questions. He had received some materials about the company prior to the seller's visit, and it was apparent that Buffett had a very clear understanding of the data that had been sent to him. As the client divulged new information, Buffett recalculated the economics on the fly. At the end of the talk, Buffett made an offer, subject to some fact finding. The banker was stunned. He had never before seen an executive make an offer on the basis of a single conversation [Lowenstein, 1996, pp. 285–286].

Arthur Rosewell, a trader who worked for Buffett, remembers how he arrived at the conclusion that Buffett was the greatest investor ever. Once, in a conversation at which Buffett was present, one of the participants mentioned Dunkin' Donuts. Rosewell thought that he knew the company well until he heard Buffett speak about it. Buffett had "in mind all the facts and figures." He knew Dunkin' Donuts "up one side and down the other." In Buffett's view, the company would have benefited from moving its property into a REIT. As a result of listening to Buffett, Rosewell sold his Dunkin' Donuts shares and bought Berkshire at $300 to $500 a share [Kilpatrick, 2005, pp. 980–981].

Buffett develops and maintains his "knowledge database." One analyst who has studied Buffett's managerial methods in depth describes how the famous "five-minute" decisions are made: "When that phone rings [this is a phone call from a business owner who is looking to sell his company], he usually knows the economics of the business (he has already analyzed every company that fits his acquisition criteria). He knows that it is being run by people who act like owners (he's checked out their capital allocation record and their reputations)" [O'Loughlin, 2003, p. 104]. Importantly, within "five minutes," Buffett lets the person know only whether or not he is potentially interested. The price is provided one or a few days later after he reviews further information about the business. In essence, Buffett is an intelligence agency, in as much as an investment company. Though, he also tells stories of how his acquaintances found interesting companies that he either had not previously considered to be attractive targets or had never heard of altogether.

Charlie Munger

Junior partner in good years and senior partner in bad years.
—WARREN BUFFETT [CITED IN LOWE, 2000, P. 75]

There is another interesting element in Buffett's success that would be hard to replicate. Over the course of his career so far, Buffett has made relatively few mistakes. His knowledge of the experiences of other investors has allowed him to learn from their errors and not make his own. In addition to Graham and Fisher, there is at least one other intellectual relationship in Buffett's professional life that has played, arguably, an extremely important role in his overall accomplishment. The oldest of Buffett's sons comments that his father is the second-smartest man he knows. Charlie Munger is the first [Lowe, 2000, p. 5]. Buffett views his relationship with Munger as that between "Siamese twins, practically" [cited in Schroeder, 2008, p. 24]. Once Buffett admitted that he had been "shaped tremendously" by Charlie [cited in Lowe, 2007, p. 55]. Munger explains the synergy of their relationship: "Everybody engaged in complicated work needs colleagues. Just the discipline of having to put your thoughts in order with somebody else is a useful thing" [Lenzner and Fondiller, 1996]. A friend of Buffett and Munger describes the collaboration between the two colleagues: "Warren uses Charlie as one last litmus test: if Charlie can't think of a reason for not doing something, they will do it" [cited in Lowe, 2000, p. 76]. A *Forbes* journalist also comments on their rapport: "Munger is the foil that makes Buffett's down home image believable. His 'tough style approach makes possible Buffett's Mr. Nice Guy'" [cited in Lowe, 2000, p. 5].

Charlie Munger, a lawyer and businessman, was born into a family of German immigrants that had settled in Nebraska. Like Warren,

Charlie spent his childhood in the state capital, Omaha. Although the future partners lived near each other and young Warren worked in the store that Munger's family owned, Buffett and Munger were not acquainted during their school years. After finishing school, Munger left Nebraska. He entered the University of Michigan to study mathematics. Eventually he decided to change his area of study, turned to law (he comes from a family of lawyers), and entered Harvard Law School. After graduation, he moved to California with his family and relatively quickly became a well-established lawyer. Together with a group of partners, he created his own law firm—Munger, Tolles & Olson LLP. Once he accumulated some capital, he began to invest in development projects in addition to practicing law.

Buffett and Munger met in 1959, when Charlie was visiting Omaha to attend his father's funeral. Munger was 35 years old, while Buffett was 29. They instantly established a friendship and began discussing various investment ideas. It turned out that at times both of them had independently invested in the same companies; for instance, each had bought shares of Blue Chip Stamps [Lowenstein, 1996, p. 163]. One of Munger's law firm partners felt that Munger was "cultivating" Buffett and that he wanted to become Buffett's partner [Lowenstein, 1996, p. 163]. Munger is Buffett's equal partner despite the fact that Buffett is considerably better known to the wider public.

Buffett's wider popularity is also partially the result of his share in the partnership being approximately 14 times higher than Munger's (before Buffett started to transfer his shares into a trust, their shares were 42 percent and approximately 3 percent, respectively). Although their shares were set at different levels at the outset of the partnership, this discrepancy is also partially the result of personal circumstances. Buffett raised three children, while Munger supported nine—his own from his two marriages and his second wife's from her first marriage. One of his sons was diagnosed with leukemia, and Munger had to cover considerable medical expenses. The personal savings that he had available to invest were not as substantial as Buffett's. It has been widely observed that Buffett lives modestly. When journalists asked him why he bought cheap suits, he responded: "I buy expensive suits. They just look cheap on me." [Buffett, Clark, 2006, p. 92] In contrast, Munger has been involved in a number of status projects. For instance, in the 1980s, he developed Mungerville, a residential project in Santa Barbara for 32 houses with original architecture. The houses sold with difficulty, and the buyers were mostly friends and acquaintances. He also built a nonmetal passenger catamaran that was described as the largest in the world at the time of its construction [Kilpatrick, 2005, p. 1211]. Buffett started working for himself very early in his career. He spent relatively little time being employed by his father and then by his teacher, Ben Graham. When Graham retired, Buffett inherited the pool of investors whose funds Graham had managed and was able to start his own business—Buffett Partnership. Munger spent a considerable period of time as an employee, although during this time he developed connections and a client base and established relationships with future partners for his businesses.

As *éminence grise*, Munger has not just assisted Buffett in putting his thoughts in order. Many of Buffett's early investments—Wesco Financial Corporation, See's Candies, and others—were introduced to him by Munger, who by the time of his meeting with Buffett already had a circle of partners with whom he had invested and whom he bounced off investment ideas.

Munger may also have been able to offer a kind of educating experience, allowing Buffett to learn from someone else's errors without making them part of Berkshire's track record. Buffett was one of the few investors who avoided the temptation to overinvest in the "new economy." It is possible that he was able to rely on Charlie Munger's history of investing in technology. In the 1950s, Munger bought a small California company that manufactured highly specialized transformers for military rockets. That company, in turn, acquired a producer of complicated cathode-ray recording oscillographs. Fortunately, the California company was able to divest the latter acquisition before this technology became outdated and was replaced by magnetic tape technology. The speed with which technology became obsolete was very fast, even in the 1950s. Munger decided not to invest in technology in the future: "I never went back to high-tech mode. I tried it once and found it to have many problems. I was like Mark Twain's cat that, after a bad experience, never again sat on a hot stove or on a cold stove either" [cited in Lowe, 2000, p. 59].

Munger's life experience would have been useful in many other situations as well. By the time he met Buffett, Munger had already served on the board of directors of International Harvester, a company specializing in the manufacture of trucks and agricultural machinery. During his tenure on the board, Munger was able to experience firsthand how challenging it was to steer toward success a business whose fundamentals were, by its nature, difficult. On the other hand, Munger may have been able to observe that the *Los Angeles Times* was flourishing. One of the clients of Munger's law practice and consequently a partner in his development projects occupied a senior post at the paper.

Arguably, the core of Munger's intellectual influence was that he taught Buffett to pay more for a business with fundamentally good economics. If, until the relationship between Buffett and Munger was established, Buffett had primarily followed Graham's advice and searched for undervalued, in Graham's terms, companies that traded at a lower price than the balance sheet value of the assets, then the first transactions in which Munger participated were executed at higher prices as a matter of principle. For example, See's Candies was purchased at three times the net asset value.

Two Images of Warren Buffett: The "Forrest Gump of Finance" and the "Oracle of Omaha"

> Birds of a feather flock together.
>
> **—PROVERB**

Buffett's social circle has played an important role in his success. One's acquaintances are always a channel for gathering information when it comes to both looking for investment opportunities and researching those that have presented themselves. Some of Buffett's transactions emerged through the network of his personal connections, which has naturally grown and evolved over the years. For instance, the idea of buying FlightSafety International was first thought of by Richard Sercer, one of Berkshire's shareholders, who was also a shareholder of FlightSafety [Kilpatrick, 2005, p. 611]. Sercer did not know Buffett personally, but he was able to initiate a conversation with Buffett through a common acquaintance. The idea of acquiring MidAmerican Energy Holdings Co.—the company that owned the electrical and gas distribution networks in Iowa—was brought to Buffett by Walter Scott, who owned a large stake in MidAmerican and was also on the board of directors of Berkshire. The idea of buying Clayton Homes was suggested by business school students whose professor had brought them to meet Buffett [Schroeder, 2008, p. 746]. Charlie Munger finds that Buffett has used his contacts mostly not to generate deals but to investigate prospects after he acquires a lead [Lowenstein, 1996, p. 331]. As for portfolio investments, Buffett tends to come up with ideas himself. He is known to have asked his brokers not to disturb him with "hot" tips (although brokers' ideas may be uninteresting to him for different reasons).

In popular books, the significance of Buffett's social circle is often omitted from the discussion of his investment strategy. For example, Mary Buffett and David Clark, the authors of *The New Buffettology*, invite investors to do their homework as "Warren would do it"—to learn as much as possible about the business of the company whose shares the investor is planning to acquire. If the company is manufacturing consumer goods, then it is advisable for the investor to visit a store that sells the goods and talk to the sales personnel. This is, of course, a reasonable recommendation. There are many well-known anecdotes illustrating this aspect of Buffett's research style. He spent a considerable amount of time sitting near the cashier at the Ross—Buffett's favorite steak restaurant in Omaha—and evaluating the proportion of clients that paid with an American Express card (prior to investing in the company) [Lowenstein, 1996, p. 81]. He counted discarded bottle caps at vending machines to assess the popularity of various soft drinks and observed the numbers of railroad cars to track shipments of oil additives [Matthews, 2009, p. 81]. Nevertheless, the sources of information that are available to Buffett are distinctly different from those that are at the disposal of an average investor.

A simple example of this difference in the quality of the information that would be available to Buffett and to a retail investor is the difference in the answer to a question that could be provided by a salesperson in a store and by a close friend of Buffett, Bill Gates. Let us imagine that the question concerns the future of Kodak. Buffett asked Gates this question in 1991, during their first meeting. Gates advised him that

Kodak was "toast." How many people would have understood this at that time, when Kodak itself may not have appreciated that the Internet and digital technologies would destroy conventional cameras and photo film? In 1991, Kodak was trading at $40. The company's stock price reached its peak of $80 only in 1996 [Schroeder, 2008, pp. 623, 625].

Buffett had comparable answers to similar questions asked by Gates. In the course of the same conversation, Gates wondered about the future of the newspaper industry. Buffett opined that it "had gotten worse, because of other media" [Schroeder, 2008, pp. 623, 625].

Whom does Buffett talk to? He speaks to the CEOs of large companies, investors, and political leaders. Buffett's circle of connections changed considerably after he became friends with Katharine Graham, the former owner and chief editor of the *Washington Post*. Katharine's husband, Phil Graham, who managed the paper from 1946 to 1967, was an advisor to two presidents: John Kennedy and Lyndon Johnson. It is said that the friendship between Phil Graham and John Kennedy was so close that they exchanged lovers [Schroeder, 2008, p. 371]. Katharine's social circle included Jackie Kennedy, Richard Nixon, Lyndon Johnson, Margaret Thatcher, Henry Kissinger, Indira Gandhi, the prince of Wales, Ronald Reagan, George Bush, and Bill Clinton, among others. Katharine organized dinners at her home, to which Buffett was invited. She liked to seat him between her and one of her guests who would be somebody from this list [Kilpatrick, 2005, p. 187]. Buffett is acquainted with Christie Hefner, the CEO of Playboy; Michael Dell, the founder of Dell; and Diane von Furstenberg, a well-known designer, among others [Schroeder, 2008, pp. 11, 12]. He gave investment advice to Nancy Reagan [Kilpatrick, 2005, p. 933]. The Getty family used his advice, in particular, in 1984 with respect to the merger of Getty Oil and Texaco. Jeffrey Immelt, the CEO of General Electric, who took over from the legendary Jack Welch, is known to have sought Buffett's opinion on occasion [Kilpatrick, 2005, p. 186]. Buffett has also counseled Barack Obama and Hillary Clinton on economic policy [Matthews, 2009, p. 215].

Buffett is a member of the elite Alfalfa Club, whose members, which number about 200, meet once a year. The 100-year-old club counts among its members a mix of politicians, top executives, military brass, and administration officials [Roberts, 2014]. In 1997, Bill Clinton invited the club members to dinner. Among the attendees were Colin Powell, who was then the chairman of the Joint Chiefs of Staff, Supreme Court Chief Justice William Rehnquist, Walt Disney's Michael Eisner, and Jack Valenti, head of the Motion Picture Association of America [Kilpatrick, 2005, p. 189].

Another prestigious club was created by Buffett himself. It emerged from social gatherings with Benjamin Graham, the author of *The Intelligent Investor*. Buffett and Munger organized this club for businessmen they knew. After Graham's death, the meetings continued. It was before precisely such a gathering that the owner of Borsheim's presented his jewelry. The membership in this informal organization is very small—approximately 12 people who meet only twice a year. At these meetings, a member of the club organizes an interesting trip, for instance, around Alaska. The "cultural program" includes discussions on a broad range of topics—global geopolitical threats, among others. The subjects are sometimes personal as well. During one meeting, each member talked about the biggest failure of his life; at another, each member talked about the most important factor or life event that had formed his character. Investment issues are also discussed. For instance, one of the meetings was devoted to analyzing the 10 most expensive companies as of 1950, 1960, 1970, 1980, and 1990 and the changes that this list of companies underwent [Schroeder, 2008, p. 625]. Aside from this club, Buffett has also created a charity golf tournament, the Omaha Classic, whose participants are a small circle of CEOs—acquaintances and friends of Buffett's and some celebrity figures [Schroeder, 2008, p. 631]. Many of these celebrities use NetJets.

Buffett's network of connections in the media has grown to include a broad range of people. We have already discussed some of his relationships with members of the staffs of the papers and journals that Berkshire owns. Carol Loomis used to be an editor at large of *Fortune* magazine. Buffett continues to be a friend of Katharine Graham's son, Donald. Steve Forbes, the heir of the Forbes publishing family and twice a candidate for the Republican presidential nomination, mentions that Buffett and his father were good friends [Kilpatrick, 2005, p. 911]. Thomas Winship, the former editor of the *Boston Globe*, described Buffett as a "great collector of friends" [cited in Lowenstein, 1996, p. 357].

Charlie Munger has also developed a unique network of connections, as Janet Lowe observed in her biography of Munger. Carla Hills, who served as Assistant U.S. Attorney General in the Nixon and Ford administrations and as secretary of the U.S. Department of Housing and Urban Development, used to work at Munger's law firm. Carla's husband, Roderick Hills, one of the founding partners of Munger's law firm, was chairman of the Securities and Exchange Commission under President Ford [Lowe, 2000, p. 87].

In the 1970s, Buffett seriously considered running for president, but then gave up the idea because he had concluded that he was "far too private" and "thin-skinned" for that "carnival test." Being a believer in liberal and democratic causes, Buffett has actively supported Democratic candidates during elections. He has developed relationships with many politicians, including those in both national and state governments [Lowenstein, 1996, p. 141]. It has been mentioned that Buffett was considered for the post of secretary of the Treasury in the Clinton administration.

A biographer of Buffett describes his social network:

> Already towards the end of the eighties Buffett was acquainted with anyone almost of any fame. He would constantly attend board meetings, sporting events, parties, where he would mingle with various celebrities or politicians. He played bridge as a member of an elite group, consisting of top CEOs. When once asked, what advice he would give to the President, he mentioned that he had been at a dinner with the President just recently. [Lowenstein, 1996, pp. 357–358]

The treasurer of Berkshire Hathaway comments that he never would have predicted that Buffett would enjoy the limelight and publicity [Lowenstein, 1996, p. 277]. Being part of these elite circles became very much second nature to him. In 1993, a journalist mentioned that Buffett had declined Bill Clinton's invitation to dinner [Lenzner, 1993].

Buffett's fortieth birthday was celebrated at a golf club in Omaha— at that age, he was relatively little known in New York. Ten years later, when relatively wide celebrity had become part of Buffett's life, his fiftieth birthday was marked at the Metropolitan Club in New York—one of the most prestigious clubs of the financial capital of the United States. At the same time, Buffett has remained faithful to his image and inner core of being a provincial, down-to-earth common man. Lowenstein observed, "Buffett likes to portray himself as a sort of provisional traveler in high society" [Lowenstein, 1996, p. 358].

This image of being a simple man ended up being of assistance not only in business, but also in political circles. It was very effective when Buffett was defending Salomon Brothers from the threat of liquidation. Roger Lowenstein reports that the organization's reputation had been undermined by the publication of *Liar's Poker* by Michael Lewis; in addition, the regulators and members of Congress were inclined to take a tough stance against the bank to make an example of it. Buffett, who had taken over the chairman of the board position at Salomon during the crisis, had to testify before the congressional committee investigating the transgressions at the bank. Buffett was simply the ideal candidate to represent the bank at the hearings. First, he had no connection with the scandal, since he had been only a passive investor. Second, his image was completely untainted by anything that could have been viewed as unlikable by any politician. Roger Lowenstein described the hearings with Buffett's participation. Buffett was kind and humble. He mentioned that he was a congressman's son and joked that he had indeed ended up in a dreadful situation. It was of help that he was on friendly terms with some politicians and, more importantly, that he was not a believer in small government and his views were widely known. The members of the hearing committee were careful not to challenge such a popular figure as Buffett too aggressively. He was seen as a person who was not an insider in Wall Street. The common opinion seemed to be that Omaha was still a provincial farm town.

Buffett was also positively characterized by others who spoke at those hearings. A congressman from Omaha commented that Buffett was "a man who is typical of the people we grow and nurture in the Midwest. . . . He continues to live in a quiet, tree-lined street in Omaha" [cited in Lowenstein, 1996, p. 394]. It is arguable that it was

Buffett's reputation and image and his participation in the hearings that rescued the bank, and with it his investment in it. Buffett was, of course, aware of the significance of his image and communication style. He started his first press conference as chairman of the board of Salomon with the words: "I will attempt to answer questions in the manner of a fellow who has never met a lawyer" [cited in Kanner, 1991]. This immediately won the hearts of the journalists, as the same observer reports. When in 1995 *Vanity Fair* called Buffett a Forrest Gump of finance, he probably liked it.

Conclusion

BUFFETT STARTED HIS CAREER IN THE 1950S AS AN ORTHODOX follower of Graham. At the time, Graham's investment system was working and was probably beating the market by a considerable margin. When Buffett began investing, the market had finally recovered from the crisis of 1929–1932 and was starting to grow gradually. The next serious market fall, in 1973–1974, was still in the distant future. The beginning of Buffett's career coincided with a long bull market.

During these years, a whole group of investors showed excellent results. However, what are the reasons that allowed Buffett to leave his competitors behind? One of the reasons involves the organizational side of things. Other managers continued to run investment funds that were mutual in structure, whereas Buffett liquidated his fund and set up his investment vehicle as a joint stock company. A mutual fund manager is far more limited in her actions than the controlling shareholder of a conglomerate. The manager of a mutual fund is constantly at the mercy of the participants and has to sell her investments if the participants want their funds back. She is often unable to use periods of panic in the financial markets as opportunities for inexpensive acquisitions of good companies. Buffett has had no limitations in this regard. The structure he set up was able to show better returns over the long term. A study that we discussed [Frazzini, Kabiller, and Pedersen, 2012] placed Berkshire in first place in terms of rate of return, adjusted for the risk level of the portfolio, compared with mutual funds that existed from 1976 to 2011, but only in eighty-eighth place among companies that existed over the same period. In my view, this statistic might be an indication that it is relatively easier to achieve good investment results if the investment vehicle is a company and not a fund.

Structuring his investment vehicle as a joint stock company permitted him to use the insurance business as the foundation stone for the whole edifice. As we discussed in Chapter 6, the insurance business, and specifically insuring against supercatastrophes, is a way of raising long-term capital. Intelligent organization of this business allows Buffett to raise this capital at very low cost. Over the 1976–2011 period, Buffett's cost of "borrowing" in the form of insurance premiums was 2.2 percent on average, which is 3 percentage points lower than the return on T-bills and 4.8 percentage points lower than the return on 10-year bonds. In addition, this evaluation probably exaggerates the capital cost, as the proportion of years when the cost of capital was negative amounted to 60 percent and in these years the cost of capital was set to zero for the purposes of the cost-of-capital calculation. Buffett finds that the company's obligations are much smaller than the accounting rules indicate them to be [Buffett, 1977–2013, 2013]. In essence, another fund is concealed within Berkshire, with the returns on the former benefiting the shareholders of the latter and not the "shareholders" of this internal structure.

By the 1980s, the financial world had changed. A large number of retail investors had come into the market and contributed to the rising trend. The number of investment funds, mutual funds, and other market participants had risen sharply, and the environment became considerably more competitive. By that time, Buffett had acquired a reputation as an investor who was loyal to his managers. He has guarded this reputation all his life so far. It is, of course, difficult to say whether this positioning has been an intentional plan from the start. His acquisition of Berkshire in the 1960s was hostile toward some of the company's manager-owners. Since the purchase of Berkshire, however, Buffett has remained largely amicable toward the selling owners who have stayed on as managers.

Buffett's image and the development of his reputation were assisted by his connections among the owners and managers of leading American business publications. To some of them, he was a friendly shareholder; to others, he was a friend of the owners or editors. It is interesting to note that perhaps the only openly anti-Buffett article, in which he was called "the local miser," was published by the *Financial Times* in 2002 [Jackson, 2002].

Buffett was often offered profitable deals at levels that a less friendly investor would not have been shown. Also, Buffett was acting on behalf of a company, not a mutual fund. Therefore, he was in a position to guarantee that he would not sell his shares under any circumstances. A mutual fund, because of its institutional organization, is not able to promise anything of the kind. In connection with this, it is critically important to note not only the organizational difference between a company and a fund, but also that Buffett is the controlling shareholder of the company. If this were not the case, he would be limited in terms of what guarantees he could offer.

Second, Buffett has guaranteed a friendly attitude. His acquisitions of a minority stake have never been a Trojan horse aimed at buying the entire company. The unique combination of a friendly investor with a great reputation who can promise specific conduct toward companies in which he invests has led to his acquisition of a considerable number of valuable minority stakes, many of which were a defense against nonfriendly takeovers. Buffett stresses that Berkshire is comprised of "toothless tigers" in terms of their influence on CEOs of public companies [Buffett, 2004b].

Berkshire's unique corporate culture, in which everything other than money is decentralized, has attracted to Buffett numerous owners of private companies who wanted to sell their businesses. Charlie Munger argues that Berkshire has built up a reputational advantage that "gives you shortcuts." He felt that the deal with Johns Manville was a good example of this [Loomis, 2001].

Why did this culture end up being unique to Berkshire? Why have no competitors entered the same market niche? Why has the model not been borrowed and copied? Buffett has given answers to some of these questions. He finds that he was able to create such an ecosystem because he started at a relatively young age and did not have to retire at 65. He had the time to develop the niche and the business. Many CEOs inherit a culture that is hard to reshape. Often they do not have a long enough horizon in which to implement the changes that they view as desirable. Often the businesses they inherit are so large that they are hard to change, even if the CEOs are very competent. Achieving this understanding became a "major management discovery" for Buffett [cited in Miles, 2002, p. xii].

One other factor that has helped Buffett enter into transactions at profitable levels and save resources is Berkshire's strong financial position. First, Buffett is able to pay 100 percent of the purchase price in cash. Second, the seller has Buffett's assurance that once he has made an offer, the deal will take place on precisely the terms that were offered. It is not Buffett's habit to change the promised conditions, and since he has financing available, he has no need to raise funds on the open market, and so nothing can compel him to alter the terms. Those who wish to sell their business in exchange for stock because of tax considerations find Berkshire stock ideally suitable—the conglomerate's business is reliable and stable, and the shares are highly liquid.

These two features of Berkshire—its unique culture and its financial muscle—provide a strong competitive advantage. In 2002, Buffett admitted that he attracts two types of buyers: one type "want their businesses to become Berkshire companies," while the other type "only want cash—and fast." Berkshire is "the buyer who can come up with cash over a weekend" [cited in Serwer and Boorstin, 2002]. In 2006, Buffett mentioned that Berkshire had become "the buyer of choice" and that at last Berkshire had also become internationally famous ("globe-trotting got under way") [Buffett, 1977–2012, 2006].

Buffett's supreme intelligence expresses itself not only in his mastery of the technical and quantitative side of investing, but also in his success in consistently applying the "right" theory, even though it is well known to everyone. This theory states that it is most profitable to invest in companies that have a stable competitive advantage. This involves either having a brand that allows the company to price its products at a premium to the price of nonbrand products or having a competitive advantage in costs. Buffett has made himself into such a brand: many people insist on transacting with him even if he is not paying the highest price. Also, Buffett is competitive in acquisitions not just from the standpoint of price. Any other buyer who tried to outbid him would not receive as high a return on the invested capital, since the business would have been acquired more expensively. In summary, Buffett aims to buy companies with a competitive advantage, but as a buyer, he has an equivalent competitive advantage with respect to other buyers. He is the only widely known investor in his niche, and therefore his costs of entry into a business are relatively modest. Buffett's name works as a brand.

Buffett acknowledges the role of his reputation. When he was asked to step in as chairman of the board of Salomon Brothers and subsequently defend the bank before the regulators, Buffett talked about how he intended to run the bank: he would be understanding if the firm lost money, but he would be ruthless if the firm's reputation was affected negatively [Schroeder, 2008, p. 603]. In one of his letters to the managers of Berkshire subsidiaries, he formulated similar principles that the managers had to abide by: "We can afford to lose money—even a lot of money. We cannot afford to lose reputation—even a shred of it" [Buffett, 2001]. This is why: "In many areas, including acquisitions, Berkshire's results have benefited from its reputation, and we don't want to do anything that in any way can tarnish it" [Buffett, 2001].

Did Buffett have a thought-out strategy for creating his own brand from the start? Perhaps yes. Continual declaration of his principles may amount to a strategy. Buffett constantly advertises his theoretical principles of investing and never fails to emphasize that his key divergence from Graham's ideas is that he is not looking for undervalued companies. Indeed, the world has changed, and Graham's strategy may have become outdated; also, there may be another reason why advertising his change from Graham's methods may be important. Publicly announcing that he aims to underpay slightly would turn away many business owners who wanted to sell their businesses. Buffett practically maintains an elite club of businesspeople who have sold their companies to him. It is very prestigious to be a member of this club. Susan Jack, who became the CEO of Borsheim's after the former owner's death, said that she felt very honored that Buffett had picked the business where she worked. Being part of Berkshire gave her a sense of pride [cited in Miles, 2002, p. 292]. It is even more prestigious for a member of this club to be perceived not as a vehicle that allows Berkshire to create excellent returns, grow his empire, and realize his ideas, but as an individual who entered into a financial transaction that was beneficial for her. Often Buffett adds to the debate about who are the winners and who are the losers in his acquisitions. When Bill Child, the former owner of RC Willey, wanted to build a furniture store in Idaho, he was not confident that the new store would be successful because he did not want to keep it open on Sundays. He suggested to Buffett that he would build the store using his own funds, and if the store ended up being successful, then he would sell it to Berkshire at cost. The store was built, became successful, and was transferred to Berkshire. When Child subsequently offered the same scheme for opening another store in Las Vegas, Buffett's reaction was: "No, I only take advantage of a guy once" [cited in Miles, 2002, p. 191].

The press has been discussing the possible fall in Berkshire returns. Buffett has been anticipating this fall. What factors are really to blame? Perhaps, given Buffett's age, his retirement is expected in the foreseeable future, and this is making it more difficult for him to sell the idea of offering the right home for the right companies and guaranteed noninterference into the business of companies in which he purchases minority stakes. The future will show whether the market associates Berkshire's culture with Buffett personally or whether the market will think that Buffett's culture has been implanted sufficiently firmly for subsequent CEOs to follow it. Will Berkshire's culture resist attempts to change it, should such attempts materialize? Will it remain as prestigious to sell to Berkshire in the future, when Buffett will no longer be at the helm? How closely intertwined and interchangeable are Berkshire's and Buffett's brands? For how many years will Buffett's effect last? If Buffett's effect persists after his retirement, will he end up being not only the greatest manager ever, but also the only manager who indeed retires, if at all, only many years after actually stepping down?

Appendix

Research, examining investment strategies into value and glamour stocks.

Paper	Multipliers	Years	Markets	Methodology and Findings
[Basu, 1977]	P/E	1957–1971	NYSE	One dollar invested into a stock in the lowest P/E ratio quintile would have increased to 8.28, and one dollar invested into a stock in the highest P/E ratio quintile would have increased to 3.47.
[Oppenheimer, 1984]	P/E	1974–1981	NYSE, AMEX	Stocks with earnings yield at least twice as high as the AAA bond yield were selected, and only in those companies where total debt was less than the book value of the shareholder equity. Portfolio was rebalanced annually. Securities were held for two years, or until a 50 percent appreciation occurred, whichever took place first. Investment in the portfolio returned 38 percent annually. NYSE-AMEX Index returned 14 percent.
[Oppenheimer, 1986]	P/Current Asset Value	1970–1983	NYSE, AMEX, over-the-counter	Stocks selling at or below 66 percent of net asset value were selected for the portfolio. Return was calculated and portfolio was reset at the end of each year. The mean return of all the yearly returns amounted to 29.4 percent as opposed to 11.5 percent a year for the NYSE-AMEX Index.
[DeBondt & Thaler, 1987]	P/BV	1966–1984	NYSE, AMEX	Companies were grouped into quintiles by P/BV at the end of each odd-numbered year. The investment return was computed for the following four years for each group of quintiles. These four-year returns were averaged for every quintile of every portfolio. The compound annual return of the stocks in the lowest P/BV quintile was 8.91 percent above the market return.
[Levis, 1989a]	P/E	1961–1985	LSE	The annual investment return in the lowest P/E quintile was 17.76 percent; in the highest P/E quintile it was 10.7 percent.

Reference	Metric	Period	Market	Description
[Levis, 1989b]	DIV/P	1955–1988	LSE	The annual investment return in the highest dividend yield decile was 19.3 percent; in the lowest it was 13.8 percent.
[Keppler, 1991a]	P/CF	1970–1989	Morgan Stanley Capital International National Equity Indexes (18 countries)	Investments in 18 countries were equally weighted and rebalanced quarterly. Each quarter the country indices were ranked according to price to cash-flow and grouped into quartiles. The return was measured over the three subsequent months for each quartile. The average compound annual investment return in the countries with the lowest price to cash-flow stocks was 20.3 percent in dollar-terms for the 20-year period; stocks in the highest price to cash-flow quartile produced 5.63 percent in dollar-terms.
[Keppler, 1991b]	DIV/P	1969–1989	Morgan Stanley Capital International National Equity Indexes (18 countries)	The same methodology as in [Keppler, 1991a] was used. Investment in the highest yielding stocks returned 19.1 percent in dollar terms; in the lowest yielding stocks returned 10.3 percent.
[Fama & French, 1992]	P/BV	1963–1990	NYSE, AMEX, NASDAQ	Stocks were ranked and grouped into deciles according to P/BV. Then each P/BV decile was ranked and sorted into deciles according to market capitalization. Annual equal-weighted investment returns for each of the 10 market capitalization deciles were assessed. Small caps with the lowest P/BV delivered the best returns. Within each market-cap category the best returns were provided by stocks with the lowest P/BV.

(continued on next page)

Research, examining investment strategies into value and glamour stocks. *(continued)*

Paper	Multipliers	Years	Markets	Methodology and Findings
[Capaul, Rowley & Sharpe, 1993]	P/BV	1981–1992	France, Germany, Switzerland, UK, Japan, USA	Stocks in each country were ranked according to P/BV every six months. Within each country ranking the stocks were grouped into two groups so that each group would represent 50 percent of the market cap. Stocks, representing 50 percent of the market capitalization with high P/BV, were named as growth stocks; stocks with the lowest P/BV were known as value stocks. The cumulative difference between the investment returns on value and growth stocks for the 11.5-year period was 31.9 percent for European countries, 69.5 percent for Japan, and 15.6 percent for the United States.
[Lakonishok, Shleifer & Vyshny, 1994]	P/BV, P/E, P/CF	1968–1990	NYSE, AMEX	Decile portfolios for each multiplier were formed and updated each year. Average annual five-year and total five-year returns were calculated. Average annual return over the five-year period of a portfolio with the lowest P/BV reached 19.8 percent; annual return of a portfolio with the highest multiplier reached 9.3 percent; the returns in the P/E groups were 19 percent and 11.4 percent, respectively; P/CF groups returned 20.1 percent and 9.1 percent. The authors also studied portfolios on two-dimensional classifications of the same multipliers against growth rate of sales and comparable patterns were observed.
[Chan, Jegadeesh & Lakonishok, 1995]	P/BV	1963–1991	Largest NYSE and AMEX companies	Quintiles were formed based on the basis of book to market value each year. Book and market values were measured at the end of each fiscal year. Equal-weighted returns were measured over the 12-month period after the portfolio formation and over each of the five years after formation. In the first year after formation portfolios with the lowest book to market ratio generated 11.3 percent. The stocks with the highest book to market ratio returned 16.8 percent. The five-year average returns were 11.4 and 16.4, respectively.

Reference	Factors	Period	Sample	Description
[Caj, 1997]	BV/P, C/P (cash flow yield), E/P, SG (sales growth)	1971–1993	Tokio Stock Exchange	Value stocks outperformed glamour stocks by between 6 and 12 percent per annum over the five years after portfolio formation.
[Fluck, Malkiel & Quandt, 1997]	P/BV, P/E	1979–1995	1,000 U.S. large-company stocks	The lowest P/BV decile rebalanced quarterly produced 1.89 percent excess return quarterly or 7.56 percent annualized above the average return of the full data sample. The lowest P/E decile produced 1.82 percent excess return quarterly or 7.28 percent annualized.
[La Porta, Lakonishok, Shleifer & Vyshny, 1997]	BV/P, C/P, SG	1971–1991	NYSE, AMEX, NASDAQ	Portfolios were formed on the basis of two classifications: stocks were sorted into deciles by P/BV, and a two-way classification where stocks were ranked and divided into groups of three based on C/P and, independently, on SG. Value stocks in the first classification were those with the lowest P/BV, while in the second—with the highest cash flow to price and lowest sales growth. Stock price reactions were measured around earnings announcements over a five-year period after portfolio formation. Earnings surprises were found to be systematically more positive for value stocks.
[Gregory, Harris & Michou, 2001]	BV/P, E/P, C/P, SG	1975–1998	LSE	In the first year after the portfolio formation, the difference in returns between the extreme value decile and glamour decile was 22.18 percent for BV/P, 20.22 percent for C/P, 11.50 percent for E/P, and 9.36 percent for SG. The difference declines subsequently but is significant in all postformation years. Value portfolio, constructed on the intersection of the lowest SG and the highest BV/P, E/P, C/P, delivers the annualized return of 25.72 percent over the five-year period, when glamour portfolio (the highest SG, the lowest BV/P, CP, E/P) returns 13.19 percent.
[Chan & Lakonishok, 2004]	BV/P, C/P E/P, S/P (Sales/Price)	1969–2001	Largest NYSE and AMEX companies	A large-cap portfolio was constructed and rebalanced each year. Stocks were ranked and grouped into deciles based on a composite measure, including BV/P, C/P, E/P, S/P. For the large-cap stocks buy-and-hold returns for the year, following portfolio formation, were 16.4 percent for the value stocks and 4.5 percent for the glamour stocks.

Bibliography

Abelson, Reed. "Buffett's New Shares Probably Won't Deter the Copycats." *New York Times*, May 8, 1996.

"Ailing Fruit of the Loom Files for Bankruptcy Protection." Dow Jones Business News, December 1999.

Alm, Richard. "Dallas-Based Investment Firm Makes Deals to Buy Roof Maker, Sell Food Company." *Texas*, June 24, 2000.

Altucher, James. *Trade Like Warren Buffett*. Hoboken, NJ: John Wiley & Sons, 2005.

Andersen, Erika. "23 Quotes from Warren Buffett on Life and Generosity." *Forbes*, February 12, 2013.

Anderson, Katie, and Josh Kosman. "Buyout Firms Want Fruit of the Loom." *Daily Deal*, August 10, 2001.

Ansberry, Clare. "Scott & Fetzer to Be Acquired for $402 Million—Berkshire Hathaway Accord for $60 a Share Edges Offer by Equity Group." *Wall Street Journal*, October 30, 1985.

Asquith, Paul, David Mullins, and Eric Wolff. "Original Issue High Yield Bonds: Aging Analyses of Defaults, Exchanges, and Calls." *Journal of Finance* 44, no. 4, 1989.

Baker, George. "Beatrice: A Study in the Creation and the Destruction of Value." *Journal of Finance* 47, no. 3, 1992.

Barsky, Robert, and Bradford DeLong. "Bull and Bear Markets in the Twentieth Century." *Journal of Economic History* 50, no. 2, 1990.

Bary, Andrew. "Searching for the Bottom." *Barron's*, December 25, 2000.

Basu, Sanjoy. "Investment Performance of Common Stocks in Relation to Their Price-Earnings Ratios: A Test of the Efficient Market Hypothesis." *Journal of Finance* 32, no. 3, 1977.

Berg, Joel. "Asbestos Trusts Control Companies." *Central Penn Business Journal*, December 22, 2000.

Berger, Philip, and Eli Ofek. "Diversification's Effect on Firm Value." *Journal of Financial Economics* 37, no. 1, 1995.

Berkshire Hathaway Annual Shareholders' Meeting, 1988.

Berkshire Hathaway Annual Shareholders' Meeting, 1992.

Berkshire Hathaway Annual Shareholders' Meeting, 1993.

Berkshire Hathaway Annual Shareholders' Meeting, 1995.

Berkshire Hathaway Annual Shareholders' Meeting, 1997.

Berkshire Hathaway Annual Shareholders' Meeting, 1998.

Berkshire Hathaway. Annual Reports, 1995–2013. http://www.berkshire hathaway.com/reports.html.

Berkshire Hathaway. "Benjamin Moore to Be Acquired by Berkshire Hathaway," News Release. November 8, 2000, http://www.berkshirehathaway.com/news/nov0800.html.

————. "Berkshire Hathaway to Acquire Fruit of the Loom's Apparel Business," News Release. November 1, 2001, http://www.berkshirehathaway.com/news/nov0101.html.

————. Form 8-K. Current report pursuant to Section 13 or 15(d) of the Securities Exchange Act of 1934. February 28, 2003, http://www.sec.gov/Archives/edgar/data/870213/000087021303000008/mar8k0303t.txt.

————. Clayton Homes News Release. July 15, 2003, http://www.berkshireha thaway.com/news/jul1503.pdf.

————. "Warren E. Buffett, CEO of Berkshire Hathaway, Announces the Resignation of David L. Sokol," News Release. March 30, 2011, http://www.berkshirehathaway.com/news/MAR3011.pdf.

Bevelin, Peter. *Seeking Wisdom: From Darwin to Munger.* Malmö: Post Scriptum AB, 2003.

Bianco, Anthony. "The Warren Buffett You Don't Know." *BusinessWeek*, July 5, 1999.

Boroson, Warren. *J.K. Lasser's Pick Stocks Like Warren Buffett.* New York: John Wiley & Sons, 2008.

Boseley, Saraph. "Mexico to Tackle Obesity with Taxes on Junk Food and Sugary Drinks." *The Guardian*, November 1, 2013.

Bottermiller Evich, Helena. "Mexico Soda Tax to Re-ignite U.S. Debate." January 1, 2014, http://www.politico.com/story/2014/01/mexico-soda-tax-101645.html.

Braine, Bob. "Fruit of the Loom Holds Risks for Buffett." Dow Jones News Service, November 7, 2001.

Brandom, Russell. "Jeff Bezos: 'I Didn't Seek to Buy the Washington Post.'" *Verge*, December 2, 2013.

Brenner, Robert. *The Boom and the Bubble: The U.S. in the World Economy.* London: Verso, 2003.

Browne, Christopher. *The Little Book of Value Investing*. New York: Wiley, 2006.

Buffett, Mary, and David Clark. *The New Buffettology*. London: Free Press Business, 2002.

———— and ————. *The Tao of Warren Buffett: Warren Buffett's Words of Wisdom: Quotations and Interpretations to Help Guide You to Billionaire Wealth and Enlightened Business Management*. New York: Scribner, 2006.

Buffett, Peter. *Life Is What You Make It: Find Your Own Path to Fulfillment*. Three Rivers Press, 2011.

Buffett, Warren. Letters to the Buffett Partnership Partners, 1957–1970.

————. Chairman's Letter to Shareholders. Berkshire Hathaway Annual Reports, 1977–2013, http://www.berkshirehathaway.com/letters/letters.html.

————. "The Superinvestors of Graham-and-Doddsville." *Hermes: The Columbia Business School Magazine*, Fall 1984.

————. "Study the Failures. Buffett Recounts Most Unforgettable Business Lessons." *Omaha World-Herald*, May 21, 1991a.

————. "Three Lectures by Warren Buffett to Notre Dame Faculty, MBA Students, and Undergraduate Students. Lecture to Faculty." Spring 1991b.

————. "Three Lectures by Warren Buffett to Notre Dame Faculty, MBA Students, and Undergraduate Students. Lecture to MBA Students." Spring 1991c.

————. "Three Lectures by Warren Buffett to Notre Dame Faculty, MBA Students, and Undergraduate Students. Lecture to Undergraduate Students." Spring 1991d.

————. "J. E. Faulkner Lecture to University of Nebraska-Lincoln Students." October 10, 1994a.

————. "A Tribute to Benjamin Graham." Special Meeting of New York Society of Security Analysts, December 6, 1994b.

————. "Letter to the Editor." *Forbes*, October 7, 1996a.

————. Warren Buffett Talks Business. The University of North Carolina. 1996b. https://www.youtube.com/watch?v=LmWWRT3fknQ&list=PL400DA4CA04EE365E.

————. Warren Buffett to Jeff Raikes: E-mail letter. August 21, 1997, http://www.tilsonfunds.com/BuffettRaikesemails.pdf.

————. *An Owner's Manual*. A Message from Warren E. Buffett, Chairman and CEO, January 1999.

————. "If We Could Finagle Golf Scores the Way Companies Finagle Restructuring Charges, We'd All Be Playing in the Masters: A Disgraceful Magic Wand." *Investment News*, April 26, 1999.

————. "Memo. From Warren Buffett to Berkshire Hathaway Managers ('The All-Stars')," August 2, 2000.

————. "Memo from Warren Buffett to Berkshire Managers ("The All-Stars")." September 26, 2001, http://www.berkshirehathaway.com/manager.html.

————. "Stock Options and Common Sense." *Washington Post*, April 9, 2002.

————. "Talk with Wharton MBA Students." October 10, 2003.

————. "Directors Who Put the Company First." *Korea Herald*, March 16, 2004.

————. "Warren Buffett Responds to Questions from 85 Wharton Students on November 12, 2004." http://www.tilsonfunds.com/BuffettWhartonspeech. pdf, 2004b.

————. "A Discussion of Mr. Warren Buffett with Doctor George Athanassakos and Ivy MBA and HSA Students." Omaha, March 31, 2008.

————. *Berkshire Hathaway Letters to Shareholders (1965–2013)*. Edited by Max Olson. Omaha, NE: Berkshire Hathaway, 2013, http://www.berkshireletters. com/#insurance.

———— and Lawrence Cunningham. *The Essays of Warren Buffett: Lessons for Corporate America*. 3d ed. Durham, NC: Carolina Academic Press, 2013.

———— and Thomas Jaffe. "What We Can Learn from Phil Fisher." *Forbes*, October 19, 1987.

———— and Carol Loomis. "Mr. Buffett on the Stock Market. The Most Celebrated of Investors Says Stocks Can't Possibly Meet the Public's Expectations. As for the Internet? He Notes How Few People Got Rich from Two Other Transforming Industries, Auto and Aviation." *Fortune*. November 22, 1999.

Buhayar, Noah. "Berkshire Hathaway's Charlie Munger Shows a Golden Touch." *Bloomberg Businessweek*. July 25, 2013.

———— and Zachary Tracer. "Buffett Expands Buyback to Pay Up to 120% of Book Value." Bloomberg, www.bloomberg.com, December 13, 2012.

Caj, Jun. "Glamour and Value Strategies on the Tokyo Stock Exchange." *Journal of Business Finance & Accounting* 24, no. 9–10, 1997.

Calandro, Joseph. *Applied Value Investing*. New York: McGraw-Hill, 2009.

Capaul, Carlo, Ian Rowley, and William Sharpe. 1993. "International Value and Growth Stocks Returns." *Financial Analysts Journal* 49, no. 1, 1993.

Caulifield, John. "Benjamin Moore to Be Added to Buffett's Plate." *National Home Center*, November 20, 2000.

Chan, Louis, Narasimhan Jegadeesh, and Josef Lakonishok. "Evaluating the Performance of Value Versus Glamour Stocks. The Impact of Selection Bias." *The Journal of Financial Economics* 38, no. 5, 1995.

Chan, Louis, and Josef Lakonishok. "Value and Growth Investing: Review and Update." *Financial Analysts Journal*, 60, no. 1, 2004.

Chan, Robert. *Behind the Berkshire Hathaway Curtain*. Hoboken, NJ: John Wiley & Sons, 2010.

Chancellor, Edward. *Devil Take the Hindmost: A History of Financial Speculation*. New York: Plume, 2000.

Cheddar, Christina. "Buffett Buys Paint; More M&A Ahead?" Dow Jones Newswires, November 17, 2000.

Chirkova, Elena. "Why Is It That I Am Not Warren Buffett?" *American Journal of Economics* 2, no. 6, 2012.

Coles, Robert. "Perelman Seeks Stake in Salomon." *New York Times*, September 29, 1987.

Condon, Christopher, "The Value Fund Manager with the $57 Million Paycheck." www.bloomberg.com, March 7, 2014.

Corner, Frances. *Why Fashion Matters*. London: Thames & Hudson, 2014.

Crippen, Alex. "Warren Buffett 'Reluctantly' Accepts Decision by NetJets Creator to Step Down." CNBC, August 9, 2009, http://www.cnbc.com/id/32289235.

———. "CNBC Transcript: Warren Buffett Explains Why He Bought $10.7B of IBM Stock (Part 5)." 2011, http://www.cnbc.com/id/45290263.

Cunningham, Thomas, and Karyn Monget. "FTL Shifts: A Call for Buyers?" *Women's Wear Daily*, September 1, 1999.

Curran, John. "Five Tips from Warren Buffett." *Fortune*, November 29, 1993.

Damodaran, Aswat, www.damodaran.com, December, 2014.

Davis, L. J. "Buffett Takes Stock." *New York Times*, April 1, 1990.

DeBondt, Werner, and Richard Thaler. "Further Evidence On Investor Overreaction and Stock Market Seasonality." *Journal of Finance* 42, no. 3, 1987.

DeLong, Bradford, and Konstantin Magin. "The U.S. Equity Premium: Past, Present and Future." *Journal of Economic Perspectives* 23, no. 1, 2009.

"Department of Labor Ruling May Delay Scheduled Closing of Proposed Leveraged Buyout of Scott Fetzer Co." PR Newswire, August 7, 1985.

Dimson, Elroy, Paul Marsh, and Mike Staunton. *Triumph of the Optimists: 101 Years of Global Investment Returns*. Princeton, NJ: Princeton University Press, 2002.

Dorfman, John. "Six High-Profit, Low-Debt Stocks Come Out of Hiding." *Los Angeles Business Journal*, November 6, 2000.

Doyle, Jack. "Celebrity Buffett, 1960–2010." www.PopHistoryDig.com, February 26, 2010.

Dunbar, Nicholas. "How the *Ought* Became the *Is*." *Dynamic Hedging*, Black-Scholes-Merton Supplement, June 1998.

———. *Inventing Money: The Story of Long-Term Capital Management and the Legends Behind It*. New York: John Wiley & Sons, 2000.

———. *The Devil's Derivatives: The Untold Story of the Slick Traders and Hapless Regulators Who Almost Blew Up Wall Street . . . and Are Ready to Do It Again*. Boston: Harvard Business Review Press, 2011.

Eisner, Michael, and Tony Schwartz. *Work in Progress: Risking Failures, Surviving Success*. New York: Hyperion, 1999.

Elder, Laura. "Star Furniture Sale Solves Estate Tax Dilemma." *Houston Business Journal*, June 29, 1997.

Faber, Mebane. "How to Ride Seth Klarman's Coattails." *Forbes*, February 25, 2010.

Fabrikant, Geraldine. "Potential Successor to Buffett Has Tough Task." *New York Times*, December 3, 2009.

Fama, Eugene. "Efficient Capital Markets: A Review of Theory and Empirical Work." *Journal of Finance* 25, no. 2, 1970.

———— and Kenneth French. "The Cross-Section of Expected Returns." *Journal of Finance* 47, no. 2, 1992.

Fisher, Philip. *Common Stocks and Uncommon Profits*. New York: Wiley Investments Classic, 1996.

————. *Path to Wealth Through Common Stocks*. Hoboken, NJ: John Wiley & Sons, 2007.

Fluck, Zsusanna, Burton Malkiel, and Richard Quandt. "The Predictability of Stock Returns: A Cross-Sectional Simulation." *Review of Economics and Statistics* 79, no. 2, 1997.

"For Buffett, Amex Is a Great Place to Stash Cash." *BusinessWeek*, August 18, 1991.

Fox, Justin. *The Myth of the Rational Market. A History of Risk, Reward and Delusion on Wall Street*. New York: Harper Business, 2001.

Frazzini, Andrea, David Kabiller, and Lasse Pedersen. "Buffett's Alpha." Mimeo, 2012, http://www.econ.yale.edu/~af227/pdf/Buffett's%20Alpha%20-%20 Frazzini,%20Kabiller%20and%20Pedersen.pdf.

Fridson, Martin. *It Was a Very Good Year: Extraordinary Moments in Stock Market History*. New York: John Wiley & Sons, 1998.

Fromson, Brett Duval. "A Warm Tip from Warren Buffett: It's Time to Buy Freddie Macs." *Fortune*, December 19, 1988.

————. "And Now Look at the Old One." *Fortune*, October 30, 1989.

"Fruit of the Loom Back as Farley Makes Changes." Dow Jones News Service, March 4, 1987.

"Fruit of the Loom Initial 27 Million Class A Priced at $9." Dow Jones News Service, March 2, 1987.

"Fruit of the Loom Is Ripe for Picking." *Toronto Star*, December 6, 2001.

"Fruit of the Loom Name—Stock Sale." Dow Jones News Service, March 2, 1987.

Fruit of the Loom, Forms 10-K, 10-Q (annual and quarterly reports pursuant to Section 13 or 15(d) of the Securities Exchange Act of 1934), 1999–2000, http://www.sec.gov/Archives/edgar/data.

Fuerbringer, Jonathan. "A Wall Street Behemoth: The Big Investor; Using Fancy Footwork, Buffett Makes a Go of It." *New York Times*, September 25, 1997.

Gad, Sham. *The Business of Value Investing*. New York: Wiley, 2009.

Gasparino, Annie. "Tightfisted New Owners Put Heinz on Diet." *Wall Street Journal*, February 10, 2014.

Gates, Bill. "What I Learned from Warren Buffett." *Harvard Business Review*, February 1, 1996.

Goodman, Andrew. "Top 40 Buffett-isms: Inspiration to Become a Better Investor." *Forbes*, September 25, 2013.

Graham, Benjamin. Letter to the Stockholders of Graham-Newman Corporation. 1946.

————. Testimony to the Committee on Banking and Commerce Senator William Fulbright, Chairman, March 11, 1955.

————. *The Intelligent Investor.* New York: HarperCollins, 2003.

————. *The Memoires of the Dean of Wall Street.* N.Y.: McGraw-Hill, 1996.

———— and David Dodd. *Security Analysis.* New York: McGraw-Hill, 2009.

Graham, Katharine. *Personal History.* New York: Vintage Books, 1998.

Grant, Linda. "The $4-Billion Regular Guy: Junk Bonds, No. Greenmail, Never. Warren Buffett Invests Money the Old-Fashioned Way." *Los Angeles Times*, April 7, 1991.

————. "Taming the Bond Buccaneers at Salomon Brothers." *Los Angeles Times Magazine*, February 16, 1992.

————. "Striking Out at Wall Street." *US News & World Report*, June 20, 1994.

Green, Leslie. "Hicks Muse, Bear Stearns Abandon Johns Manville Deal." *Buyouts*, December 20, 2000.

Greenblatt, Joel. *You Can Be a Stock Market Genius (Even if You Are Not Too Smart).* New York: Simon & Schuster, 1997.

Gregory, Alan, Richard Harris, and Maria Michou. "An Analysis of Contrarian Investment Strategies in the UK." *Journal of Business Finance & Accounting* 28, no. 9–10, 2001.

Gubernick, L. "Raiders in Short Pants." *Forbes*, November 18, 1985.

Hagstrom, Robert, Jr., *The Warren Buffett Way.* Hoboken, NJ: John Wiley & Sons, 2005.

Hart, Oliver, and John Moore. "Debt and Seniority: An Analysis of the Role of Hard Claims in Constraining Management." *American Economic Review* 85, no. 3, 1995.

Haughney, Christine. "Newsweek, Sold in 2010, Is Changing Hands Again." *New York Times*, August 3, 2013.

Hays, Constance. *The Real Thing: Truth and Power at the Coca-Cola Company.* New York: Random House, 2005.

Helzberg, Barnett. *What I Learned Before I Sold to Warren Buffett. An Entrepreneur's Guide to Developing a Highly Successful Company.* New York: John Wiley & Sons, 2003.

Hoerr, John, Gelvin Stevenson, and James Norman. "ESOPs: Revolution or Ripoff? They Can Spread the Wealth to Workers—or Withhold It from Them." *BusinessWeek*, April 15, 1985.

"Homespun Wisdom from the 'Oracle of Omaha.'" *BusinessWeek Online*, July 5, 1999.

Huey, John. "The World's Best Brand." *Fortune*, May 31, 1993.

Hughey, Ann. "Omaha's Plain Dealer." *Newsweek*, December 13, 1985.

Ibbotson, Roger and Rex Sinquefield. "Stocks, Bonds, Bills and Inflation: Year by Year Historical Return (1926–1974)." *Journal of Business* 49, no. 1, 1976.

Ikkenberry, David, Joseph Lakonishok, and Theo Vermaelen. "Market Underreaction to Open Market Share Repurchases." *Journal of Financial Economics* 39, no. 2–3, 1995.

Jackson, T. "Rich Beyond Reason." *Financial Times*, May 6, 2002.

James, Frank. "Farley Apparel to Go Public in Share Offer." *Wall Street Journal*, August 27, 1986.

Janjigian, Vahan. *Even Buffett Isn't Perfect.* New York: Portfolio, 2008.

Jargon, Julie, and Serena Ng. "Heinz Sold as Deal Takes Off." *Wall Street Journal*, February 15, 2013.

Jensen, Michael. "Agency Costs of Free Cash Flow, Corporate Finance and Takeovers." *American Economic Review* 76, no. 2, 1986.

Kahn, Irving, and Robert Milne. "Benjamin Graham: The Father of Financial Analysis." Occasional Paper No. 5, Financial Analysts Research Foundation, 1977.

Kanner, Bernice. "Saving Salomon." *New York*, December 9, 1991.

Kaplan, Steven, and Jeremy Stein. "The Evolution of Buyout Pricing and Financial Structure in the 80s." *Quarterly Journal of Economics* 108, no. 2, 1993.

Keppler, Michael. "Further Evidence on the Predictability of International Equity Returns." *Journal of Portfolio Management* 18, no. 1, 1991a.

———. "The Importance of Dividend Yields in Country Selection." *Journal of Portfolio Management* 17, no. 2, 1991b.

Kilpatrick, Andrew. *Of Permanent Value: The Story of Warren Buffett.* Birmingham, AL: AKPE, 2005.

Klarman, Seth. *Margin of Safety: Risk-Averse Value Investing Strategies for the Thoughtful Investor.* New York: HarperCollins, 1991.

Klott, Gary. "When Warren Buffett Talks, 15,000 Shareholders Listen." *SunSentinel*, www.sun-sentinel.com, May 10, 1999.

LaFon, Holly. "Buffett's Billion Dollar Mistake with Moody's." GuruFocus, November 24, 2011, www.gurufocus.com/news/137224/buffetts-billion-dollar-mistake-with-moodys.

Lakonishok, Josef, Andrew Shleifer, and Robert Vyshny. "Contrarian Investment, Extrapolation, and Risk." *The Journal of Finance* 49, no. 5, 1994.

Langley, Monica. *Tearing Down the Walls: How Sandy Weill Fought His Way to the Top of the Financial World . . . and Then Nearly Lost It All.* New York: Simon & Schuster, 2003.

La Porta, Rafael, Josef Lakonishok, Andrew Shleifer, and Robert Vyshny. 1997. "Good News for Value Stocks: Further Evidence on Market Efficiency." *The Journal of Finance* 52, no. 2, 1997.

Leeson, Nick. *Rough Trader*. London: Sphere, 2007.

Lenzner, Robert. "Warren Buffett's Idea of Heaven: 'I Don't Have to Work with People I Don't Like.'" *Forbes*, October 18, 1993.

_____ and David Fondiller. "Not-So-Silent Partner: Meet Charlie Munger." *Forbes*, January 22, 1996.

Levis, Mario. "Market Size, PE Ratios, Dividend Yield and Share Prices: The UK Evidence." A Reappraisal of the Efficiency of Financial Markets NATO ASI Series. Volume 54, 1989a.

_____. "Stock Market Anomalies: A Re-assessment Based on the UK Evidence." *Journal of Banking* 13, no. 4–5, 1989b.

Levitt, Arthur. *Take On the Street*. New York: Vintage Books, 2003.

Lewin, Tamar. "Scrutiny Takes Toll on For-Profit College Company." *New York Times*, November 9, 2010.

Lewis, Michel. "The Temptation of St. Warren." *New Republic*, February 17, 1992.

Loeb, Gerald. *The Battle for Investment Survival*. CreateSpace Independent Publishing Platform, 2009.

Loomis, Carol. "The Inside Story of Warren Buffett." *Fortune*, April 11, 1988.

_____. "Tap Dancing to Work: Warren Buffett on Practically Everything." *Fortune*, September 11, 1989.

_____. "A House Built on Sand: John Meriwether's Once-Mighty Long-Term Capital Has All but Crumbled. So Why Did Warren Buffett Offer to Buy It?" *Fortune*, October 26, 1998.

_____. "The Value Machine: Warren Buffett's Berkshire Hathaway Is on a Buying Binge. You Were Expecting Stocks?" *Fortune*, February 19, 2001.

_____. "The Wit and Wisdom of Warren Buffett." *Fortune*, November 19, 2012.

_____. "Buffett: Why I Didn't Buy the Washington Post." CNN Money, 2013, http://finance.FORTUNE.cnn.com/2013/10/23/warren-buffett-washington-post.

_____ and Maria Atanasov. "Warren Buffett's Wild Ride at Salomon: A Harrowing, Bizarre Take of Misdeeds and Mistakes That Pushed Salomon to the Brink and Produced the 'Most Important Day' in Warren Buffett's Life." *Fortune*, October 27, 1997.

Lowe, Janet. *Damn Right! Behind the Scenes with Berkshire Hathaway Billionaire Charlie Munger*. New York: John Wiley & Sons, 2000.

_____. *Warren Buffett Speaks: Wit and Wisdom from the World's Greatest Investor*. Hoboken, NJ: John Wiley & Sons, 2007.

Lowenstein, Roger. *Buffett: The Making of an American Capitalist*. New York: Broadway Books, 1996.

———. *When Genius Failed*. London: Fourth Estate, 2002.

Lynch, Peter. Interview on PBS (http://www.pbs.org/wgbh/pages/frontline/shows/betting/pros/lynch.html).

——— and John Rothchild. *Beating the Street*. New York: Simon & Schuster, 1994.

——— and ———. *One Up on Wall Street*. New York: Simon & Schuster, 2000.

"Making a Merger—$1.3 Billion Play." *New York Times*, April 16, 1985.

Mallory, Maria. "Behemoth on a Tear." *BusinessWeek*, October 3, 1994.

Mandelbrot, Benoit, and Richard Hudson. *The (Mis)behavior of Markets: A Fractal View of Financial Turbulence*. New York: Basic Books, 2006.

Marcus, Alan. "The Magellan Fund and Market Efficiency." *Journal of Portfolio Management* 17, no. 1, 1990.

Markowitz, Henry. "Portfolio Selection." *Journal of Finance* 7, no. 1, 1952.

Martin, Gerald, and John Puthenpurackal. "Imitation Is the Sincerest Form of Flattery: Warren Buffett and Berkshire Hathaway." Working Paper, 2008.

Matthews, Jeff. *Pilgrimage to Warren Buffett's Omaha*. New York: McGraw-Hill, 2009.

McGhee, Tom. "Manville Officials Say Buffett Sought Buyout." *Denver Post*, December 22, 2000.

Mehra, Rajnish, and Edward Prescott. "The Equity Risk Premium: A Puzzle." *Journal of Monetary Economics* 15, no. 1, 1985.

Merced, Michael, and Andrew Sorkin. "Buffett Bets Big on Railroads' Future." *New York Times*, November 3, 2009.

Miles, Robert. *The Warren Buffett CEO: Secrets from the Berkshire Hathaway Managers*. New York: John Wiley & Sons, 2002.

Munger, Charlie. Wesco Financial Corporation, Letter to Shareholders, 1989.

———. "A Lesson on Elementary, Worldly Wisdom as It Relates to Investment Management and Business." Lecture at the University of Southern California, April 14, 1994. In Charlie Munger, *Poor Charlie's Almanack*, PCA Publication L.L.C., 2007a.

———. "Practical Thought About Practical Thought," July 20, 1996. In Charlie Munger, *Poor Charlie's Almanack*, PCA Publication L.L.C., 2007b.

Murphy, Austin, Robert Kleiman, and Kevin Nathan. "The Value of Convertible Preferred Stocks in Transactions with Relationship Investors Like Warren Buffett." *International Review of Financial Analysis* 6, no. 3, 1997.

Murphy, Kevin. "Executive Compensation." In Orley Ashenfelter and David Card, eds., *Handbook of Labor Economics*, vol. 3B, Amsterdam: Elsevier, 1999, chap. 38.

Neff, John. *John Neff on Investing*. New York: John Wiley & Sons, 1999.

Nocera, Joseph. *A Piece of the Action. How the Middle Class Joined the Money Class*. New York: Simon & Schuster, 2004.

"Northwest Industries OKs $1.4-Billion Merger Offer." *Los Angeles Times*, April 11, 1985.

O'Loughlin, James. *The Real Warren Buffett: Managing Capital, Leading People*. London: Nicolas Brealey Publishing, 2003.

Olson, Max. "Warren Buffett and the Washington Post." Csinvesting, 2006, http://www.futureblind.com/2006/12/warren-buffett-washington-post.

"Online Data Robert Shiller." www.econ.yale.edu~shiller/data.htm.

Oppenheimer, Henry. "A Test of Ben Graham's Selection Criteria." *Financial Analysts Journal* 40, no. 5, 1984.

———. "Ben Graham's Net Current Asset Values: A Performance Update." *Financial Analysts Journal* 42, no. 6, 1986.

Pardoe, James. *Warren Buffett Has Spoken, The Question Is Who is Listening?* Complied by James Pardoe. Los Angeles: Pardoe & Associates, 2003.

Pare, Terence. "Yes, You Can Beat the Market." *Fortune*, April 3, 1995.

Pratt, Shannon. *Business Valuation. Discounts and Premiums*. New York: Wiley & Sons, 2009.

"Questions Concerning Warren Buffett and Investing." www.fusioninvesting/gurus/buffett.

Rabinovich, Eli. "Going Out on Top: Walter and Edwin Schloss." *The Bottom Line*, April 17, 2003.

Rasmussen, Jim. "Hometown Deal Pleases Buffett: Central States Management Team to Stay Intact after Purchase." *Omaha World-Herald*, October 21, 1992.

———. "Billionaire Talks Strategy with Students: Columbia University Group Hears from Famous Alumnus Berkshire Hathaway." *Omaha World-Herald*, January 2, 1994.

"Recap: The 2014 Berkshire Hathaway Annual Meeting." *Wall Street Journal*, May 3, 2014.

Ricardo-Campbell, Rita. *Resisting Hostile Takeovers: The Case of Gillette*. Westport, CT: Praeger, 1997.

Roberts, Roxanne. "The Alfalfa Club: Still a Place for the Powerful to See and Be Seen." *Washington Post*, January 24, 2014.

Roll, Richard. "The Hubris Hypothesis of Corporate Takeovers." *Journal of Business* 59, no. 2, 1986.

Ross, Nikki. *Lessons from the Legends of Wall Street*. Chicago: Dearborn Publishers, 2000.

Rotbart, Dean. "Scott & Fetzer Is Still Weighing Takeover Bids and May Yet Accept Buyout Plan from Kelso." *Wall Street Journal*, November 21, 1984.

Rothchild, John. "How Smart Is Warren Buffett?" *Time*, April 3, 1995.

Rowe, F. "Rowe as Buffett?" *Forbes*, August 6, 1990.

Ryan, Thomas. "Fruit of the Loom, Burdened by Debt, Files for Bankruptcy." *Women's Wear Daily*, December 30, 1999.

Saba, Jennifer. "Amazon's Bezos Pays Hefty Price for Washington Post." Reuters, August 7, 2013, www.reuters.com.

Samuelson, Paul. Foreword to *Continuous Time Finance*, by Robert Merton. New York: Wiley-Blackwell, 1992.

Sandler, Linda. "Buffett's Savior Role Lands Him Deals Other Holders Can't Get," *Wall Street Journal*, August 14. 1989.

Schlender, Brent, Warren Buffett, and Bill Gates. "The Bill & Warren Show," *Fortune*, July 20, 1998.

Schloss, Walter. Columbia Upper Level Seminar in Value Investing. November 17, 1993.

———. Sixty-Five Years on Wall Street. Grant's Interest Rate Observer. Fall Investment Conference. November, 1998.

———. *The Memoirs of Walter J. Schloss: A Personal and Family History*. September Press, 2003.

Schroeder, Alice. *The Snowball: Warren Buffett and the Business of Life*. New York: Bantam Books, 2008.

"Scott & Fetzer Co. Agrees to Be Acquired by Kelso at $62 a Share." *Wall Street Journal*, February 15, 1984.

Sellers, Patricia, and Natasha Tarpley. "Crunch Time for Coke: His Company Is Overflowing with Trouble. But CEO Doug Ivester Says He's in Firm Control of 'the Most Noble Business on Earth.'" *Fortune*, July 19, 1999.

Serwer, Andy, and Julia Boorstin. "The Oracle of Everything: Warren Buffett Has Been Right About the Stock Market, Rotten Accounting, CEO Greed, and Corporate Governance." *Fortune*, November 11, 2002.

Setton, Dolly. "The Berkshire Bunch." *Forbes*, October 12, 1998.

Shiller, Robert. *Irrational Exuberance*. New York: Broadway Books, 2005.

Siegel, Jeremy. *Stocks for the Long Run*. New York: McGraw-Hill, 2008.

Smith, Adam [George Goodman]. *The Money Game*. New York: Random House, 1967.

———. *Supermoney*. New York: John Wiley & Sons, 2006.

Smith, Edgar. *Common Stocks as Long Term Investments*. New York: The Macmillan Company, 1924.

Snyder, David. "Hungry for Fame, Farley Goes Madison Ave." *Crain's Chicago Business*, June 16, 1986.

Sorkin, Andrew. *Too Big to Fail*. New York: Viking, 2009.

Spragins, Ellyn. "Northwest Industries: The Acid Test for Bill Farley's Offbeat Style." *BusinessWeek*, September 9, 1985.

Stempel, Jonathan. "Buffett Defends Using Stock in Burlington Takeover." Reuters, February 27, 2010, www.reuters.com.

Taleb, Nassim Nicolas. *Fooled by Randomness: The Hidden Role of Chance in the Markets and Life*. New York: W.W. Norton & Company, 2001.

_____. *The Black Swan: The Impact of the Highly Improbable*. New York: Random House, 2007.

_____. "The Future Has Thicker Tails than the Past. Model Error in Branching Counterfactuals." Paper presented at Benoit Mandelbrot's Scientific Memorial, Yale University, April 29, 2011, www.fooledbyrandomness.com/errors.pdf.

Tavakoli, Janet. *Dear Mr. Buffett: What an Investor Learns 1,269 Miles from Wall Street*. Hoboken, NJ: John Wiley & Sons, 2009.

"Telecommunications: Buffett Company Cuts Level 3 Stake." *New York Times*. November 14, 2003.

"The Money Man. Making Money Out of Junk." *Forbes*, August 15, 1973.

Train, John. *The Midas Touch: The Strategies That Have Made Warren Buffett America's Pre-Eminent Investor*. New York: HarperCollins, 1987.

Tsai, Catherine. "Analysts View Berkshire-Manville Deal Favorably." Associated Press Newswires, December 20, 2000.

Tyco International (A). Harvard Business School, February 2001.

Ueltschi, Albert. *The History and Future of FlightSafety International*. New York: FlightSafety International, 1999, https://www.flightsafety.com/html/book.

Vermaelen, Theo. "Common Stock Repurchases and Market Signalling." *Journal of Financial Economics* 9, no. 2, 1981.

Washington Post Company, Forms 10-K (annual reports pursuant to section 13 or 15(d) of the Securities Exchange Act of 1934), 2005–2012, http://www.sec.gov/Archives/edgar/data.

Wiggins, Robert, and Timothy Ruefli. "Sustained Competitive Advantage: Temporal Dynamics and the Incidence and Persistence of Superior Economic Performance." *Organization Science* 13, no. 1, 2002.

Williams, John. *Theory of Investment Value*. Cambridge, MA: Harvard University Press, 1938.

Winter, Ralph. "Scott & Fetzer Co. Rejects Boesky Bid, Asks Other Offers." *Wall Street Journal*, May 25, 1984.

Wismer, David. "Billionaire Fund Manager Mario Gabelli: 'I Like PHD's: Poor, Hungry and Driven'." *Forbes*, December 10, 2012.

Index

About the Author

ELENA CHIRKOVA GRADUATED WITH HONORS FROM THE ECONOMICS faculty of Moscow State University in Russia. She later studied at the Claremont Graduate School in California (United States) as an Edmund S. Muskie Graduate Fellow. Elena holds a PhD in economics.

She has 17 years of practical experience in financial advisory services and investment banking. She has worked at the Financial Advisory Services Department at Deloitte and at the investment bank N. M. Rothschild in Moscow, where she specialized in M&A.

Elena was also a visiting scholar at Harvard University through the Fulbright Scholar Program. She is an associate professor in the finance division of the economics department at the Higher School of Economics in Moscow, the leading finance and economics school in Russia. Her sphere of interest includes the theory of financial bubbles, corporate finance, value investing, valuation of shares, and, in particular, the use of multipliers in the valuation of shares.

Elena is an experienced and active investor, investing in U.S. and western European markets. She relies on value investing principles.

Elena is also the author of six books on finance in Russian. Her articles are frequently published in the popular Russian economics and finance magazine *Kommersant Money*. She covers the subjects of financial markets and the economics of totalitarian regimes. She also writes a column "Economics in Literature," in which she discusses economic history through examples of events portrayed in well-known and popular classical works.

Elena is the mother of a pair of twins, a boy and a girl. Her daughter is studying to be an architect and her son to be a programmer and mathematician.